William Miller, William Miller

Jottings of Kent

A Series of Historical, Ecclesiastical, Topographical and Statistical Sketches

William Miller, William Miller

Jottings of Kent
A Series of Historical, Ecclesiastical, Topographical and Statistical Sketches

ISBN/EAN: 9783743417694

Manufactured in Europe, USA, Canada, Australia, Japa

Cover: Foto ©ninafisch / pixelio.de

Manufactured and distributed by brebook publishing software (www.brebook.com)

William Miller, William Miller

Jottings of Kent

BEING A SERIES OF

HISTORICAL, ECCLESIASTICAL,

TOPOGRAPHICAL,

AND

ATISTICAL SKETCHES,

BY

LIAM MILLER

The ea

GRAVESE

THOMAS HALL, 4a, WI

LONDON:

V HITTAKER & CO., AVE MARIA

1864.

——

GRAVESEND,

PRINTED BY THOMAS HALL,

4a, WINDMILL STREET.

PREFACE TO THE FIRST EDITION.

————::————

IT was not contemplated, whilst contributing these Sketches to a Kentish Journal, that a desire would be manifested for their re-production in a collected form, neither that the compiler's incognito should be disclosed; still it is a gratifying fact to him, that however simple their garb,— divested as they are of pretentious phraseology, — the purpose has been served.

Without desire to claim merit, and in perfect disregard of all pecuniary interest, he has selected his materials from the highest authorities, re-written them in a familiar style, and brought them down to the present time as a simple epitome of Historical and Topographical Sketches, as their title indicates,—JOTTINGS OF KENT; and however imperfectly rendered, neither praise or censure belongs to him for re-producing much that has emanated from other minds.

It is the compiler's pleasing duty to tender to the Most Reverend Prelate, whose name graces the Patron's page, his warmest thanks for the honour he has conferred on the Work, as well as upon him, in accepting the Dedication;—a high compliment also to the people of Kent, his Grace being a native of that County, and the highest Ecclesiastical Personage in England. Neither can he omit expressing his kind acknowledgments to Mr. Thomas Hall, the respected Proprietor of the " Gravesend Free Press," for the pains-taking manner in which they were presented,—in the first instance,—through the columns of that excellent Journal, and subsequently, in the present neat pocket volume.

————::————

PREFACE TO THE SECOND EDITION.

It would be discourteous in the Compiler of the " JOTTINGS OF KENT," to allow a Second Edition to appear without a few words, in acknowledgment of the patronage extended to his simple labours.

Long before the First Edition was published the whole were sold, and a widely expressed desire evinced, for a second issue. Mr. Hall readily acceded to this request, and, at considerable outlay, reprinted the work in its present form.

The Compiler,—desirous of manifesting his appreciation of such favour,—has retouched many portions, and introduced several interesting facts that have transpired subsequent to their first appearance in the pages of the " Gravesend Free Press;" not only from a desire to render the work more complete, but also to secure to the spirited Proprietor of that excellent Journal, a remunerative return for the large expense he has incurred to meet the wishes of Kentish people and others.

Dalston, N. E.,
13*th Dec.*, 1864.

CONTENTS.

—::—

—::—

** *An Index will be found at the end of the Volume.*

JOTTINGS OF KENT.

KENT, the garden of the Home Counties, so rich in natural beauty and historical interest, possesses advantages peculiarly its own, foremost amongst which is the coast line, the grand highway of trade and commerce to the port of London.

The unbounded wealth borne upon the Thames and Medway far surpasses that of any other nation, whilst on their banks stand four of the docks of the Royal Navy—that of Woolwich, the 'Mother Dock of England,' being pre-eminent in attractions for foreign and distinguished visitors. Some of the finest ships of the British Navy were built here:—the 'Henry Grâce de Dieu,' launched in 1515,—the 'Queen Elizabeth' in 1559, launched in the presence of the Queen whose name she bore,—the 'Royal Sovereign,' of 100 guns, in 1637, designated by the Dutch, from her naval successes, the 'Golden Devil,'—the 'Royal George,' sunk at Spithead, 29th of August, 1782, and, in our own time, some of the noblest vessels that ever nation boasted. The appliances of steam-power and delicacy of machinery are amongst the wonders to be witnessed at Woolwich, especially that of a huge hammer, which can snap asunder a thick bar of iron or, at the will of the engineer, crack the shell of a filbert nut without injury to the kernel.

Anterior to the Christian era, the inhabitants of Kent were known to have intercourse with other nations, for Cæsar in his 'Commentaries' records them as far more civilized than those of any other part of Britain, which gave them a status amongst foreigners they still continue to merit.

History further tells us that the natural bravery of the people of Kent preserved it an entire kingdom during nearly *four centuries*, and ever afterwards the Kentishmen, being distinguished for their valour, especially against the incursions of the Danes, were placed foremost in battle in acknowledgment of their natural bravery.

Early in the Saxon Heptarchy the Christian religion was established in Kent, and its principal city, Canterbury, has the honour of holding the primatial see of all England.

B

When Julius Cæsar invaded England, fifty-four years before
Christ, Kent was largely inhabited by the Belgic Gauls, who
evidenced considerable progress in civilization, by the cultivation
of the lands and the growth of corn, contrary to the practice of the
inhabitants inland, who lived mostly on milk and flesh procured by
the chase ; they had also established a mode of government like that
in Gaul, which had spread over great part of the island, for
even at that early period there were four princes or chiefs govern-
ing it.

Their vessels, however, were small and fragile, suited only for
river excursions, with keels of slight timber laced with wicker-work
and covered with hides.   The towns or villages, if such they may
be called, were little more than groups of huts placed at short dis-
tances from each other, and mostly in the middle of a wood, defended
with earth-mounds, or trees that had been cut down to clear the
ground: they bred abundance of cattle, and their cash was of brass
and iron in rings, which currented by weight.   As before remarked,
from their origin and intercourse with the Continent, the inhabitants
were the most civilized of the ancient Britons ; and whilst the use of
clothing was scarcely known in any other parts of the island, those
of Kent wore garments made of the skins of wild beasts.   Plutarch
describes them as, from their regular and temperate habits, remarkable for longevity, and only beginning to grow old at one hundred
and twenty years.

The Britons, after the departure of the Romans, having suffered
severely from the ravages of the Picts and Scots, who had driven
them to precarious shelter in the woods and mountains, convened a
General Assembly in the year 445, at which they elected Vortigern
king ; but he proved ill-qualified to restore the nation's fallen condition, and, regardless of the welfare of his subjects, became cruel,
avaricious, and debauched, living in equal dread of his enemies and
of his own people.   To free himself from the danger of the one, and
the plots of the other, he called a National Assembly, and propounded
the necessity of bringing to their assistance the Saxons, a brave and
ambitious people, settled in Germany upon lands of the Romans ;
when it was determined to invite Hengist and his brother Horsa to
defend them, in return for the Isle of Thanet, and to allow the
Saxon soldiers pay, to be settled by mutual agreement.

Hengist, then 35 years old, gladly accepted the terms : he was the
son of Wetgiffel, great-grandson of WODEN, from whom descended
all the Saxon royal families.

Hengist and Horsa arrived with three ships and fifteen hundred
men, and landed on the Isle of Thanet, where they were welcomed
with demonstrations of great joy by Vortigern.

Thus in possession of the Isle of Thanet, the Saxons did not
long remain inactive, but, being united to the British forces, boldly
marched to Stamford in Lincolnshire, and gave the Picts and Scots

battle, in which the latter were entirely routed, leaving the Saxons and British masters of the spoil and booty taken.

In A.D. 450, Hengist, ambitious of a permanent settlement for his countrymen in Britain, and sensible of the fertility of Kent in comparison to his own barren country, persuaded Vortigern of his danger of a fresh invasion of the Picts and Scots, and of the necessity for an augmentation of Saxons to strengthen him against enemies, to which Vortigern readily assented.

Hengist thereupon invited over great numbers, to become sharers in their new expedition, and, during the same year, upwards of 5,000 Saxons, exclusive of wives and children, were landed from sixteen ships. With this reinforcement came Œsc or Escus, Hengist's son, and, according to Nennius, Rowena his daughter, whose beauty and elegance of manner captivated Vortigern, for whom he divorced his wife and married her, settling upon her father Hengist the fertile province of Kent.

In 452 a further reinforcement of Saxons arrived in forty ships, and ravaged the countries of the Scots and Picts; while Hengist, emboldened by their success, sent for more men and ships, until his native country was left almost uninhabited. Thus multiplied, they purposely quarrelled with the Britons and, after secretly concluding peace with the Scots and Picts, turned their arrows against Vortigern.

In 455 a great battle was fought between the Britons and Saxons at Eglesford (now Aylesford), Kent, in which Horsa, Hengist's brother, was slain. Immediately after the battle Hengist took upon himself the title of KING OF KENT, from which time the Saxons spread rapidly over the face of Britain. Hengist fixed his royal seat at Canterbury, where he governed thirty-three years : he died in 488, aged 69 years, 39 of which he passed in Britain. He was one of the bravest generals of his age, but his love of bloodshed, fraud, and treachery remain indelible blemishes on his memory.

Hengist left two sons, Escus and Andoacer. Escus, the eldest, took possession of the kingdom, and ascended the throne as Escus, (second) King of Kent (A.D. 488). Escus possessed neither the valour nor bravery of his parent, preferring ease and luxury to the fatigues and privations of warfare. During the first three years of his reign little transpired to disturb the peace between the Saxons and Britons, but in the following year (492) Ella, a Saxon general of the posterity of Woden, erected his standard in Sussex, where he was established as King of Sussex, or of the South Saxons. He was also elected general of the Saxons in the room of Hengist, who, beyond his title as King of Kent, was head of all the Saxons in Britain. This was the second Saxon kingdom, answering to the present counties of Sussex and Surrey.

The year 495 was remarkable for the arrival in Britain of Cerdic, a noble Saxon general, with a long train of distinguished Saxons ; more especially he being the progenitor of the Kings of England to

Edward the Confessor, and downwards in the female line to George III.   Cerdic was further famous as the founder of a kingdom to which, ultimately, all became subject,—that glorious line of which our beloved Queen is the exalted representative.   He landed with his nobles and forces at a place called ' Cerdic's Ora.'

Of Escus, King of Kent, little can be traced.   His apathy allowed the powers of Hengist to be usurped by Ella, whose successful warfare against the Britons founded a new kingdom.   Thus content to possess in tranquillity the crown of Kent, Escus died in 512, after a reign of twenty-four years, memorable only for leaving his name to succeeding Kings of Kent, who, from him, were called ' Escingians.'

OCTA, (third) King of Kent (A.D. 512), succeeded his father Escus, and reigned twenty-two years. . During the second year of his reign Ella, King of the Saxons, died, after considerably enlarging his kingdom.   Octa, like his father, was wanting in the energy of purpose and indomitable bravery of Hengist, who had peopled Essex and Middlesex as well as Kent, which he governed by a prefect, or deputy, but which were wrested from his successor in 527 by Erchenwin, another descendant from Woden, who assumed the title of King of Essex, or of the East Saxons.   We have no record of the right by which he claimed this kingdom, although historians ascribe it to Octa's weakness, of which he took advantage.   In 532 Cerdic invited great numbers of his countrymen with their families to settle in his territory.   They came over from Germany in eight hundred vessels, whereby Cerdic's powers were largely increased.   He was afterwards crowned at Winchester as King of Wessex or the West Saxons, and died in 534, thirty-nine years after his arrival in Britain.

Octa died the same year, and was succeeded by his son—

HERMENRIC, (fourth) King of Kent (A.D. 534).   In the thirteenth year of his reign (547), Ida, a noble Saxon chief, embarked from Germany in forty vessels, and landed his forces at Flamborough in Yorkshire, then in possession of the Northumbrian* Saxons, who had inhabited that country since the time of Hengist, to whom they were tributary.   Ida was at once acknowledged sovereign, under the title of King of Northumberland, which was the fifth Anglo-Saxon kingdom.   He was a prince of great fame, and built a city in honour of his queen Bebba (Bebbanburgh), of which the Castle of Bamborough still remains.   He died in 559.   Thus the apathy and neglect of Hengist's successors seriously curtailed the powers and territory of the Kings of Kent, which Hermenric made no efforts to arrest.   Three years before his death he admitted his son Ethelbert sharer with him in the kingdom.   Hermenric died in 564, after a reign of thirty years.

ETHELBERT, (fifth) King of Kent (A.D. 564), ascended the throne

* From North Humber.

immediately after the death of his father. He was one of the most celebrated monarchs not only of Kent but of the whole heptarchy, more especially as being the first Christian king of his nation. This prince beheld with regret the superiority of Hengist lost by the apathy of his successors : he attempted by force of arms to establish his own dignity, but unsuccessfully until, in conjunction with other kings, he defeated Ceaulin, King of Wessex, after whose death Ethelbert was elected monarch of the Anglo-Saxons, and exercised an almost absolute power over all the kingdoms south of the Humber. Besides being formidable to his neighbours from his conquests, his alliance with Bertha, daughter of Caribert, King of Paris, brought the friendship of France, Italy, and other continental nations, as well as the respect and dread by his people of the introduction of the French into Britain.

The most memorable fact which gave lustre to his reign was the founding of Christianity in Britain through the instrumentality of Queen Bertha, who brought over a French bishop to the Court of Canterbury, and employed her best powers to induce Ethelbert to embrace the Christian faith.

In 597 Pope Gregory the Great sent Augustine with forty companions to propound the tenets of the Church of Rome. Ethelbert assigned them residence in the Isle of Thanet, already prepared by the care of the Queen. Augustine preached the gospel with earnestness : numbers of Kentishmen were baptized. The king viewed with secret pleasure a religion which could inspire so much piety and disinterestedness, and on the feast of Pentecost in the year 597 he professed himself a Christian and was baptized. The following Christmas ten thousand of his subjects followed the example of their sovereign. Ethelbert exerted all his influence to second the efforts of the missionaries. As soon as Augustine was consecrated archbishop, by the Archbishop of Arles, the king gave his royal palace at Canterbury to Augustine as a dwelling for himself and clergy, and out of the Roman ruins at Reculver built himself another palace. Ethelbert also converted many of the heathen temples into churches, the first of which was dedicated to St. Pancrace (St. Pancras). During this reign the foundation of Canterbury Cathedral was laid, and a monastery erected in honour of Augustine, whose name it bore.

In 604 Ethelbert endowed the Augustine monastery with large revenues : the laws he made, which are the most ancient, are still extant in the Saxon language. He was the husband of two wives : by his first wife, Bertha, he had a son, Eadbald, who succeeded him, and a daughter, Ethelburga, who married Edwin, King of Northumberland.

Ethelbert died in the year 616, after a brilliant reign of fifty-two years, and was buried in Canterbury Cathedral, near his consort Queen Bertha.

EADBALD, (sixth) King of Kent (A.D. 616). This prince, upon ascending the throne, forsook the Christian faith and turned to idolatry, in which his whole people followed. Hume tells us Laurentius, the successor of Augustine, found the Christian religion wholly abandoned, and Mellitus and Justus, Bishops of London and Rochester, already departed the kingdom. Eadbald had married his mother-in-law : his vices rendered him slothful and inactive ; all the English sovereigns cast him off with the yoke they had borne during the life of Ethelbert, as he had neither the power nor courage to maintain the kingdom his father had so firmly established; hence Laurentius, Archbishop of Canterbury, after preaching the gospel without fruit to a nation of infidels, resolved on returning to France, but before which he determined on a last effort to reclaim the king. Eadbald, deeply moved by his eloquence, was brought to a sense of his errors, and, divorcing himself from his mother-in-law, returned with his people to the faith of the gospel, and spent the remainder of his life in the practice of its precepts: but he had lost for ever the fame and authority of his father.

Eadbald left two sons, Ermenfride and Ercombert, and a daughter, Eanswith, who became a nun and founded the nunnery at Folkestone. He died in 640, after a reign of twenty-four years, and was buried at Canterbury, near his father, in a chapel which he himself had built.

ERCOMBERT, (seventh) King of Kent (A.D. 640). Ercombert was famed for piety and love of his country. Although the youngest son of Eadbald (by Emma, daughter of the King of France), he ascended the throne to the prejudice of his eldest brother. It was this monarch who first established in Britain the fast of Lent. He caused the heathen temples to be destroyed and the idols broken in pieces, lest they should prove a future snare. He had issue two sons, Egbert and Lothair, and two daughters, Ermenilda and Domnona. The eldest daughter married Wulpher, King of Mercia; the youngest was a nun. Ercombert reigned twenty-four years, and left the crown to his son Egbert. He died in the year 664, and was buried in St. Augustine's monastery.

EGBERT, (eighth) King of Kent (A.D. 664). This prince is renowned for his encouragement of learning and the liberal arts, but infamous for putting to death the two sons of his uncle Ermenfride, lest they should disturb him in the possession of the crown. Egbert gave to his youngest sister, Domnona, some lands in the Isle of Thanet, where she founded a nunnery ; he afterwards (669) gave the palace and lands of Reculver to build a monastery. Egbert reigned nine years, and died in 673, leaving two sons, Edric and Widred, who were not his immediate successors, for his uncle Lothair usurped the throne.

LOTHAIR, (ninth) King of Kent (A.D. 673). Lothair, having reigned some years unmolested, made his son Richard partner with him in the kingdom, which at once obliged Edric, his nephew, to withdraw from court, and seek aid from Edelwalch, King of Sussex. Edelwalch placed under his command a formidable army, which marched into Kent. Edric gave his uncle battle, in which Lothair was vanquished, and died of his wounds in 684–5. He was buried in St. Augustine's monastery, near King Ercombert. Richard, son of Lothair, fled to Germany, where he married the sister of the Archbishop of Mentz, and was afterwards elected King of Suabia.

EDRIC, (tenth) King of Kent (A.D. 684–5). Edric, the eldest son of Egbert, then ascended the throne. His reign was a continued scene of warfare with his subjects, by whom he was slain within two years, leaving the kingdom weakened and embroiled.

WIDRED and SWABERT, (joint) Kings of Kent (A.D. 686). Widred succeeded his brother Edric, but, not having the general approbation of the people, was obliged to admit one Swabert as partner in the kingdom. During the reign of these two kings, Cedwalla, King of the West Saxons, imagining from intestine divisions that the kingdom of Kent would prove an easy conquest, sent an army under command of his brother Mollo, who overran the country and committed great ravages. In this extremity Widred and Swabert joined forces; the natural courage of the Kentishmen was aroused, and, after a sanguinary battle, they put Mollo and his troops to flight. Mollo with twelve of his officers, being sorely pressed, took shelter in a house, but the Kentish soldiers fired the house and they all perished in the flames. Cedwalla soon revenged the death of his brother Mollo, whom he tenderly loved. He entered Kent with a formidable army, and devastated the whole country with fire and sword. The two kings had no repose until the year 691—indeed, the horrors of the invasion had so enfeebled Kent as a nation that it never again recovered its superiority in the heptarchy.

Swabert died in 695, and Widred reigned alone in peace to his death in 725, leaving three sons—Ethelbert, Eadbert, and Aldric. Widred was buried near the body of St. Augustine, in the porch of Our Lady's Chapel, Canterbury, built by King Eadbald.

ETHELBERT. (twelfth) King of Kent (A.D. 725). According to some writers, Ethelbert associated his brothers Eadbert and Aldric with him in the government, whilst others assert that he reigned alone. Rapin tells us that Ethelbert and Eadbert reigned together until 748, when Eadbert died, and Ethelbert reigned alone until his death in 760, after reigning thirty-six years.

ALDRIC, (thirteenth) King of Kent (A.D. 760). Aldric, the only surviving son of Widred, succeeded to the crown. The enfeebled state of the kingdom exposed it to the incursions of neighbours—Offa, King of Mercia, most prominent amongst them. Offa entered Kent with a large army, and gained a great victory over Aldric, which still more seriously impoverished the affairs of Kent. Jealousy, however, on the part of other kings would not allow Offa to

usurp the kingdom, for he was drawn from Kent by a Welsh invasion of his own territory, but for which Offa would in all probability have united Kent to Mercia. Aldric associated his only son,
Alemand, with himself in the government, but that prince died
before his father, and, as Aldric left no heir, the race of Hengist
became extinct with his death in the year 794.

EADBERT-PREN, (fourteenth) King of Kent (A.D. 794). The
death of Aldric, the last of the Royal House of Kent, had thrown
the State into considerable confusion, when Eadbert, or Edilbert
(surnamed Pren), took possession of the throne. His reign was of
brief duration, for Cenulph, successor of Offa, King of Mercia,
taking advantage of the enfeebled state of the kingdom, ravaged it
throughout, and, having defeated Eadbert, whom he took prisoner,
carried him to Mercia, where he caused his eyes to be put out and
his hands to be cut off.

CUDRED, (fifteenth) King of Kent (A.D. 798). Cenulph, having
subdued Kent, placed his brother Cudred on the throne, but only as
the vassal of Mercia, to whose king he paid tribute. Cudred died
in the year 805, after reigning eight years.

BALDRED, (sixteenth) King of Kent (A.D. 805). Baldred was
the son of Cudred, and, like his father, paid tribute to the King of
Mercia. He reigned eighteen years, after which he was driven out
of Kent in 823 by Egbert.

Egbert, who commenced his reign as King of the West Saxons
in 800, ultimately subdued the Britons, and in the space of nineteen years extended his authority over the greater part of the island.
He finished his conquests in the year 828, from which time is to be
dated his title of King of England, and the dissolution of the Saxon
Heptarchy, as well as the kingdom of Kent, which during four
centuries was a distinct and noble nation, whose history will be
read to latest posterity with pride and admiration by every Anglo-
Briton.

Kent, now part of the kingdom of England, remained without
material alteration as to government, but from its situation was
especially exposed to the incursions of the Danes, and came succes-
sively under the power of their kings—SWEYN, EDMUNDS, CANUTE,
and HARDICANUTE.

In 832 a numerous fleet of Danes invaded Kent: they landed on
the Isle of Sheppey, and after plundering the neighbouring country
returned to their ships, but still continued their ravages in various
other parts of England, burning churches, destroying towns, and
cruelly wasting the lands; again, in 838, the Danes landed in
Lincolnshire, East Anglia, and Kent, extending as far as Canterbury
and Rochester, and even to London.

The civil jurisdiction of counties now subject to the King of
England was confided to an Eoderman or Earl, frequently persons
invested with great military power. The first created was—

ALCHER, or AUCHER, Earl of Kent (A.D. 850). He was a distinguished warrior, and displayed great bravery in 853, when the Danes again harassed the country. He was killed, with Earl Huda, in a great battle fought on the Isle of Thanet.

CEOLMUND, Earl of Kent (A.D. 897). ALFRED THE GREAT created Ceolmund Earl of Kent, to resist the Danes, who still continued to annoy this coast; little is recorded of him, beyond that he was a brave general and a faithful subject.

GOODWYNE, Earl of Kent (A.D. 1020). Goodwyne was of noble birth, and brother to Edric, Earl of Mercia. King Canute appointed him commander-in-chief of his forces in an expedition against the Vandals in Denmark, over whom he gained a triumphant victory, for which he was created Earl of Kent. On the death of Canute in 1036, Goodwyne directed with absolute sway; he had risen to an eminence scarcely admitting of any addition. He was the favourite of King Harold, at whose death, and the accession of Edward the Confessor, he usurped so great authority as to receive almost equal deference with the king. Edward would have obstructed Goodwyne's advancement, but his power was so unbounded that it might have proved dangerous had not death removed this formidable subject, for he died suddenly at the king's table the 15th April, 1053, and was buried at Winchester.

HAROLD, Earl of Kent (A.D. 1053). Harold, Earl of Kent and Duke of Wessex, the second son of Goodwyne, was in temper more courteous and conciliatory than his father, with a much higher sense of honour, which secured him the respect of both nobles and people. The peace of England was somewhat disturbed in the year 1055, from a quarrel with Macbeth, King of Scotland, who had seized upon Cumberland; but King Edward, espousing the cause of Malcolm, one of the royal family of Cumberland, speedily expelled him. In 1057 Leofric, Earl of Mercia, died: he is memorable from his wife Godiva freeing the inhabitants of Coventry of a heavy tax by submitting to ride in a nude state through the town. Leofric and Godiva built a monastery at Coventry, to which they gave such vast treasures of gold, silver, and precious stones, that it was said to be the richest in the kingdom.

Edward the Confessor had set apart the tenth of his revenue, and rebuilt from its foundation the Church of St. Peter (Westminster Abbey), which was the great object of his solicitude during his latter years: it was finished in 1065, when the king summoned all the bishops and great men of the nation to assist at the dedication, Harold being prominent amongst them. Harold reached the metropolis on the 30th November, 1065, five weeks before the king's death: the Festival of the Innocents was the day appointed for the dedication of Edward's church, but he was unable to be present at the ceremony. King Edward died on the 5th January following, and was buried with great pomp in the church which he had erected.

Edward the Confessor was the last king of Egbert's race, though not the last of the Saxon monarchs, since his successor was of that nation.

The same year, 1066, Harold, Earl of Kent, ascended the throne of England, according to some historians by the unanimous voice of the nation, although he had previously bound himself to the Duke of Normandy not to attempt the throne of England : it is, however, evident that after his coronation he was universally acknowledged sovereign, and possessed the esteem of his people.

William, Duke of Normandy, enraged at Harold's breach of faith, invaded England with a large fleet, landed without opposition at Pevensey in Sussex, and marched to Hastings. Harold, who was in the north, little expecting this invasion until the following spring, hastened to London, where he received ambassadors from Duke William requesting the surrender of the crown, and charging him with breach of faith. Harold sent a haughty reply, and marched his forces to Senlac, seven miles from Hastings, where he massed them on a declivity ; in the centre of his army floated the royal standard, by which stood Harold and his brothers Gurth and Leofwin. William, perceiving that a battle was inevitable, advanced to an advantageous position.

On the following morning—Saturday, October 14th, 1066 (Harold's birthday)—the two armies were ranged in line of battle at daybreak : in front of the English were the brave Kentishmen. The conflict continued from six in the morning until night, when Harold was slain by an arrow shot through his head, and his troops entirely routed : on the side of the victors, of an army of nearly sixty thousand, more than one-fourth were left on the field ; while of the vanquished the loss is unknown.

The great and decisive battle of Hastings was worthy of the heroic valour displayed by both armies. The bodies of Harold and his brothers being found, William the Conqueror sent them to their mother, who gave them honourable burial in Waltham Abbey, which was founded by King Harold. Thus ended in England the empire of the Anglo-Saxons, founded 600 years before by HENGIST, first King of Kent.

William, Duke of Normandy, now forty-two years old, having subjugated the kingdom, ascended the throne of England, and advanced to honour and distinction those who had displayed valour in his late struggle for the crown: amongst these was his half-brother Odo, Bishop of Bayeux, who, although an ecclesiastic, was created—

ODO, Earl of Kent (A.D. 1067). Odo was amiable of disposition,— eloquent, courtly, and courageous; he honoured religion, and defended his clergy as well with his sword as his tongue. He was vested with great powers by the king, and having amassed large wealth, formed the utopian idea of buying the Papal See, which project reaching the knowledge of the king, he was arrested and sent prisoner to Normandy, where he remained until 1087, when William the Conqueror released him shortly before his death. Odo afterwards undertook a journey to Rome accompanied by his nephew, which he never reached, but died at Palermo, in Sicily, in the year 1096, at an advanced age : he was thirty years Earl of Kent, and upwards of fifty years Bishop of Bayeux.

WILLIAM DE IPRE, Earl of Kent (A.D. 1141). This earl had given great proofs of his courage in Flanders and Normandy during the closing years of the reign of Henry I., as well as in the beginning of that of Stephen, which Stephen rewarded by creating him Earl of Kent in the sixth year of his reign. After the death of Stephen, in 1154, the Flemish were expelled the kingdom,—Earl William their leader, and the confidant of Stephen, with them ; they returned to Flanders, where William de Ipre became a monk: he died in the Abbey of Laon, in the year 1162.

HUBERT DE BURGH, Earl of Kent (A.D. 1213). This earl was in high favour with King John, as well as with his successor, Henry III. He was considered the richest subject in England, which excited the envy of Peter, Bishop of Winchester, his rival at court, who spared no means to destroy his popularity, which he ultimately effected by estranging the king's favour from him, through which Hubert suffered great persecution : he was deprived of all his dignified offices and emoluments, after which he was thrust into prison, and his vast stores of treasure and jewels of immense value seized, and carried to the king's treasury. He died at Banstede, in Surrey, the 12th May, 1243, in the 27th year of the reign of Henry III. Camden says of this great man—' *He was an entire lover of his country, and amidst the storms of adversity discharged all the duties that could be demanded from the best of subjects.*'

EDMUND, Earl of Kent (about A.D. 1285). Edmund was second son of Edward I. After the accession of Edward III. he was accused of plotting the restoration of Edward II. and cruelly adjudged to die for high treason, which was carried into execution the same day at Winchester.

EDMUND PLANTAGENET, Earl of Kent. This prince was the eldest son of Edmund, second son of Edward I., and the King's ward, but he died the next year without issue.

JOHN PLANTAGENET, Earl of Kent. He was brother of the last earl, but only lived a year after his creation ; he died on St. Stephen's day following, and was buried at Winchester.

THOMAS DE HOLAND, Earl of Kent. He assumed the earldom in right of his wife Joane, sister and heir of the last-named John Plantagenet, Earl of Kent: there is no record of his having been so created, although he was summoned to Parliament by that title. He died in 1359, the thirty-fourth year of Edward III., and left issue three sons—Thomas, Edmund, and John. John was afterwards

created Duke of Exeter, and married Elizabeth, second daughter of
John of Gaunt, Duke of Lancaster, by whom he had three sons, and
a daughter Constance. Constance, after the death of her first
husband, married John, Lord Grey of Ruthven, from whom the Earls
of Kent of that family descended.

THOMAS, Earl of Kent. He was the eldest son of Thomas de
Holand, and was knighted by Edward the Black Prince in 1365.
Edward had married his mother, by whom he had a son, Richard
II., his half-brother. This earl, who was made Constable of the
Tower in 1389, died the 25th April, 1396, leaving issue four sons
and six daughters: of his sons, Thomas and Edmund only survived.

THOMAS, Earl of Kent (A.D. 1396), succeeded to the title in his
own right as heir of the last earl. He was in high favour with his
kinsman, Richard II., who conferred on him a royal grant of land.
The same year he was created Duke of Surrey, and afterwards
invested with the Order of the Garter and made Marshal of England.
The king gave him the famous Arras hangings of Warwick Castle;
and in 1398 he became Lieutenant of Ireland and Baron of Norrhage
in that kingdom, having previously founded the Priory of Car-
thusians at Montgrace, in Yorkshire.

In 1399 the Irish, taking advantage of the small number of troops
left in their country, revolted, and took up arms against the powers
of England. Richard II. resolved to chastise the rebels in person;
he was accompanied by the Earl of Kent, with whom he returned to
England when Henry Duke of Lancaster's arrival became known.

Richard II. was deposed 30th April, 1399, after which the Earl
of Kent was deprived of all his honours: he then plotted with others
the murder of Henry IV. and the restoration of Richard II., of
which Henry became privily advised by the Duke of York. The king
was at Windsor, but at once hastened to London; the conspirators,
in ignorance of Henry's departure, came to Windsor on the same
night, headed by the Earls of Kent and Salisbury. Thus foiled in
their design of seizing the king, they went to Wallingford and
Abingdon, where they importuned the people to join them, and
passed on to Cirencester for the same purpose. At the latter place
they took lodgings, the Earls of Kent and Salisbury at one inn, the
Duke of Exeter and Earl of Gloucester at another. The mayor of
the town during the night assembled a number of townsmen and
seized upon the Earls of Kent and Salisbury, whom the mayor
caused to be beheaded immediately; the head of the Earl of Kent
was sent to London and elevated upon the Bridge, but it was afterwards taken down and given over to his widow, to be buried with
his body in the priory that he had founded in Montgrace.

EDMUND, Earl of Kent (A.D. 1400). Edmund, brother of the last
Earl of Kent, succeeded to his title; his loyalty not being questioned, he had restitution of all the estate possessed by his brother
within a year.

In the sixth year of Henry IV. (A.D. 1405) the Earl of March came to England and challenged Edmund to single combat; they fought with great skill and bravery, but the Earl of Kent won the field. He married Lucy, daughter of the Duke of Millaine, but died without issue.

In the ninth year of Henry IV. (A.D. 1408) the Earl was shot through the head by an arrow whilst besieging the castle of Briac, in Brittany: his body was brought back to England and buried with those of his ancestors.

WILLIAM NEVILL, Earl of Kent (A.D. 1461). William Nevill, the second son of the Earl of Westmoreland, was created Earl of Kent by Edward IV.: he was a distinguished soldier, and fought at the siege of Orleans in the 26th Henry VI. (1448); he again displayed great valour in the wars of France, and was made Governor of Roxburgh Castle in Scotland. During an embassy into Normandy to negociate peace he was taken prisoner by the French, and remained their hostage several years. In the first year of Edward IV. (1461) he highly distinguished himself in the battle of Touton, and overthrew the Lancastrians: his bravery was handsomely rewarded, and he was created Earl of Kent and Lord Admiral of England, but did not long enjoy his honours, for he died in 1462, leaving three daughters, and was buried in the Priory of Gisborough, York.

EDMUND GREY, Earl of Kent (A.D. 1465). This scion of an ancient and noble house bore the titles of Lord of Hastings, Weysford, and Ruthven, and was created Earl of Kent by Edward IV. in the fifth year of his reign. He was' descended from Anschetil de Grai, recorded in Domesday Book as holding many lands during the reign of William the Conqueror. He died in 1489, the fourth year of Henry VII., and left four sons, of whom only one survived.

GEORGE GREY, Earl of Kent (A.D. 1489). George, the only surviving son of Edmund Grey, succeeded his father with all his titles, and was a chief leader in the king's forces during those tumultuous times, more especially in 1497. He died in the year 1507, in the twenty-second year of the reign of Henry VII., and left issue four sons,—Richard, Henry, George, and Anthony.

RICHARD GREY, Earl of Kent (A.D. 1507). This nobleman inherited the titles and estate of his father, and was elected a Knight of the Garter. He accompanied Henry VIII. to France as the king's personal attendant, and distinguished himself at the siege of Terrouenne in 1513. He died without issue in 1524, and was buried at the Whitefriars, Fleet-street, London.

SIR HENRY GREY, Earl of Kent (A.D. 1524). Sir Henry, brother of the last earl, succeeded to the title and estate, which, having been wasted and encumbered by Richard, he declined taking up. He died in 1562, the fourth year of Queen Elizabeth, and was buried in the Church of St. Giles, Cripplegate, London, leaving a son and a daughter.

HENRY GREY, Earl of Kent (A.D. 1562). Henry, like his father declined taking up the titles. He married Margaret, daughter of John of Bletsoe, and left issue three sons—Reginald, Henry, and Charles.

REGINALD GREY, Earl of Kent (A.D. 1571). Reginald was of frugal habits, by which he greatly recovered his father's estate, and in the thirteenth year of Queen Elizabeth assumed his full titles, being the sixth earl of this family. He died in 1573, without issue, and was buried in Cripplegate Church, near his grandsire Sir Henry Grey.

HENRY GREY, Earl of Kent (A.D. 1573). According to Camden, this earl was '*a person plentifully endowed with all the ornaments of true nobility.*' He died without issue in 1614, and was buried in a chapel he founded adjoining Flitton Church, in Bedfordshire, in which a handsome monument was erected to his memory.

CHARLES GREY, Earl of Kent (A.D. 1614). Charles Grey, the surviving son of the first Henry Grey, succeeded to all the titles: he had issue a son Henry, and a daughter Susan. This earl died September 1625, and was buried near his brother in the chapel at Flitton.

HENRY GREY, Earl of Kent (A.D. 1625). Henry Grey, the ninth Earl of Kent of this family, married Elizabeth, second daughter of Gilbert Talbot, Earl of Shrewsbury, and died in London, without issue, November 1639. After his death the barony of Ruthven was conferred by Charles I. on his sister Susan's son Charles.

ANTHONY GREY, Earl of Kent (A.D. 1639). Anthony, Rector of Burbache in Leicestershire, great-grandson of George, second Earl of Kent of this name, succeeded to the titles, but upon being summoned to Parliament excused himself from age and indisposition. He left five sons—Henry, John, Job, Theophilus, and Nathaniel— and five daughters: he died in the year 1643, and was buried in his own parish church.

HENRY GREY, Earl of Kent (A.D. 1643). This earl was the husband of two wives : his first, Mary daughter of Sir William Courteene, bore him a son, who died in 1644, and was buried near his mother in Westminster Abbey, who had died shortly before. He afterwards married Amabella, daughter of Sir Anthony Ben, Recorder of London, widow of Anthony Fane, third son of Francis, Earl of Westmoreland. She brought him great wealth, and thus restored the lustre of this noble family : by her he had two sons, Anthony and Henry, and a daughter Elizabeth. Henry died a youth, and Elizabeth married Lord Maynard. Nothing remarkable is recorded of this earl: he was amiable of disposition, and by his second marriage restored the fallen fortunes of his house. He died in 1651, and was buried with his ancestors in the chapel at Flitton. His countess erected a handsome monument to his memory : she attained the age of 92, and died in 1698.

ANTHONY GREY, Earl of Kent (A.D. 1651). Anthony, the eldest and only surviving son of Henry, the last-named Earl of Kent, inherited the title: he married Mary, heiress of Lord Lucas, Baron of Shenfield in Essex; she was created Baroness Lucas in 1663 (13th Car. II.), with succession to her heirs male and female by her husband Anthony Grey, Earl of Kent. They had issue one son Henry, and a daughter Amabella. The Earl died August 19th, 1702, and was buried in the family mausoleum in Flitton Church.

HENRY GREY, Earl of Kent (A.D. 1702). Henry, the only son of the last Earl, took his seat in the House of Peers as Earl of Kent 20th October, 1702, being the thirteenth of that noble family; his mother died the same year, when he added to his titles that of Lord Lucas of Crudwell. He became Lord Chamberlain in 1704, and in the fifth year of Queen Anne (December 1706) was created Viscount Goodrich, Earl of Harold, and Marquis of Kent.

In 1707 he was made Lord Lieutenant of Bedford and a Knight of the Garter. His amiability endeared him to all with whom he was associated; although laden with honours, he was never wanting in sympathy for suffering humanity. He enjoyed the favour of his Queen, and after her death, in 1714, was received into the confidence and esteem of George I., who, in acknowledgment of his exemplary services, constituted him Lord Steward of the King's Household and Lord Privy Seal, as well as Constable of the Tower. He was twice married—first to Jemima, eldest daughter of Lord Crew of Stene, and had issue four sons and seven daughters. His son Anthony assumed the title of Earl of Harold, and took his seat as a peer by the title of Lord Lucas of Crudwell, but he died without issue in the year 1723: his other sons died young. Amabella, his eldest daughter, married Viscount Glenorchy, but she died at Copenhagen in 1726. Jemima married the Earl of Ashburnham, Anne Lord Charles Cavendish, and Mary Dr. Gregory, Canon of Christchurch; the remaining daughters died in infancy.

In 1729 the Duke of Kent married his second wife Sophia, daughter of William Bentinck, Earl of Portland: she died in 1748, leaving a daughter Anne Sophia, who married Dr. John Egerton, son of the Bishop of Hereford. This venerable duke, who lived to a ripe old age, died 5th June 1740, but without a male heir, by which the titles of Duke of Kent, Earl of Harold, and Viscount Goodrich passed from his house. His granddaughter Jemima, only surviving child of his daughter Amabella, inherited the titles of Marchioness Grey and Baroness Lucas of Crudwell: she married Philip Yorke afterwards Earl of Hardwicke, and left issue two daughters.

EDWARD, Duke of Kent (A.D. 1799). This beloved prince was the fourth son of George III. He was born the 2nd of November 1767, and educated in England, at Gottingen, and Geneva; he remained at Geneva until the year 1790, when he proceeded to Gibraltar in military command; subsequently he went to America, from whence he returned to England in 1799, and was created

Duke of Kent and Strathern and Earl of Dublin the 23rd of April of the same year. In 1802 he was made Governor of Gibraltar, which he resigned the following year.

On the 11th of July 1818, his Royal Highness married Victoria Mary Louisa, sister of Leopold King of the Belgians, and fourth daughter of Francis Frederick Anthony, Duke of Saxe-Coburg. His superior talents, amiability of disposition, and wide-spread benevolence elicited universal admiration, but above all his magnanimous efforts for the improvement of society. He died 23rd of January 1820, in the fifty-third year of his age, leaving his good name and inestimable character to adorn the pages of British History. His only issue was a daughter, our beloved

QUEEN VICTORIA,

whose reign has indeed been glorious, as shedding blessings throughout the length and breadth of her vast Empire : as the mother of her people, so she lives, treasured for her virtues ; a people who have mourned as well as rejoiced with her, and who, while holding her sacred in their best affections, mingle united prayers for Heaven's guidance and support, and that she might be brought through the bitter trial that has riven her heart, to the full enjoyment of health and happiness.

With the death of His Royal Highness ended the long line of Kings, Earls, and Dukes of Kent, covering a period of 1365 years, during which the men of Kent figured more conspicuously in history than almost any other of the inhabitants of our English counties, and who had, before the Christian era, elicited the admiration of Julius Cæsar, when he pronounced them as possessing knowledge of tillage and agriculture, and from whose progress in civilization was manifested an amount of intelligence and friendliness to foreigners over every other part of the island.

ROMAN ANTIQUITIES.

ALTHOUGH we possess little to enlighten us as to the aborigines of the British Isles, more especially of the Welsh, yet Herodotus, who flourished five centuries before Christ, tells us of intercourse between distant nations and the Tin Islands, or Cassiterides (Cornwall), and that merchant vessels traded there from Phœnicia and Carthage many centuries before the invasion of Julius Cæsar, which proves beyond doubt that metallurgy was known in Britain even at that remote period. Thus it may be fairly assumed that the discovery of metals was not only the first means for bringing the nations of the East into intercourse with the ancient Britons, but also an important medium towards civilization.

KENT, as already shown, occupies the early chapters of British History; and as all the events identical with Cæsar's invasion of Britain previous to the Christian era were enacted in this county, when Kent was governed by four kings or chiefs, some notice of the Roman Antiquities still remaining may not inappropriately form the subject of our present sketch.

Under the Roman dynasty Britain was divided into four divisions, and was governed by Roman laws, dispensed mostly by Roman officers. Kent was included in that division called *Britannia Prima*, in which several permanent stations, occasional encampments, and military roads were established.

Julius Agricola, the better to secure his conquests against the inroads of the Caledonians, built during the first century a chain of forts between the Frith of Forth and the Clyde, as was supposed had been previously done between the Solway Frith and the Tyne. Early in the second century, the Emperor Adrian erected a rampart or wall of earth, sixty-two miles in length, from the Tyne to Solway Frith, to intercept the inroads of the Scots and Picts, by whom the Romans were much harassed—all south of that line being civilized and within the Roman pale. This rampart having proved wholly insufficient, the Emperor Severus undertook the stupendous task of building a wall twelve feet high, eight feet thick, and sixty-eight miles in length, of which some grand remains are still to be seen. This magnificent work was accomplished in the incredibly short period of two years, and bore the name of *'Picts' Wall.'* The Emperor Severus lived in Britain several years, his chief residence being at York (*Eboracum*), where he died in the year 211. After

c

his death the Southern Coast—KENT—suffered severely from the incursions of the Franks and Germans, and not less from the exactions of the Roman governors.

Whilst Britain was under Roman rule, their Emperor Constantius married the British Princess Helena, by whom he had a son. Constantius died at York in the year 274, when this son (Constantine the Great) became emperor: a memorable fact, inasmuch as Constantine the Great was the *first* Christian emperor,—his mother a Briton, and he born at York, one of the archiepiscopal sees of England.

Rome, harassed by the inroads of neighbouring states, withdrew from Britain the larger portion of her troops, after which the Emperor Honorius, finding it impossible to maintain possession of the nation without a powerful army, finally abandoned the island, A.D. 410.

The great Roman line of road passing through KENT was called Watling Street; it commenced at Dover (*Dubris*), and extended to London (*Londinium*), with stations at Canterbury (*Durovernum*), Rochester (*Durolevum*), and Southfleet (*Vagniacæ*). A second road branched from Canterbury to Reculver (*Regulbium*), another from Canterbury to Richborough (*Rutipium*), and the *Portus Lemanis*, called Stone-way: beyond these others have been discovered in Kent, but without any distinguishing names.

Many interesting antiquities have been dug up in these lines of road, including coins, implements in brass and iron, pottery, weapons, and other interesting relics. Some remains of these Roman stations and roads still exist: a portion of the station at Reculver is to be seen, of which a large part has been washed away by the inroads of the sea. Amongst the most perfect Roman remains in Kent is Richborough Castle, covering an area of five acres within the walls, at the angles of which are round towers. Some approximate idea of the strength of this grand ruin may be formed from the structure and thickness of its walls, built of solid blocks of stone and chalk, faced within, as well as without, by other blocks of stone, making the thickness of the walls upwards of eleven feet. Near Richborough Castle are the remains of a Roman Amphitheatre, measuring upwards of two hundred feet in diameter.

The Old Church in Dover Castle is another interesting relic. According to ancient chronicles of Dover, it was built A.D. 156, and is supposed to have been a Specula or Watch-tower. The arches are of Roman brick, and the other portions of stone cut by the Romans; the style of building resembles that of Richborough Castle. A coin of Diocletian was found here during the last century.

Saltwood Castle, a mile north-west of Hythe, was supposed to have been built by the Romans for defence against the piratical attempts of the Saxons. Several Roman antiquities have, at different times, been dug up in the neighbourhood, and an anchor was ploughed up in the valley near the castle, which indicates that the sea once covered that place and formed the castle harbour. About two miles west of Hythe stood the Roman fortress ' *Ad Portum Lemanis*,' of which some remains exist, affording good evidence of its strength and stately proportions.

On a hill near Farnborough Roman coins, bricks, and tiles have been found, and the remains of a Roman encampment clearly traced.

Canterbury also has many relics. Roman bricks were used in building portions of the city walls, and several arches of Roman brick were remaining until the end of the eighteenth century ; south of Canterbury a square camp with elliptic corners was clearly defined.

At Southfleet, near Gravesend, many interesting antiquities were found. Amongst these was a Roman milestone, an earthen urn containing funeral reliquiæ, pottery, coins, and other ancient curiosities. As recently as October 1864 some walls of Roman buildings have been grubbed up in a field adjoining Springhead Gardens, composed of flints and tiles, proving that a number of Roman dwellings stood on this spot, which was probably a station— the *Vagniacæ* of Antonius. Mr. Roach Smith, in his ' *Collectanea Antiqua*,' has already given plates of Springhead antiquities ; and Mr. E. Colyer, some years since, liberally offered every facility to the British Archæological Association for regular excavations, which would doubtless unfold most interesting remains.

Between Halstow and Rainham several Roman potteries were discovered, containing numerous fragments of classic vessels, amply sufficient to illustrate the beauty of Roman art in this particular manufacture.

Rochester has liberally contributed its share of Roman antiquities, which have at various periods been dug up. In the mouldering walls of the cathedral precincts Roman bricks have been largely used.

The principal of the Roman antiquities dug up in Kent have been in the line of their Watling Street, which was little removed from the line of the old stage-coach road between London and Canterbury. Many remains of the Roman Watling Street still exist, which may be seen at Blackheath, Bexley-heath, Dartford, Stone, Southfleet, and Rochester. Again, beyond Canterbury, the Roman road known as ' *Stone Stre t*' is traceable, and of which many vestiges are distinguishable for three miles.

Comparatively few Mosaic pavements have been found in Kent, and those of indifferent execution in comparison with the elaborate and truly elegant specimens dug up in London ; but Kent was great as the stronghold of the Romans—great in castles and forts, encampments and military roads, with a barbican or watch-tower at Dover to command the Channel, and a native people, brave and generous, who learned the art of warfare while under Roman rule, and afterwards became the most distinguished warriors in Britain,—a people whose prowess is chronicled in history. and whose valour maintained KENT an independent kingdom through several centuries.

c 2

PRODUCTS AND RESOURCES.

THE county of Kent is divided into two parts : that portion comprising the laths of St. Augustine and Shipway, with the upper section of the lath of Scray, being the Eastern Division ; and the laths of Sutton-at-Hone and Aylesford, with the lower portion of Scray, forming the Western Division.

Kent, geologically considered, presents considerable varieties of soil, the principal of which are chalk, flint, gravel, and clay, mostly found in parallel strata, to attempt a full description of which would far exceed the limit and purpose of these desultory scraps : suffice it therefore to remark, that this fertile county possesses in a high degree natural, as well as acquired, advantages over most of our English counties.

Early in the Saxon Heptarchy the Weald (Saxon for *woody country*) was a wild desert without human habitation, but well stocked with deer and wild hogs. According to HASTED, royal donations of the pannage of hogs in the wealdy country were granted to the cathedral churches of Canterbury and Rochester.

When parishes extend into the wealdy country and their churches stand above the hill, the land is distinguished as Upland and Weald—thus, ' Seven Oaks Upland,' ' Seven Oaks Weald.' Perhaps one of the grandest scenes that can be contemplated on a fine autumn day is the Weald of Kent when viewed from the Upland, which presents the illusive appearance of an immense level country, carpeted with rich verdure of every hue, stretching to the farthest extent of vision ; bold lofty oaks, growing luxuriously, cover the surface,— mansions, villas, farmhouses, cottages, and quaint old churches, illumed by the sun, dot the distance ; whilst cattle browsing under shady trees in rich pastures, the golden crops nodding to the passing zephyr, and the feathered songster of the wood carolling forth in beauty and variety of melody, combine to form a picture surpassingly beautiful.

The Oak may be considered as indigenous to Kent from the suitability of the soil. The British navy has for ages drawn large supplies from this source. Some of these trees attain gigantic proportions, instanced by HASTED, who describes an oak felled in

Penshurst Park as producing twenty-one tons of timber, equal to eight hundred and forty feet.

Kent, according to history, was celebrated for the number and extent of ancient parks. Of fifty-three, however, during the reign of Elizabeth only about eight remain.

Although the soils of Kent are mostly of chalk, gravel, and clay, yet they exist in such variety as to be adapted to almost every purpose of agriculture. Thus the Isle of Thanet, with a rich mould on a chalk foundation, produces abundantly wheat, barley, oats, and other valuable grains; filberts are grown successfully on gravelly and rocky soils; other districts grow freely on a heavy clay mixed with shells from the sea-shore, each having their distinctive value under the culture of Kentish farmers, who have won considerable reputation.

The London markets are largely supplied from Kent with the finest of fruits and vegetables. Where is the visitor to this health-restoring county who, whilst luxuriating in its picturesque beauties, has not felt tempted when beholding its orchards borne down with magnificent fruits ?

Hops are cultivated to an immense extent; nearly half the consumption of the entire nation is grown in Kent, which gives employment to great numbers of the neighbouring poor, as well as in the manufacture of bags or pockets. During harvest many thousands of men, women, and children are imported from Ireland, and all parts of the United Kingdom, as pickers of this valuable product,—called, during the reign of Henry VIII., ' The wicked weed.'

Romney Marsh has been from time immemorial devoted to grazing. The maintenance of its embankments is vested in lords of neighbouring manors, who are designated ' The Lords of the Marsh.' It consists of some twenty thousand acres of rich soft loam, intermixed with shells and sand. From one hundred and fifty to two hundred thousand sheep, besides oxen, are annually grazed on this level, a number by far exceeding that of any other district in England of like dimensions. Sheep fed on this marsh are much celebrated for excellence of flavour and superiority of wool. The trunks of immense trees have been frequently dug up, resembling, both in colour and hardness, the wood known as Lignum vitæ.

Every luxury that can be desired is produced in Kent and sent to London in large quantities. The meats, as already shown, especially mutton, are in large demand, and secure the best of prices; poultry large and well fattened ; fish excellent, caught on its own shores and promptly sent to market ; oysters superior to all others ; venison and game abundant; luscious fruits and vegetables, including asparagus, second to none ; and if we add hops (without which where would be our sparkling ' October?'), nothing is wanting that can gratify the palate of the epicure, or of the less craving of mankind.

MARBLE is a product of Kent, known as Bethersden marble, the name of the place near Ashford where found. It was formerly in considerable request for pillars in churches, tombs, monuments, and ornamental chimneypieces. It is mostly grey and turbinated, and said to be brittle and easily broken after a few years' exposure to the atmosphere—hence the demand has become inconsiderable.

RAGSTONE is quarried near Maidstone, and carried to market on the Thames and Medway. It is a valuable product, and in good request for public building in London and elsewhere. The new church of St. Philip, Kennington, lately consecrated by the Bishop of London, is built of Kentish ragstone, with carved facings, and presents a handsome appearance.

SALT is another natural product of Kent, obtainable at Sandwich and the Isle of Thanet.

PYRITES and LIMESTONE abound in Kent, the former in the rocks of the Isle of Sheppey, and the latter in green sand formations, as well as in quarries at Maidstone.

CHALK for ages has been an article of commerce, dug from the long range of hills in the central and eastern parts of Kent, terminating in the cliffs at Dover. These formations contain nodules of flint and fossilised organic remains. The chalk is either made into lime, and shipped on the Thames or Medway, or supplied to numberless craft leaving the port of London, as ballast, at either Northfleet or Gravesend.

LIME was from a very early date an article of commerce. We read that the Danes and other foreign nations, many centuries since, purchased lime in Kent; and also that, when the old wall of London was thoroughly repaired between Aldgate, Cripplegate, and Aldersgate, in the year 1477, the lime was brought from Kent, near Northfleet.

FLINT was extensively used by the ancients as well as chalk for building, of which we have ample evidence in the grand ruins spread over the face of this county; it was also used in the ceramic art, and in the manufacture of glass, and is still in request for building purposes, for decorative walls, and for the ornamentation of garden walks and grotto-work.

IRON ORE, which is found in the Weald, or lowlands, was formerly extensively worked and manufactured between the Homesdale Vale and the Hastings Ridge, until sea-coal became the substitute for charcoal, when, the cost of labour not being compensated, it was abandoned as a failure in commerce.

The people of Kent may be distinguished as nobility, gentry, yeomen, tradesmen, artificers, seafaring men, and labourers, whose possessions in it were at first described as 'Knights Fee' and 'Gavelkind;' the former relating to the soldier, and the latter to the husbandman.

The Yeomanry comprehend the principal farmers and landowners, who are mostly rich, and are generally styled '*gentlemen farmers.*' The common yeomanry, as implied, are working farmers ; this class generally hire a single farm, in addition to the land they may have inherited ; from these come the labourers, the eldest son succeeding to the homestead, and the rest sharing in their father's land by the custom of '*Gavelkind.*' Hence, from the wide distribution and number of freeholds belonging to all grades, a good feeling generally exists between the gentry and yeomanry, their lands being everywhere intermixed.

GAVELKIND, or the common law of Kent, refers to the tenure of land. When the kingdoms of the heptarchy were united in the ninth century, Kent retained much of its former importance, through which it is said that William the Conqueror, after his victory at Hastings, entered into a convention with the people of Kent, securing to them their ancient rights and privileges, as the condition of their admitting his claim to the crown ; thus the custom of '*Gavelkind*' has been preserved in this county, while it has been abolished in almost every other part of England, and cannot be taken away by any change of tenure, or by any other means than by Act of Parliament.

The customs incident to '*Gavelkind*' are,—that the husband, after the death of his wife, enjoys a moiety of her inheritance in courtesy, whether he has children by her or not, until he again marries ; the wife also in like manner claims a moiety of his lands so long as she remains unmarried. Lands in '*Gavelkind*' are not forfeited to the Crown, even if the tenant be convicted of felony. *Gavelkind* lands descend in equal shares to all the sons, and if no sons, then to the daughters in just proportions : formerly it was part of the custom, after payment of debts and funeral expenses, to divide the residue into three parts,—one for the payment of legacies, a second for the education of the children, and the remainder for the benefit of the widow. It is from this law, doubtless, that Kent boasts its long race of yeomen, which exempted the natives from the tenure of bondage generally imposed in olden times, when it was only necessary for a man to prove that his father was born in Kent to establish his freedom.

TOPOGRAPHICAL SKETCHES.

CANTERBURY.

Chapter I.

The city of Canterbury, as the capital of Kent and the see of the Primate of All England, claims the foremost place in our topographical sketches.

Canterbury (the Roman *Durovernum*, and the Saxon *Cantwarabyrig*) is about fifty-five miles S.E. of London by road; in history it is famous as the scene of many battles during the wars with the Romans, Saxons, and Normans.

According to some writers, a castle was erected here in the time of Ludhudibras, who, Stow says, lived eight hundred and thirty-six years before Christ, and founded this city. Kilburn, on the other hand, ascribes to Julius Cæsar the first castle, which Hengist (King of Kent) gave to Lodias, a Saxon, who resided therein, and named it after himself as Lodias' Castle. It was afterwards destroyed by the Danes when they burned Canterbury, and remained a ruin until the Conquest. William built on the ancient foundation another castle, which he garrisoned with seven hundred men, and surrounded by a wall six feet in thickness and nearly two miles in circumference, with a deep ditch in front, called ' the Ditch of the Ballium,' or advanced work.

The passage from the city lay over a bridge, and beyond that through a gate, built at the entrance of the castle; little of the outworks are remaining except the foundations. The ruined body of the castle, however, is still standing; it is built of rough stone, and is nearly square, each external side measuring about eighty-seven feet in length, ten feet in thickness, and fifty feet in height.

Worthgate is universally acknowledged to be of great antiquity. Leland says, ' *The most ancient building of the towne appeareth yn the Castel, and at Ryder's-gate, where appere long Briton brikes.*'

Grose, in his 'Antiquities,' adds, 'The old way to London was along Castle-street, and through this gate,' which Somner considers took its name from the castle—*Worth* signifying fort or castle. The height of the gate, from the crown to the ground, is thirteen feet; seven feet is of brick, the remainder of squared stone.

The ruins of the Chapel of St. Pancrace stand south-east of the Abbey-close, and are considered to be of great antiquity. Thorn supposes it to have been a place of idol worship before Augustine came, and afterwards consecrated to the service of God. The Venerable Bede questions Thorn's accuracy; while Grose, remarking on the east window as being of pointed architecture, invalidates any pretensions to that portion being of very remote antiquity. Batteley, in his additions to Somner, pronounces this chapel as built by King Eadbald in honour of the Virgin Mary, and that St. Dunstan spent, at midnight, much time therein at his devotions.

Augustine founded a monastery in the year 605, which was dedicated to the Apostles Paul and Peter. It will be remembered that Augustine was the instrument by which the Saxon King of Kent, Ethelbert, was converted from paganism to Christianity, and who gave lands for the erection of a monastery, which he designed to be the future place of sepulture for the Kings of Kent; he also gave his palace at Canterbury, it being prohibited by the law of the Twelve Tables to bury in any city. Archbishop Dunstan, in 987, added St. Augustine to the former dedication of this monastery, by which name it has since been commonly known. Grose asserts that it possessed 9,862 acres of land; that benefactors, royal, noble, and private, vied with each other in enriching this the parent of our universities, which was, as Black phrases it, 'the seat of letters and study at a time when Cambridge was a desolate fen, and Oxford a tangled forest in a wide waste of waters.'

Amongst its many privileges and immunities was the right of magistracy, or the power of judging thieves taken within its jurisdiction, and, for a long period, the liberty of mintage.

It possessed the exclusive right of cemetery for the Kings of Kent, until the days of Archbishop Brightwald, during which period Kings Ethelbert, Eadbald, Ercombert, Lothair, Edelbert, and Widred were buried there.

In 1011 this monastery was plundered by the Danes; in 1168 the church was almost destroyed by fire, and a fearful storm in 1271 nearly ruined the entire monastery by inundation.

The numerous buildings constituting this religious house were the creations of different individuals, at different periods: Ethelbert's tower, so called from a bell of that name hanging in it, was built by Archbishop Eadsin; a church built by Eadbalden was taken down and rebuilt by the Abbot Wido in 1099; the dormitories and chapter-house were erected by Hugo Florie, a kinsman of William Rufus, and the cemetery gate by a monk.

At the resignation of this monastery to Henry VIII. in 1539, the
establishment comprised a lord abbot and sixty monks, after which
it remained in possession of the crown until the end of the reign of
Edward VI. (1553), when a portion became the mansion of Lord
Wolton—at which palace, it is said, Charles I. consummated his marriage with the Princess Henrietta of France, A.D. 1625.

Some of the exterior walls of this monastery still remain, as well
as traces of buildings evidently erected at different periods, demonstrating that a large surface was once covered by them. In 1765
the tower was ordered to be taken down for the value of the material,
but time had so hardened the cement that the cost of labour by far
exceeded the worth of the stone, when the project was abandoned.
The precincts of the Augustine monastery described an area of
sixteen acres, and the length of the west front alone of the abbey
measured 250 feet.

After the dissolution many of the buildings were pulled down;
still some were left to moulder and decay, of which a few choice
relics remain, to mark the spot where Christianity was first propounded to a nation of idolaters—that spot where King Ethelbert,
in the sixth century, built the first Christian church, the precursor
of the present cathedral of Canterbury, amidst the most formidable
of impediments, and from which sprung the light of Gospel truth—
that Gospel which Britons have sent to every land and tribe in their
native tongue, which, like good seed, may lie long in the soil, but
which germinates, though in darkness, and rises at last into day-
light, and ripens into the nutritious grain, blossoms in the beautiful
flower, and expands into the vast and majestic monarch of the forest.

CHAPTER II.

CANTERBURY CATHEDRAL stands the proud ornament of the city,
a glorious relic of early Church history, the grand mausoleum of
kings, princes, and the most distinguished of our early ecclesiastics.
It is built in the form of a double cross, and displays in beauty of
architecture every variety of style, from the eleventh to the sixteenth century. The length of this magnificent structure, from east
to west is 514 feet; length of the choir, 180 feet; height of great
tower, 235 feet; north-west tower, 100 feet; and of the south-west
tower, 130 feet.

The present cathedral stands on the site of a church built in the
ninth century, which was partially destroyed by fire by the Danes
in 1011 and afterwards restored, but again became nearly a ruin
from a like conflagration. Archbishop Lanfranc caused the ruins
to be cleared towards the close of the eleventh century, and founded
the present gorgeous pile.

Archbishop Anselm, his successor, continued the work, and built the choir and the eastern end on a scale of greater magnificence ; Anselm's successor, Archbishop Ralph, completed the whole ; which according to Gervase, was dedicated in 1130 ' *with a splendour and magnificence which had never been heard of on earth since the dedication of Solomon's Temple,*' in the presence of Henry I. and his Consort, King David of Scotland, and nearly the whole of the nobles and prelates.

The principal entrance is from the south. The west window is rich in painted glass, with full-length figures of Canute, Edward the Confessor, Harold, William the Conqueror, William Rufus, Henry I., and Stephen, with other figures of the Apostles and Saints ; the north window of the west transept is filled with stained glass, and another window to correspond at the south end. The Dean's chapel is an exquisite example of pointed architecture : the north division of this transept is called the ' *Martyrdom*,' being the spot where Becket was murdered ; the choir aisles are interesting from the fact of the walls being those built by Lanfranc eight centuries since, at the end of which is a semicircular aisle surrounding the chapel of the Holy Trinity : here was formerly the venerated Shrine of Becket, where pilgrims crowded to pay their devotions and enrich the treasury of the Church. To form some approximate idea of the immense value of the shrine, we quote STOW's description, wherein he says :—' *It was built about a man's height, all of stone ; then upwards of timber, plain ; within the which was a chest of iron, containing the bones of Thomas Becket, skull and all, with the wound of his death, and the piece cut out of his skull laid in the same wound ;— these bones, by command of Lord Cromwell (September 1538) were there and then burned : the timber-work of this Shrine, on the outside, was covered with plates of gold, damasked with gold wire, which ground of gold was again covered with jewels of gold, as rings ten or twelve crumped with gold wire into the said ground of gold, many of those rings having stones in them ; broaches, images, angels, precious stones, and great orient pearls ; the spoil of which shrine in gold and precious stones filled two great chests, requiring six or seven strong men to convey each one from the church.*'

Anterior to the dissolution there were nearly forty altars in the cathedral, many of which were splendid in an eminent degree. The high altar especially is said to have been ' *ornamented as richly as gold, silver, jewellery, and costly art could adorn it,*' and that the '*richest monarchs might be considered as mere beggars in comparison with the abundance of silver and gold which it exhibited.*' The Sacristy, according to HASTED, '*was filled with jewellery and with candlesticks, cups, pixes, and crosses of every size, made of silver and gold.*' The pomp attendant on their religious ceremonies in those times may in some degree be estimated, for, according to BATTELEY, '*seven wax candles in seven branches weighed fifty pounds—procession candles weighed ten pounds each, and the weight of the Pascal taper was three hundred pounds.'*

The vestments and copes of the priests were beyond number, and of the richest damask and velvet gorgeously embroidered with gold and silver, and of immense value, as shown by the inventory taken at the dissolution, when they were carried away for the king's use. We have no estimate of the value or number of the relics, although ' DART'S CANTERBURY ' fills eight folio pages with a partial description of them.

The east transept has a window filled with fine painted glass, representing Ezekiel, Daniel, Isaiah, and Jeremiah; the Norman architecture in this transept leaves little doubt of its being a portion of Archbishop Lanfranc's building early in the eleventh century.

The nave has an aisle on each side, from which it is separated by eight bays, supported on columns. The choir-screen was constructed very early in the fourteenth century, and is a grand specimen of rich carving and niched statues. The organ, formerly on the screen, is now hidden ' in the triforium of the south aisle of the choir ;' still it is played in the choir, the action being brought down the south wall, and then under the pavement to the manuals, upwards of ninety feet from the instrument.

The monuments in the choir are mostly of black and white marble and alabaster, richly sculptured and otherwise decorated by gilding and painting; amongst them are those of Archbishops Meopham, who died in 1333 ; Stratford, died 1341 ; Bradwardine, died 1349 ; Chicheley, died 1443 ; Kemp, died 1454 ; Bourchier, died 1486 ; Reynolds, Walter, and that of Archbishop Sudbury, who was cruelly beheaded, in 1381, by the infamous Jack Cade.

In the chapel of the Holy Trinity are numerous tombs and monuments, rich in sumptuous sculpture and high decoration ; amongst the most noteworthy is the tomb of William the Conqueror, supporting a full-length figure in armour, the head resting on a helmet, the hands clasped, and the whole gilded. The monument of Henry IV. and his Queen Joan of Navarre (1413) ; their figures, in royal robes crowned, rest on the tomb. The tomb of Edward the Black Prince next arrests attention, supporting the figure of himself as a warrior in full armour. A rich cenotaph to the memory of Archbishop Courtenay represented in his pontificals ; this tomb is a highly decorated specimen of pointed Gothic architecture. The most ancient tomb is opposite to the cenotaph, and supposed to be that of Archbishop Theobald, probably erected after the rebuilding of this part of the cathedral.

We must now, however reluctantly, take leave of this gorgeous sanctuary, so full of interest as an historical monument, marking the grandeur of the past, in beauty of architecture, richness of decorations. and, above all, as a temple dedicated to God almost from the dawn of Christianity in Britain.

CHAPTER III.

ANCIENT historians assert that at the time of the Conquest (A.D. 1066) Canterbury exceeded London in its buildings, and that by the bounty of its prelates it rose to such splendour, as even, for the beauty of its private buildings, to equal any city in Britain, but for the magnificence of its churches, and their number, to surpass the best of them.

The prelates in those days were remarkable for hospitality, and lived in common with their monks, until Archbishop Lanfranc came to the see in 1070, when he abolished community of living, and built a distinct palace for his separate residence, of which a few remains may be traced. Archbishop Hubert built in the thirteenth century a new palace, and a noble hall, in which his hospitality, as well as that of his successors, was dispensed with great liberality.

It was in this hall that the nuptials of Edward I., in the year 1299, were kept in great splendour, after the king's marriage to Margaret, sister of the King of France; we read that the feast lasted four days, and that most of the nobility were present. Archbishop Warham also was distinguished for the festivities of his time; he gave a magnificent ball, during the Whitsuntide of 1520, to the Emperor Charles V., who danced with the Queen of England, and Henry VIII. with the Emperor's mother, the Queen of Arragon. Queen Elizabeth partook of a grand banquet in this hall on the 7th September, 1573, being the anniversary of her birth, at which were present a brilliant assemblage of the leading nobility. This hall was taken down during the Commonwealth.

St. Martin's Church calls for special notice from its remote antiquity; it is built mostly of Roman and British bricks, which are invariably considered proofs of very early date; it has a nave and chancel. This venerable sanctuary stands about half a mile from the wall of the city, on the side of a hill, and is supposed to have been one of two churches built by the Christians of the Roman army in the time of Lucius, who lived in the year 182; if so, and historians are fairly agreed, this must be one of, if not the oldest church in the kingdom.

Gostling tells us that the materials and the architecture of this most simple church fully warrant this conclusion; he further assumes that Queen Bertha might find it more convenient to pay her devotions in this obscure chapel than to erect one more suitable to her rank, while her husband, King Ethelbert, and his subjects were idolaters.

Here, therefore, was a Christian church and congregation settled, with a queen and her chaplain (Luidhard, Bishop of Soissons), before St. Augustine and his monks made their appearance in England, and where, according to Somner, did he and his fellow-labourers resort to their devotions on their first arrival, by the license of King Ethelbert. The visitor to this venerable piece of antiquity must not omit noticing the font, probably of the same date as the structure, where seventeen hundred years since children were baptized in the Christian faith. During the last century, a Roman tessellated pavement was found in Canterbury four feet below the surface; it was a fair specimen of mosaic, of a diamond pattern, the *tessellæ* of burnt earth, red, yellow, black, and white; their shapes and sizes varying, some being an inch across, others exceedingly small, laid on a bed of thick hard mortar almost sufficient to allow of its removal entire : some three feét by five was recovered. Further portions were buried under party-walls, which prevented their dimensions being ascertained : in 1824, however, while digging the foundations of some houses, other parts of this pavement were discovered, which are now in the possession of a gentleman resident in Canterbury.

Dane John Hill is supposed to be the work of the Danes when they besieged Canterbury during the reign of King Ethelbert. This immense mound has been carefully planted and laid out as a promenade, with walks and beautiful shrubs; the lower part of the enclosure is shaded with poplar trees; upon the top is a round gravelled plat and a stone pillar terminating with an ornamental urn, which was erected by subscription in 1803, and £60 per annum voted in perpetuity by the corporation, as the salary of a gardener for keeping the whole in repair. From this eminence, the city, the majestic cathedral, the surrounding villages, and the gently rising hills form a most beautiful and pleasing landscape. Formerly a deep and wide ditch encircled the base, in which were found Roman coins, the head of a spear, spurs of brass, and other interesting relics.

We shall conclude our chapters on Canterbury by culling from Hasted, Madox, Ireland, and others, some of the remarkable events that occurred in this city :—

King Henry I., in 1129, kept his court at Canterbury with great splendour.

King Stephen was supposed by Hasted to have died here, 25th October 1154.

William King of Scotland, in 1189, paid homage to Richard I. at Canterbury.

King John, in 1204, kept the festival of Christmas here with great splendour, as also did King Henry III. in 1263.

In the reign of Edward I., in the year 1272, a fearful tempest burst over this city, when the inundations submerged many dwellings and drowned several persons.

In 1299 Canterbury received a shock from an earthquake, which was felt many miles distant.

In 1347 a famous tournament was celebrated in this city, when Thomas de Grey received from Edward III. 'a hood of white cloth richly embroidered with figures, which buttoned before with costly pearls.'

At mid-day on the 21st May, 1382, another earthquake shattered the eastern window of the chapter-house, and damaged many buildings of note.

In 1469 Edward IV. repaired to Canterbury, when the mayor, Nicholas Faunte, and others were executed for having abetted Falconbridge.

Henry VIII. met the Emperor Charles V. at Canterbury (1520) with the nobility of England and Spain, when they were entertained at a grand banquet and ball by Archbishop Warham.

In 1573 Queen Elizabeth kept her court at the Palace of St. Augustine, where she was sumptuously feasted by Archbishop Parker.

In 1625, as already stated, Charles I., with his consort, celebrated their marriage at the Palace of St. Augustine's Monastery.

Charles II. with his brothers, the Dukes of York and Gloucester, sojourned three days at the Palace of St. Augustine on their way to London in 1660.

George IV., when Prince of Wales, in 1798, was presented with the freedom of Canterbury, and dined with the mayor; he afterwards patronised a public ball, in aid of funds for the relief of the widows and children of those who had fallen in the victory just gained by Nelson.

———◆◇◆———

ROCHESTER.

CHAPTER I.

THE city of Rochester may appropriately follow that of Canterbury, as being an episcopal see, as well as a place of considerable importance during the Roman dynasty, when it was the accustomed pass over the River Medway.

Most of our antiquaries are unanimous in allowing it to be the *Durobrivæ* of Antonius, situated twenty-seven miles from London. The remains of the Roman road (*Watling Street*), visible from Shinglewell, by Cobham Park, though lost in the coppice, is again to be traced on Chatham Hill, on its way to Canterbury and Richborough.

There is no evidence of a bridge at Rochester over the Medway for centuries after the Romans; probably a ferry was the mode of conveyance. There was, however, a bridge before the Conquest, and certain lands were made chargeable for its maintenance, and which bridge, like the present, was in the line of street between Rochester and Strood. Being built of wood it required frequent reparation, and becoming dangerous for passengers, Sir Robert Knolles and Sir John de Cobham built a bridge of stone in the fourteenth century.

King Ethelbert built the church of St. Andrew in 597, and made it a bishop's see, which gave it a distinguished place in ecclesiastical and civil history.

When Ethelred, King of Mercia, invaded Kent in 676, he destroyed this city, and returned with the plunder to his own kingdom. Rochester frequently suffered from the ravages of the Danes, and at length submitted, with the rest of the nation, to the yoke of these marauders. Henry III., however, resolved to augment its strength, when he repaired and restored the city walls, and commenced a large ditch.

Rochester, from lying in the direct route from the Continent to London, was famous for royal and illustrious visitors. Without plunging deeply into history for early instances, it may suffice to commence with Queen Elizabeth, who in 1573 abode in this city five days, attended Divine service at the cathedral, and dined with Mr. Watts at his house on Bully Hill.

King James I. and the King of Denmark were present at a sermon preached in the cathedral in 1606 by Dr. Parry, Dean of Chester, who was esteemed as the most eloquent preacher of his time.

King Charles II., on his restoration in 1660, was sumptuously entertained by the mayor and corporation, who presented him with a costly silver bason and ewer.

King James II., on his abdication, came to Rochester (December 19th, 1688), and resided with Sir Richard Head until the 23rd of that month, when he embarked on board a tender in the Medway.

Her late Royal Highness the Duchess of Kent, with Her Majesty, then Princess Victoria, visited Rochester 29th November 1836, where they remained until the following day.

In the year 1856 Her Majesty, with that sympathy so beautifully adorning her character, frequently passed through Rochester on her way to the military hospital at Chatham, when visiting the sick and suffering soldiers from the Crimea.

William the Conqueror gave Rochester to his half-brother Odo, Bishop of Bayeux, on whose disgrace, in 1083, it was confiscated to the crown.

Henry I. let the city to farm at pleasure to the townsmen, at an annual rent of £20, and granted to Bishop Gundulph and the church at Rochester one fair, yearly.

Henry II., by charter, also granted the city for £20 a year, with sundry other privileges.

Richard I. commanded that no person, except his own servants, should purchase food in the city until after the monks of St. Andrew's had been supplied, much to the disgust and inconvenience of the citizens.

Formerly a toll called Maltolt was received from all persons passing through the city to embark for the Holy Land, which was abolished by Richard I.

Henry III. confirmed the charter of Henry II., and in recompense for the faithful services of the citizens, remitted part of their annual fee, and extended their privileges.

Edward I., in the eighth year of his reign (A.D. 1280), granted Rochester to John de Cobham at a like annual rental; but Edward III., in 1331, reconfirmed to the citizens King Henry III.'s charter.

Henry VI. granted to the Bailiff and Citizens the passage of the ferry between the city and Strood, the bridge being broken.

Edward IV., in 1460, in consideration of the loyalty and services of the citizens of Rochester, confirmed to them former charters, and granted that, instead of a bailiff, they should be constituted as the ' Mayor and Citizens.' These charters and privileges were again confirmed by Henry VIII. and Charles I.

The City of Rochester consists of one principal street of considerable length, having several avenues of houses on either side; the new bridge over the Medway bounds it westward, and the town of Chatham towards the east. The houses are generally well-built, and inhabited by persons of wealth and condition. The Town Hall, on the north side of High Street, was erected in 1687. It is a handsome structure, built of brick, supported by stone columns of the Doric order. The ancient guildhall of the city stood on the spot where the present clock-house is erected, in which is the clock given by Sir Cloudesley Shovel in 1706.

Richard Watts, an eminent merchant of Rochester, founded, in 1579, a Hospital for six poor travellers, not being ' *rogues or procters*;' each traveller to have a lodging for the night, a supper, and fourpence on his departure next morning. Out of funds bequeathed by the same noble benefactor, new Almshouses for twenty poor men and women have been built on the Maidstone Road, over the entrance of which, under an archway, is carved in stone, ' *Watts' Almshouses*, erected A.D. 1858.' A monument containing the bust of this excellent man is placed in the south transept of Rochester Cathedral.

Sir Joseph Williamson's Free School, in High Street, was founded for the education of the sons of Rochester freemen. Many distinguished naval officers owe their early education to this school, which formerly was more devoted to the acquirement of mathematics than at present.

Rochester, from its having been a station situated at so important a passage over the Medway, might well be supposed to have been fortified by the Romans; such an opinion is strengthened by the Roman bricks still visible in several parts of the walls, and the variety of Roman coins, from the time of Vespasian downwards, which have been found in the ruins of the castle. In the time of the Saxon Heptarchy Rochester continued a fortress of considerable account. The entire city, as well as the church, was within the walls, comprehended under the name of *Castrum* and *Castellum Hrofesceastre*, by which the whole was understood, and not any particular castle or tower in it.

D

The Castle, the venerable relic of which has for many centuries attracted the attention of every traveller, is situated on an eminence joining the River Medway, at the south-west angle of the city walls; it is nearly quadrangular, three hundred feet square within the walls, which were seven feet in thickness, and twenty feet above the present level, with embrasures; three sides were surrounded with a deep ditch, the Medway flowing on the remaining side; in the angles and sides of the walls were several square towers. That noble ruin usually called Rochester Castle was the keep or large tower which stands at the south-east corner of it, so lofty as to be seen several miles distant; it is a quadrangle of upwards of seventy feet square at the base, and the walls are twelve feet thick. There were three stories of large and lofty apartments, and beneath, a vault or dungeon for prisoners; in the centre of the building a well, two feet nine inches in diameter, wrought in the partition-wall, ascends through all the stories to the top of the tower, with each of which it has a communication. This tower, with its embattlements, is upwards of one hundred feet in height; a spiral staircase of 138 steps, in one angle, leads to the summit, from which a grand view of the surrounding country is obtained.. Considering the ages this fabric has been neglected, there are few buildings, perhaps, so perfect.

Henry I., in 1127, granted the custody of the castle to the Archbishop of Canterbury. Robert, Earl of Gloucester, Henry I.'s natural son, was afterwards a close prisoner in this fortress.

Henry III., in the year 1264, greatly increased the fortifications of Rochester Castle, when it was garrisoned to resist a siege. Shortly afterwards Simon, Earl of Leicester, marched into Kent to besiege it. Arriving at the western side, he found the passage of the bridge disputed; after being twice repulsed, the bridge (being of wood) was burned, and the enemy passed the river, spoiled the church, made a furious assault on the castle, and became master of every part of it, excepting the great tower. which resisted the siege during seven days, when the earl suddenly returned to London.

Gundulph, Bishop of Rochester, who had superintended the building of the White Tower in London, erected this tower in the eleventh century, which bears his name, and has proved a lasting monument of his fame through succeeding ages.

In 1272 there were two priests (kings chaplains) officiating in the castle, whose stipends were fifty shillings a year each. Sir John de Cobham was constable of this castle in 1289.

King James I., in 1613, granted the property or fee-simple of the Castle of Rochester to Sir Anthony Weldon, since which time it has continued in the same line of ownership.

Many estates in this county, Surrey, and Essex are held of the Castle of Rochester, by the tenure of 'CASTLE-GUARD;' of these the manor of Swanscombe is the principal.

CHAPTER II.

ALTHOUGH there is no mention of a bridge over the Medway at Rochester until the reign of Henry I., yet it is evident there must have been one some years before ; for Ernulfus, Bishop of Rochester A.D. 1116, has inserted in the *Textus Roffensis* several regulations for the repair of Rochester Bridge as an ancient custom.

Lambarde has given an extract from the *Textus Roffensis*, which describes this bridge as being made of wood, with nine piers and ten spaces equal in length to four hundred and thirty-one feet, which corresponds to the breadth of the river where it stood, in the line between Rochester and Strood. It is further shown that 'the owners of the manors and lands chargeable with the repairs were used, by ancient custom, to elect two men from amongst themselves to be wardens, or overseers, and that there was a wooden tower erected on the bridge, with strong gates, as a fortification for the defence of this passage into the city.'

Stow, in his Annals, writes 'that when King John, in 1215, besieged and took Rochester Castle, he attempted to burn the bridge ; but Robert Fitzwalter put out the fire, and saved it.' In 1281 several of the piers were swept away after a sudden thaw, and passengers had to cross in boats. It was repaired, but very imperfectly, in 1311-12, for Edward III., having made war with France, found it unsafe for the passage of his army. There is mention made of a drawbridge and barbican on the west side, both of which belonged to the king ; the master and wardens of Strood Hospital being bound to repair the bridge and wharf, from the drawbridge to its western end. Sir Robert Knolles and Sir John de Cobham built a new bridge of stone nearer to the castle, where the tide ran less strong, which was completed about the fifteenth year of King Richard II. (A.D. 1392). In 1394 it was enacted in parliament 'that all who were accustomed to pay any rents or customs to the old bridge should thenceforth pay them to the new one.' The length of this substantial bridge of stone was five hundred and sixty-six feet, with a stone parapet on each side, coped and surmounted with a railing of iron. It had eleven arches, supported by massive piers. It was repaired in 1492, but afterwards wholly neglected, and became so dilapidated that decay appeared inevitable, notwithstanding a toll had been levied on all passengers and carriages towards its support in the reign of Queen Mary, and also in that of Elizabeth.

Queen Elizabeth, however, instituted a commission, in 1574, to examine into these defects and devise means for their remedy, which commission was composed of the great officers of state and nobility, with several knights and gentlemen of the county.

In the execution of this important trust, though the Lord Treasurer, Lord Admiral, and many of the aristocracy gave themselves earnestly to the work, yet Sir Roger Manwood, Chief Baron of the

Exchequer, deserves special commendation for the laborious part he took throughout the whole. First he got the leases of the bridge lands cancelled which had been granted for long terms at minimum rents ; he then devised a plan for the perfect reformation and future conduct of both officers and matters relating to it, and caused all fees from lands tributary to the maintenance of the bridge to be enforced, which had not been done for many years; and, as a climax to his laudable zeal, he procured, in 1576, a statute for the better management of the trusts, whereby the estate became greatly improved, and the bridge repaired and ornamented.

In 1832 the wardens had a reserve-fund amounting to £25,000, and an annual income of £3,000, when they proposed the construction of a new bridge, the wear of nearly five centuries having rendered it expedient to determine future proceedings from the dilapidated condition of the old one. Sir William Cubitt was instructed to prepare the design for a new bridge, which was commenced in 1850, and opened on Wednesday, April 13, 1856. This bridge, like the former wooden bridge, connects Rochester and Strood in a direct line. It is built of iron, 485 feet in length, 40 feet in width ; and has three arches, two of 140 feet span, and the centre one 170; at the west end is a swing-bridge for the passage of large vessels. The bridge-wardens have in progress considerable improvements for widening the approaches from Rochester. The ancient Crown Hotel, immortalised by Shakspeare in his ' Henry IV.,' has been demolished, and a handsome new hotel erected nearly adjoining.

Sir John de Cobham, one of the founders of the stone bridge, built, in 1369, a chapel or chantry at the east end, of which an archway and portions of the wall still remain. In 1735 the bridge-wardens erected, on part of the site, a neat stone building, where they held their meetings.

St. Andrew's Church, built by King Ethelbert, at the instance of St. Augustine, towards the close of the sixth century, had a monastery adjoining it. Augustine appointed Justus to be bishop in 604, and placed secular priests in the monastery. When Gundulph became bishop he displaced the secular priests and substituted Benedictine monks, of whom there were sixty at his death. Bishop Gundulph rebuilt the church and enlarged the priory.

From the Conquest to the reign of Henry VIII. nearly every king granted some liberties and privileges as well to the Bishop of Rochester as to the prior of the convent, and confirmed also the grants of his predecessors.

The first prior was Ordowinus, who witnessed the charter of foundation, dated September 20, 1089. The last prior of this monastery was Walter Boxley: for Henry VIII., in the 31st year of his reign, granted a commission to the Archbishop of Canterbury, Lord George Cobham, and others, to receive the surrender of this priory ; and accordingly the prior and convent, by an instrument under their common seal, dated April 8, 1540, gave and granted their monastery, churches, manors, demesnes, and messuages to King Henry VIII., which deed was executed in the presence of a Master in Chancery.

The Priory of Rochester was valued at £486 11s. 5d. annual income, the whole of which passed into the king's hands; who, although empowered by parliament to erect new sees and ecclesiastical bodies out of the estates belonging to suppressed monasteries, allowed two years to elapse before any new ecclesiastical foundation was created at Rochester.

CHAPTER III.

On the 18th of June 1542 King Henry VIII. founded, within the precincts of the late monastery, Rochester Cathedral, to be the episcopal see of the Bishop of Rochester and his successors for ever; and he appointed the late prior there the first dean of this church, and Hugh Aprice, John Wildbore, Robert Johnson, John Symkins, Robert Salisbury, and Richard Engest the six prebendaries of it, which he incorporated by the name of ' the Dean and Chapter,' and granted to them 'the site and precincts of the late monastery, the church, and all things whatsoever in it,' with the power of appointing the inferior officers of the church—the king reserving to himself the power of nominating the dean and six prebendaries.

The Cathedral Church of Rochester is situated at a short distance from the south side of the High Street, within the ancient gate of the priory. Bishop Gundulph rebuilt this church in the year 1080, of which the west front of the cathedral, with its grand entrance, and the nave as far as the transept, are portions. Here are some grand remains of Norman architecture, evidently of an early period, bearing the sacred stamp of venerable antiquity in artistic elaboration. The west front is eighty-one feet in breadth : the principal entrance is in the centre, through an arch fluted, which forms numerous pillars and statues, when you descend by steps into the cathedral. The length from west to east is 306 feet; from the western entrance to the choir, 150 feet; and from the steps leading to the choir, 156 feet.

There are two transepts; the western one measures 122 feet, in the middle of which formerly stood a steeple with a spire 156 feet in height, containing a peal of six bells. This spire was taken down and a square tower erected about 1830 : at the upper end of the choir is another cross aisle or transept ninety feet in length. Between the two transepts on the north side without the cathedral stands an old ruined tower, no higher than the roof of the church, generally allowed to have been erected by Bishop Gundulph: the walls are six feet thick, and the area on the inside twenty-four feet.

On the opposite side, at the west end of the south aisle, is a chapel of later date, now used as the Bishop's Consistory Court.

The choir is upwards of 636 years old, being first used at the consecration of Henry de Sandford in 1227. During certain repairs, about forty years since, some fine pointed arches, with clustered columns supporting a gallery under the east window, were discovered hidden behind the altarpiece, which have been carefully restored. Near the altar are two tombs—one supposed to be that of Bishop Glanville, who died 1214; the other of Lawrence de Martin, who died 1274. Another tomb, near the communion-table, is considered to be Bishop Gundulph's; if so, it dates back to 1107.

The organ stands over the entrance to the choir, upon a plain stone screen; it was built by Green in 1791, since which it has been enlarged and improved, and is now an effective instrument. The choral service here deserves commendation, as being rendered very effectively by a limited choir, uniform in attendance, and painstaking, and in all respects a laudable example, as well as a rebuke, to many of our richly-endowed cathedrals, not excepting that of St. Paul's in London.

At the north end of the upper transept is St. William's Chapel; this saint, or rather this saint's repute, was a source of great profit to the priory, which it rose from poverty to affluence and riches.

At the south-east corner of the same transept is a richly carved doorway, which formerly led to the chapter-house of the priory, but now to the library, which, although not numbering its tomes by thousands, yet possesses many rare and valuable manuscripts. Here is the well-known ' *Textus Roffensis*,' compiled in the twelfth century by Bishop Ernulfus, and also another ancient manuscript, the ' *Custumale Roffense*,' supposed to be the more ancient of the two.

Near the west end of the same aisle is St. Edmund's Chapel, behind the choir of which is a sort of stone chest sunk into the wall, and a reclining figure, much mutilated, supposed by some to be the tomb of Bishop Bradfield, who died in 1283. Formerly there were several frescoes interspersed through the cathedral, which have all disappeared; one in this chapel, near the tomb just mentioned, represented the Virgin and Child. Descending a few steps is a small room formerly a dungeon.

The crypt, which embraces three distinct orders of architecture, is very interesting. It is spacious and vaulted with stone; there are seven aisles, and traces of a chapel. The arches near the entrance are Saxon, those opposite Norman, and the remainder early English.

In taking leave of Rochester Cathedral we exhume Hasted's graphic description of the arch of the great door, now 783 years old, which he designates as 'a most curious piece of workmanship; every stone has been engraved with some device, and it must have been magnificent in its original state. It is supported, the depth of the wall, on each side the door, by several small columns, two of which are carved into statues, representing Gundulph's royal patrons, Henry I. and his Queen Matilda. The capitals of these columns, as well as the whole arch, are cut into the figures of various animals and flowers. The keystone of the arch seems to have been designed to represent Our Saviour in a niche, with an angel on each side; but the head is broken off. Under this figure are twelve others, representing the Apostles, few of which are entire.'

The parish church of St. Nicholas is near the north door of the cathedral, and was first built in 1421. In the time of Bishop Gundulph (A.D. 1076) there was no church, although it was a parochial district before the Conquest; the parishioners worshipped at an altar in the cathedral, called the ' Parochial Altar of St. Nicholas.'

When the church was built the altar of St. Nicholas was transferred from the cathedral to the church. No description of this church is to be found, beyond that it remained nearly two hundred years, but becoming ruinous was taken down in 1620. Antiquarians, however, pronounce the walls and buttresses portions of the ancient structure.

The present church was consecrated by Bishop Buckridge, 24th September, 1624. It extends in length 100 feet by 60 in breadth, and consists of a nave and two aisles, divided by columns. The church has recently been repaired and galleries erected, which detract from the architectural beauties of the building, although not obnoxious from dissimilarity. The Corinthian altarpiece of wainscot was presented by Edward Bartholomew, Esq., in 1706, with two silver flagons and a paten, of £30 value; and Mr. Edward Harlow gave a handsome gilt cup in 1629. Mr. Francis Brook gave a large silver salver for the offerings at the sacrament, in 1703; and Mr. Henry Austen gave two handsome quarto prayer-books to be placed on the altar.

The living of St. Nicholas, a vicarage, in the patronage of the Bishop of Rochester, recently vacant by the translation of the Rev. W. Conway, M.A., to a canonry in Westminster Abbey, has been conferred on the Rev. C. Bosanquet, incumbent of St. Osyth, Essex.

MAIDSTONE.

MAIDSTONE, the assize town of Kent, lies pleasantly near the middle of the county, and is reputed for the dryness of the soil and quality of its water.

Many Roman remains have been found here, that warrant the supposition of its having been a Roman station. Camden, Burton, and others considered it the station called by Antonius *Vagniacæ*;

Nennius that it was called *Cœr Meguiad*, or Medway. The Saxons named it *Medweyston*, in English *Medway's Town*, written in Domesday *Meddestane*.

The town is screened by hills rising from the valley. Through it runs the River Medway, which is of vast importance as a medium for considerable traffic from hence to Rochester, Chatham, and London. A seven-arched bridge spans the river, which affords a good view of fine old buildings and rich landscape. On the banks are numerous flour, paper, and other mills. The soil of Maidstone is rich and fertile, and covers an entire bed of Kentish ragstone, that becomes a deep sand towards the east.

Formerly Maidstone was governed by a *Portreeve and Twelve Brethren*, but in 1550 Edward VI., under letters-patent, incorporated it as the ' *Mayor, Jurats, and Commonalty*;' these privileges were forfeited in 1553, when the rebellion of Sir Thomas Wyatt began in this town. In 1559 Queen Elizabeth restored its incorporation by the title of the ' *Mayor and Aldermen*.' According to a return in the eighth year of the same reign, there were 294 inhabited houses, four landing-places, and five vessels belonging to the town; the population, which at the close of the last century numbered few more than 6,000, now exceeds 22,000.

The town consists of four principal streets, meeting at the Market Cross, from which many others diverge. The market, granted in 1261 by Henry III., is held weekly, and supplies abundantly all kinds of excellent provisions; the mayor is Clerk of the Market.

There are four fairs annually—on February 13, May 12, June 20, and October 27,—for the sale of cattle as well as wares. Maidstone was anciently part of the possessions of the see of Canterbury, and the place of residence of many archbishops. Archbishop Langton lived here in the seventh year of King John; in 1348 Archbishop Ufford commenced a new palace, which his successor, Simon Islip, finished. Archbishop Courtenay died here in 1396; he was buried at Canterbury, but a cenotaph was erected to his memory in the chancel of Maidstone Church. This palace was a favourite residence of the prelates of Canterbury down to Archbishop Cranmer. King Henry VI. visited Archbishop Morton here, in 1438. This ancient relic has been well preserved and converted into two private residences; the outer stone staircase, gothic doorways and windows are very interesting remains.

Archbishop Boniface founded, in 1260, All Saints' College on the bank of the Medway for poor travellers; it was given in 1395 to the church at Maidstone, which was then made a collegiate church. Archbishop Courtenay erected the college and buildings, and died in the year following. Of this noble pile of stone buildings, now belonging to the Marsham family (Lord Romney), much remains; the great tower gateway, clothed with ivy, is almost entire, as well as other portions of this foundation.

During the fourteenth century the inhabitants founded the Fraternity of *Corpus Christi*, in a house erected near the river; beyond the resident members, others of both sexes, to the number of 120, were admitted. Many were persons of distinction, who contributed liberally; each of the others paid an annual fee, besides which the Fraternity was enriched by many legacies and gifts, and an estate in land and houses; and on the death of members masses for the repose of their souls were celebrated, which materially added to their revenues. The chapel and parts of the cloister still remain.

A Convent of Franciscan or Grey Friars is said to have been founded here by Edward III. in 1331, which was removed in 1345, to Walsingham in Norfolk, where a convent was built for this order of friars.

When the Walloons fled to England, to escape the persecution of the Duke d'Alva, in the reign of Queen Elizabeth, they introduced into this town the manufacture of linen thread; in 1634 there were fifty Walloon families resident here, and two large manufactories of linen thread. The Free Chapel of St. Faith in the northernmost part of the town, then in disuse, was occupied by these refugees; it was afterwards used as a Presbyterian chapel until nearly the middle of the last century; a few remains still exist.

Maidstone is within the diocese of Canterbury. The Church dedicated to All Saints stands westward of the town on the river-bank, and was built on the site of a former church by Archbishop Courtenay, in 1395 (19th Richard II.). The finely carved stalls for the fellows of the college still grace the chancel, upon which are the arms of the founder: it is a noble sanctuary of considerable elevation, with nave, two aisles, and a large chancel. A spire of eighty feet in height, which surmounted the tower, was destroyed by lightning in 1730. In 1700 the church was paved and galleries erected, partly at the cost of Lord Romney: most of the beautiful monumental brasses for which this church was famous have been carried away. The supposed cenotaph of Archbishop Courtenay stands in the chancel; the portraiture of a prelate in full canonicals is still traceable on the slab from which the brass original was taken, but the inscription that surrounded it is for ever lost. In the south chancel, under a handsome monument, slumbers all that was mortal of the first principal of the college,—John Wootton, who died in 1471.

The other churches are dedicated to 'SS. Peter, Paul, John, Philip,' and the 'Holy Trinity.' the former is said to be fitted with some of the interior decorations of Archbishop Boniface's Chapel, founded in 1260.

A new Congregational Church, in the Italian style, is in course of erection, to accommodate 800 persons, with commodious schools and class-rooms beneath. The cost is estimated at £3,000, to be raised by voluntary contributions.

Maidstone has two representatives in Parliament : the right of election is vested in freemen by birth, the eldest son being born free. From its central position, Maidstone has long been the county or shire town.

The Gaol of the western division of the county formerly stood in the centre of the town ; an Act of Parliament was obtained in 1736 for its removal to the suburbs, when the present extensive stone building in East Lane was erected, since which it has been much enlarged and strengthened at considerable expense.

The County Gaol, built on the Rochester Road, is a formidable pile, occupying upwards of thirteen acres, and was finished in 1818, at a cost of £180,000. The walls are of immense thickness, built of brick, faced with ragstone; every appliance has been exhausted to render it a model prison. The prisoners are all classi-fied, having distinct yards for outdoor exercise ; each prisoner has a separate cell, and juvenile offenders, the teaching and attention of a reformatory.

The Mote, an ancient seat, stood east of the town, in a noble park ; it was castellated, and belonged to the noted family of Roger de Leyborne, during the reign of Henry III. It afterwards passed to Sir Robert Marsham, subsequently Lord Romney ; it was pulled down, and another mansion built in a more commanding situation in the park, which is richly wooded with oaks of large growth.

The land throughout the neighbourhood is prolific in hops, fruit, and filberts; much of the prosperity of Maidstone has arisen from the successful culture of hops, supposed to have been introduced here at the Reformation.

Maidstone was famous also for the distillation of spirit, well known as ' MAIDSTONE GIN.' A Mr. George Bishop erected large works here ; and in proof of the magnitude of his distillery, it is affirmed that 700 hogs were kept and fattened upon the surplus of the grain.

The barracks for cavalry, built on the river margin, are extensive and well appointed, and are capable of receiving upwards of four hundred troopers.

It was our desire to have been enabled to enlarge more fully on this the county town of Kent, seated in one of the loveliest parts, beautiful in hill and valley and in memories of early history; but our pen must drop here. We migrate to our favourite old town, GRAVESEND, for relaxation, and propose during our sojourn there to gossip of its rise and progress, with sketchy notices of excursions in its vicinity, reserving until our return to the bustle of life further Jottings of some of the many interesting spots that abound throughout this historical county.

GRAVESEND.

Chapter I.

GRAVESEND, called in Domesday Book *Gravesham*, is bounded on the north by the Thames, distant from London by the old coach-road twenty-two miles, or by water 28½ miles, and built on an acclivity extending to Windmill Hill.

The reputed site of the Roman station ' *Vagniacis* ' lies distant little more than two miles west by south-west; the Roman road called Watling-street ran two miles due south of Gravesend ; and from numerous Roman relics found at Higham, on the east, marks the Romans almost at equidistances over three sides of a square, bounded on the fourth by the Thames: it may be therefore fairly inferred that Gravesend, as the centre, was a town or village early in the Christian era.

After the departure of the Romans, when the Saxons invaded Britain in A.D. 455, the first great battle on record was fought at Aylesford, within twelve miles of Gravesend, where four thousand combatants were slain.

In 839, when the Danes committed great slaughter at Rochester, it is supposed that Gravesend was ravaged, on their way to London. It is, however, certain that in the survey instituted by William the Conqueror in 1067, Gravesend was a place of importance, so much so that Herbert, son of Ivo, was ' *Bishop of Gravesham* ' at that time.

A family of high repute took its name from this town, and were called ' *De Gravesend* ; ' they had large possessions here. Three of them were bishops during the reigns of Henry III., Edward I., and Edward II.—namely, Richard de Gravesend, Bishop of Lincoln in 1258 ; Richard de Gravesend (his son), Bishop of London in 1282 ; and Stephen de Gravesend, Bishop of London in 1318.

After the murder of Thomas à Becket, Archbishop of Canterbury, in 1170, pilgrimages were made to his tomb by multitudes from London, when stations were erected on the way, where the pilgrims halted ; these stations were called ' St. Thomas' Waterings.' One was at Gravesend, near the site of the Almshouses (so called) at the north-east corner of Windmill-street.

Taverns, or Wine-houses, were known here early in the thirteenth century ; for it is recorded that ' John Baker of Milton and James Maracall of Gravesend were, in the year 1240-41, brought before the Justice Itinerant, for selling wine against the assize.' In the year 1279 several persons were presented to the Justice Itinerant for selling sundry casks of wine ; and in the same year a murder is chronicled as having been committed in the house of ' Alexander Cook, a tavernkeeper at Gravesend.'

In the year 1268 a grant of free warren, with a market and fair, was conferred upon Robert de la Parrok, who held the manor of Parrok.

Kent suffered fearfully from a violent storm and inundation in 1286, which happening towards harvest the crops were destroyed, and the price of corn enhanced for several years, and the causeway and landing at Gravesend materially injured.

In the 21st year of Edward I. (A.D. 1293), seven years after the great storm, complaint was made to the Justice of Assize of the dangerous condition of the bridge and chalk causeway at Gravesend, through which many persons had sustained injury, and urging that the moiety or half on the riverside ought to be repaired by the lord of the manor, Henry de Cramaville, and the other half, next the town, by the men of Milton—which was accordingly so determined.

During the same presentment several boatmen of Gravesend, Milton, and London were arraigned for extorting excessive fares from passengers : the legal fare for passage to London by the Thames was one halfpenny, whereas the boatmen had been charging a penny ; it was required that in future no more than one halfpenny be taken, under a bond of forty shillings.

This nominal charge of one halfpenny to London excites surprise in the nineteenth century, until we consider the value of money at that date, which may be better understood if we give the price of provisions in London in 1300, regulated by an Act of Common Council with the king's approval ; from which we extract the following :—

	s.	d.		s.	d.
Two Pullets	0	1½	Ground Malt per Quarter	4	0
A fat Goose	0	4	A Bull	7	6
A fat Lamb from Christmas to Lent	1	4	A Cow	6	6
Ditto at other times	0	4	A fat Sheep	1	0
A Cock or Hen	0	1½	Wheat per Quarter	4	0

—thus demonstrating that the fare of one halfpenny was equivalent to a shilling of present value.

Richard II., in the year 1377, directed his writs to the Sheriffs of Kent and Essex, commanding the erection of beacons on each side of the river, opposite to each other, to be kept prepared, and fired on the approach of an enemy's vessel. One was accordingly erected at Gravesend, and the other at Farnedon, on the Essex coast ; notwithstanding which Gravesend was shortly afterwards plundered and burned by the French, who arrived in their galleys, and carried away many of the inhabitants prisoners. The king, being assured of the bold resistance of the inhabitants, and commiserating the shock that had befallen them, conferred upon the men of Gravesend and Milton the exclusive right of river-traffic between Gravesend and London; for which purpose they were to provide suitable boats, and carry all passengers at twopence each, with their personal luggage, or, for the hire of the whole boat, four shillings—a charter confirmed by several succeeding kings.

These boats, during the last century, were called '*Tilt Boats*;' the signal for their departure was the ringing of a bell for a quarter of an hour, when they left with the flood for London, and returned from Billingsgate with every ebb.

The Lords of the Manor of Gravesend had the right of holding a court for the regulation of the boats and water-carriage between Gravesend and the Port of London : this court was called '*Curia Cursus Aquæ*,' according to an old roll in the possession of Earl Darnley of the 33rd of Elizabeth, A.D. 1591.

In the year 1401, upon an alarm of invasion, writs were issued, commanding all ports to build and man barges and balingers—the barges with eighty, and the balingers with forty men; when Gravesend and Tilbury supplied one balinger, fully manned.

The navigation of the Thames was wholly stopped through a great frost, which commenced on Christmas Day 1434, when all communications and merchandise were carried to London from Gravesend by land for nearly two months.

Edward IV., in 1461, renewed the grant of Henry IV. to the inhabitants of Gravesend of the right of river-traffic, setting forth as his reason, ' *The good and gratuitous service which our dear lieges the inhabitants of Gravesend had done us.*'

During the illness of Elizabeth, Queen of Henry VII., in 1503, a special officer of His Majesty's household was despatched by boat to Gravesend to summon to her bedside Dr. Aylsworth, a famous physician. His entire expenses, including horse-hire, refreshments, guides by night and day, watermen, and other incidentals, amounted to *seven shillings and eightpence!*

Under a patent granted by Edward III., in the 30th year of his reign, A.D. 1357, the market is held twice weekly in the town of Gravesend, on Wednesday and Saturday, and two fairs annually, the profits to belong to the lord of the manor.

The Emperor Charles V. was entertained by Henry VIII. at Gravesend, on the 2nd June, 1522, after which, attended by a brilliant train of nobles, they embarked hence for Greenwich in thirty barges.

In 1539 Henry VIII. built platforms or bulwarks at Gravesend, Tilbury, and Higham, and mounted them with cannon, for the defence of the river. Five years afterwards Henry VIII. proceeded to Gravesend in state by water, and dined there the 12th of July, 1544. The cost of a royal banquet, however, in those days was comparatively insignificant. Hasted tells us that on the triumphal return of Henry V. from France, he was entertained at the Red Lion Inn, Sittingbourne, by John Norwood, Esq., with princely splendour, and that the banquet cost *nine shillings and ninepence;* but wine was then at the rate of twopence per pint.

Brewer, who wrote on the luxuries and necessaries of life during the reign of Henry VIII., gives a cartel of salaries and prices, in which we have the following:—'Salary of the chancellor, £200; the speaker of the House of Commons, £100; the king's chief surgeon, £13 10s. per annum; librarian, £10; superior workmen, 6d. per day in summer, 5d. in winter; labourers, 4d. long days; a shepherd's clothing for the year, 5s., and that of a woman-servant, 4s.

In the Navy, the admiral had 10s. a day; captains and treasurer, 3s. 6d.; under-captains, 1s. 6d.; clerks, 8d.; master and pilot, 30s. a month; master surgeon, 13s. 4d. a month; sailors and marines, 5s. a month. Beer cost 6s. 8d. per pipe; salt, 5d. a bushel; oatmeal, 10d. a bushel; and oil, 10d. a gallon.

Queen Elizabeth confirmed to the parishes of Gravesend and Milton their charter of Henry IV., and further incorporated those parishes as the ' *Portreeve,*' now the ' Mayor, Jurats, and Inhabitants of Gravesend and Milton;' the mayor to be chosen annually, on the first Monday after the Feast of St. Michael.

Queen Elizabeth further ordered that all eminent strangers and ambassadors should be received at Gravesend, and that the mayor, aldermen, and companies of London should attend them to London in their barges; or if they came by land, then they were to meet them at Blackheath.

CHAPTER II.

IN 1536 Mr. Hore, of London, originated an exploring expedition to the north-west coast of America. The route viâ the Cape of Good Hope had been discovered, and enterprise was awakened for seeking across the Atlantic a passage to China. Two ships, the ' Trinity' and ' Minion,' were chartered; and of a crew of one hundred and twenty persons thirty were gentlemen, including members of the bar and of the Court of Chancery. The whole were assembled at Gravesend, and, according to Hakluyt, received the sacrament before embarking, at the end of April of that year.

The famous circumnavigator Sir Martin Frobisher, on his first voyage to the north-west, sailed from Gravesend in 1576. After adjusting his compasses, and marking the latitude (51°33″) he returned in safety with a piece of gold ore. Thus encouraged, a second expedition sailed from Gravesend the following year (1577), when ' *all received the communion by the minister of Gravesend, and prepared, as good Christians towards God and resolute men, for all fortunes, and towards night departed for Tilbury Hope.*'

When the nation was in dread of an invasion from Spain, in the year 1588, fortifications were erected at Gravesend and Tilbury, and a fleet of battle-ships, to contest the passage of the river, moored here, whilst a large army encamped near the fort at Tilbury.

On the 8th of August Queen Elizabeth came in a state-barge to Tilbury, to review her troops, and landed under a royal salute from Gravesend and the opposite fort. Her Majesty, mounted on a white palfrey and bearing a marshal's bâton, was attended to the camp by the Earl of Leicester, a thousand horse, and two thousand infantry, to witness a sham-fight. After the review the Queen dined with the Lord Steward in his tent, and then embarked for St. James's under salutes, as on her arrival.

In the third year of the reign of King James, on Thursday the 17th of July, 1606, Christian IV., King of Denmark, arrived at Gravesend with a fleet of seven ships of war, on a visit to King James and his Queen, who was sister to the Danish monarch. They anchored at Gravesend, and remained on board until the following day, when King James, Prince Henry, and a brilliant staff embarked from Greenwich, in thirty-five barges, to meet the king at Gravesend. Cruden tells us that the barge of King James was built 'in the form of a tower or castle, enclosed with glass windows and casements, carved and gilt, the roof made with battlements, pinnacles, pyramids, and fine imagery, which was towed by another barge with thirty oars.' After the reception the monarchs, with their respective suites and the flotilla of barges, proceeded to Greenwich, leaving the Danish ships at Gravesend.

King Christian returned to Gravesend after a visit of nearly a month to the King of England, and gave a grand banquet to his Majesty and Prince Henry ; and sailed the 13th of August, attended by two British ships of war, under salutes from Gravesend and Tilbury.

Gravesend, even before the Portuguese had voyaged viâ the Cape, in 1497, was famous as a port for large shipping ; and was then, as now, deservedly a favourite market for supplies of ship-stores, fresh provisions, liquors, and all other necessaries and comforts essential to the distant voyager. For nearly two centuries the magnificent fleets of the East India Company were wont to ride at Gravesend, and crowd the town with their officers, their crews, and their friends. Alas! how many bitter tears have flowed here when fathers, mothers, wives, husbands, and beloved ones have parted, perhaps for ever ; how many fervent prayers have ascended from agonised hearts to Him who ' maketh the storm a calm, so that the waves thereof are still ;' or, on the other hand, how many the rejoicings over those safely returned from burning climes, lands pregnant with disease and death !

The King of Denmark made a second visit to England in 1612, when his ships, as before, were anchored off Gravesend. It was

on the 1st of August of this year that King James and Prince
Henry dined with the King of Denmark, at the Ship Tavern (for
merly 15 and 16 High-street), and after visiting Rochester the
following day, returned to Gravesend for dinner.

During the same year the Count Palatine of the Rhine landed
at Gravesend when he came to marry Elizabeth, daughter of King
James.   The issue of this marriage was a daughter, the Princess
Sophia, whose son was GEORGE I. King of England.

When Prince Charles was leaving England for Spain, attended
by the Duke of Buckingham, under fictitious names, both disguised
with beards, they crossed from Tilbury to Gravesend, and, not
having silver, gave the boatman a gold-piece in payment.   The
man, in his surprise, reported the fact to the officers at Gravesend
who pursued and arrested them at Canterbury, upon which the
duke, who was Lord High Admiral, removed the false beard, when
they were released with many apologies.

After the gorgeous nuptials of Charles I. at Canterbury, in June
1625, and the daughter of Henri IV. of France, the king and his
bride rode to Cobham Hall.   The way was strewn with flowers
by the people, who testified their joy by acclamations.   The next
day their majesties came to Gravesend, where they dismounted and
received the congratulations of the nobility and numberless ladies
and gentlemen, who had the honour of kissing hands; after which
they embarked on the royal barge, under a salute from the Blockhouse.

The assizes for the County of Kent were held several times
within the parish of Milton during the reigns of James I. and
Charles I.

Stage-coaches or, as they were called, Tide-coaches were in use
at Gravesend earlier than upon any other road in this country.   In
Wood's Diary the first mention of a stage-coach was in 1661, when
the journey from Oxford to London occupied two days; against
which we have an order of the Corporation of Gravesend, dated
July 21, 1647 (fourteen years before), confining the plying of
tide-coaches to the inns or houses from whence they started.

The first Town Hall of Gravesend was built in the year 1573
it was rebuilt in 1764, and considerably altered in 1836, when a new
front of the Doric order was substituted.   The handsome flute
columns, supporting a noble pediment, surmounted by sculptures of
Justice and Truth, with Minerva in the centre, give an imposing
appearance, highly creditable to the architect.   According to the
inscription, it was rebuilt during the mayoralties of M. Troughton
and R. Oakes, Esqrs.

At the period of the Revolution in 1688, when King James II
resolved to leave the kingdom, his Queen, with the infant Prince of
Wales and a female servant, disguised as Italians, drove to Gravesend on the 1st of December of that year, where a yacht, prepared

by Lord and Lady Powis, was ready to convey them to Calais. The following day the king, disguised as a country gentleman, proceeded to Gravesend on his way to Faversham, from whence he returned to London, where he remained until Tuesday the 18th December, when he again proceeded by barge to Gravesend, slept there that night, and finally embarked on the Medway for Ambleteuse, in France, the 23rd of December, 1688.

When GEORGE I., great-grandson of James I., arrived in the Lower Hope on his way to Greenwich, the 18th September, 1714, the Mayor and Corporation of Gravesend presented a loyal address to His Majesty, which was graciously acknowledged, thereby giving them priority over all corporate bodies, as being the *first* that welcomed to the shores of England the *first* prince of the illustrious House of Brunswick as King of the Realm.

On the 24th of August, 1727, a considerable portion of Gravesend was destroyed by fire, which fearful conflagration originated in a building adjacent to the church, when the parish church, one hundred and twenty dwelling-houses, and numerous stables and outbuildings, were entirely destroyed. The loss was computed by some at nearly a quarter of a million sterling, whilst others pronounced the amount an exaggeration. Other fires happened in 1731, 1748, 1779, and 1801, but the damage was inconsiderable in comparison with that of 1727. During the present century several fires have occurred in West Street, and two in High Street. The first of those in High Street was in 1845, when a tavern (the Black Horse) with several private dwellings were wholly destroyed. The second, a few years later, demolished a large amount of valuable property and houses, including the County Bank. So extensive was the conflagration that the ruins were smouldering for many days. This sad calamity to the inhabitants has proved a great improvement to the town, not only in the widening of the street, but by the erection of handsome brick structures on the site of many crazy wooden houses.

CHAPTER III.

WE find that eight hundred years since Gravesend had a parish church; but beyond this little is recorded, save that the rector, John Thorpe, who lived in the fifteenth century, directed by his will that he should be buried in the churchyard. It was situated at the extreme south of the parish, but, from the distance, was little used by the inhabitants. To meet this inconvenience a chapel was erected near the river, corresponding to the site of the present church, which was duly licensed in 1497, and consecrated in 1510, as St. George's Chapel. It became the parish church in 1544, when the old church, which was burned down in 1509 and rebuilt in 1510, was abandoned under grant of Henry VIII.

E

We have already shown that St. George's Church was burned down, with a large portion of the town, in 1727, by which the inhabitants were plunged into great pecuniary difficulty, and wholly unable, without considerable extraneous assistance, to rebuild the church; it was therefore resolved to petition Parliament for a grant. The petitions were entrusted for presentation to the members for the county, consequent upon which five thousand pounds were granted by Parliament in 1731. His Majesty George II. gave a further sum of one thousand pounds, and his Queen five hundred, making together a total of six thousand five hundred pounds.

The present church, dedicated to St. George, was commenced the same year, when Sir Roger Meredith, one of the county members, laid the first stone on the 3rd of June. It was finished in one year and eight months, and was consecrated and opened on the 11th of February, 1733. St. George's Church is a neat substantial structure built of brick, with stone groins and cornices. It has a nave, two aisles, and galleries. In the west gallery is an organ, erected in 1764. The church measures 80 feet by 50 feet. The tower contains a peal of eight bells, of which two were cast in 1771, four in 1736, one recast in 1793, and the remaining one recast in 1813, by Mears of London. A steeple of wood rises 52 feet above the tower, in which is a clock having four dials, and from its commanding elevation is of general utility.

Gravesend and Milton were incorporated under one charter, as the '*Mayor, Jurats, and Inhabitants of Gravesend and Milton.*' The High Street divides the parishes, the west side being in the parish of Gravesend, and the east side in that of Milton.

Milton Church, dedicated to SS. Peter and Paul, is built of flints and ragstone. It consists of a nave and chancel, and measures within the walls 78 feet in length and 25 in breadth. There was a church at Milton as early as the Conquest, but the present structure is certainly not of that date. There is no direct evidence to prove when the present church was built, but the architecture is neither Norman nor Early English, which brings us down to the beginning of the fourteenth century, when the Decorated English style commenced, which prevailed from 1307 to 1377—a period of seventy years—and during which there can be little doubt Milton Church was built. This conclusion is based upon the evidence of a window on the south side, next to the porch, which is a pure specimen of Decorated English in two lights, divided by a mullion, with trefoiled arches forming the heads and a sixfoiled circle rising to the apex. Again, it is supposed to have been built by the Countess of Pembroke after the death of the Earl, in 1323, who was Lord of the Manor of Milton. The Countess died in 1377; thus we have conclusive evidence that the style of architecture of Milton Church was in the ascendant while the Countess held the manor in right of her deceased lord.

Formerly the window at the east end of Milton Church was of large dimensions, of the Decorative style, since contracted to nearly one-half, and a window in the Perpendicular style substituted. The interesting sedilia on the south side of the communion remain; they consist of four niches divided by clustered columns and pointed arches with moulded soffits, the outer arches having trefoiled heads. These sedilia are to be found in many of our ancient churches, but varying in form and number, according to the clergy engaged in the service, for whom they were used as seats, with the exception of that at the extreme east, which was the piscina, for the use of the priest in washing the sacramental vessels, having a perforation in the bottom as a lavatory. A series of fourteen stone corbels, formerly supporting the roof, are distributed on each side of the church: upon the fronts of seven are sculptured heads, very grotesque for a sacred edifice; three others on the north and two on the south sides are supposed to represent distinguished benefactors. There are two niches in the south wall, and one on the outside, by the south porch, formerly receptacles for holy water.

Milton Church was formerly battled, as well as the tower, but in 1790 the battlements were demolished and the present incongruous roof substituted. The tower was built after the church, as was usual in the middle ages; but, from the style and materials, it must have been erected shortly afterwards. There are five bells in the tower, cast in 1656. Over the porch, on the south side, is a curious sun dial, constructed by James Giles, master of the Free School: it bears the following significant motto:—

' Trifle not, your time's but short.'

Aylmer de Valence, Earl of Pembroke, founded, about the year 1321–22, a chapel and chantry at Milton, and endowed it with lands and tenements in the county of Essex. It was suppressed at the Reformation, although it had been long in disuse, and become a ruin from the endowments being lost through neglect.

In 1779–80 the site of the chantry, with certain premises, including the New Tavern, of which it was part, were purchased by the Crown for the construction of a battery, which, although not very formidable, would be capable of great havoc from its embrasures being mounted with modern cannon.

King George II. embarked at Gravesend on the 13th May, 1740, for Holland, and on several other occasions when visiting Germany. Gravesend at this time was the military rendezvous for troops passing to the Continent, who embarked and landed here. War raged on the Continent, and troops were continually passing and repassing until the peace in 1748, during which period trade flourished beyond all precedent in Gravesend.

The oldest street in Gravesend is West Street. There is a deed extant, dated 4th September, 1418, wherein Mr. Thomas Bolynne assigned certain premises, with a wharf, in ' *Weste Strete, Gravy-sende.*' East Street also bears the stamp of antiquity, for by the will of William Burston, dated 10th December, 1548, certain messuages there are demised. These, with the High Street, which bore the same name three hundred years since, are the oldest portions of the town, although doubtless there were, even at that time, many other groups of dwellings not recorded under any discriminative appellation.

In the Amended Charter of Incorporation of 1568, wholesome regulations were enacted for the cleansing, paving, and lighting of Gravesend, from which we extract the following:—

' *All Innkeepers and Victuallers should nightly, between the Feast of All Saints and the Purification of Our Lady, hang up lights at their doors, upon pain to forfeit fourpence, and every inhabitant shall pave against his premises under a penalty of three shillings and fourpence, and to weekly cleanse his door for avoiding evil odours.*'

An Act of Parliament was passed in 1773 for paving and cleansing the town, which gave authority to impose rates, and for the removal of ' *signs, sign-posts, sign-irons, spouts, cellar-windows, penthouses, and other encroachments,*' which Pocock thus remarks upon :—' *Before the passing of the Act the town was most irregularly paved; the kennel then went down (uncovered) near the middle of the High Street; almost every tradesman had a sign; and in the night, when the wind blew strong, a concert of squeaking music filled your ears with sounds not the most pleasant.*'

On the 23rd of August, 1759 a melancholy accident befell the ship 'FRIENDSHIP,' just arrived from Jamaica, which blew up off Gravesend, when forty-two persons perished: of this number, eighteen were young ladies and gentlemen sent from Jamaica to be educated in England.

CHAPTER IV.

WE learn from CRUDEN and POCOCK—two clever historians—that at the close of 1784 there was but one watchman for the parishes of Gravesend and Milton, and that this important functionary, named Clifford Reed, was also town-crier, and was remunerated by the inhabitants.

The present system of police was organised in the year 1836, an institution highly creditable to the Corporation for the vigilance and respectability of its members, as well as for efficiency under the able conduct of Mr. Superintendent White.

The year 1788 is memorable for a great frost, when the river at Gravesend resembled a northern sea, covered with mimic icebergs; some men walked ashore from their ships—others. shipwrights from Mr. Pitcher's at Northfleet, amused themselves at 'ricket on a large field of ice.

The first steamboat that ran between Gravesend and London was the ' MARGERY;' her passengers embarked and landed by watermen's boats at Wates' Hotel, at fares of four shillings saloon and three shillings fore-cabin; her first trip from Gravesend was on Monday the 23rd of January, 1815.

In 1824 gasworks were erected, and the town was lighted for the first time with gas on the evening of Thursday the 9th of December. Gravesend was now rising as a popular summer resort. Londoners came down in large numbers, trade gave evidence of considerable improvement, and building to meet the influx commenced in the suburbs.

In 1827 popularity had set in, passengers from London by steamboat arrived in masses : the Steam Navigation Company alone conveyed, on the average, 5,000 per week. In 1828 the Gravesend and Milton Steamboat Company was formed, and during the following year three boats were launched—the ' KENT,' ' PEARL,' and ' ESSEX.' The old Company built a new boat, the ' ECLIPSE ;' then came the fast and elegant boats of the Diamond Company, carrying from nine to fourteen hundred passengers. We well remember those bright days of water-carriage, when the weekly average of visitors to Gravesend rose to 20,000 ; when the merchants and citizens of London could enjoy an early picturesque walk amongst the beauties of the suburbs, and find a 7 or 8 o'clock boat ready to bear them to the Great Metropolis within two hours; boats remarkable for cleanliness, saloons capacious and replete with every comfort, breakfasts abundantly supplied with hot rolls, ham, eggs, and an array of etceteras ; and after business, either at 4 or 5 o'clock, return-boats, which provided excellent hot dinners of the best description, unlimited in quantity, at moderate cost.

The Town Pier was opened on the 29th of July, 1834, when the chairman of the committee congratulated Earl Darnley on the completion of the work he had so zealously promoted. The company, numbering nearly 300 of the gentry and principal inhabitants, embarked on board the ' MERCURY ' steamboat, and after a short excursion down the river returned to a banquet on the Pier, which was tastefully decked and draped with canvas and numerous flags.

During that year nearly 300,000 passengers had passed between London and Gravesend, which induced the formation of the ' Star Company,' who launched four boats that year—the ' MEDWAY,' the ' COMET,' the ' MERCURY,' and the ' STAR.'

In 1840 Brunswick Wharf, Blackwall, was opened, and extra packets launched to run between Blackwall and Gravesend, when the passage was effected in from one hour to one hour and a quarter, according to the tide. The new boats were the ' BLACKWALL,' ' RAILWAY,' and ' BRUNSWICK ;' the other company's boats also called here, and we have, with favourable tide and by catching the train, been in London within an hour and a half of leaving Gravesend.

The Blockhouses at Gravesend, erected by Henry VIII. in 1539-40, were both within the parish of Milton ; one was built on the chapel field near the ancient chantry, the other in front of the Terrace. In 1834 the Board of Ordnance announced this property for sale by public auction; a committee of the inhabitants was formed to treat with the Government for its purchase, which was finally effected for £7,000 on the 31st of March, 1835, when a temporary pier was commenced, and opened on the 7th of June following, on which day the 'STAR' steam-packet landed 524 passengers.

The Terrace Gardens were commenced at the close of this season; they justly rank amongst the attractions here, being laid out with excellent taste in pleasant walks, choice shrubs, and gay flowers ; a commanding river-frontage, and abundance of seats in shady retreats.

The temporary pier was used until 1842-3, when the present elegant structure was erected and for years landed flights of excursionists from London. Now alas ! its vocation is gone, through railways and diminished popularity ; still in its individuality, there is the proud boast that HER MAJESTY, with the many members of Her Illustrious House, have made it their favourite place for embarkation and reception ; a distinction merited by the town and corporation, who have won the admiration of all loyal subjects from their munificent and highly successful efforts to demonstrate their devoted affection for England's beloved Queen.

The name of the late James Harmer, Esq., of Ingress Abbey, must have a place here from his zeal in the furtherance of improvements, and the formation of the Gardens and Pier on the old Blockhouse land, in which enterprise he was the largest shareholder. To effect those improvements it became necessary to purchase three houses on the Terrace, and several acres of land south of the Gardens, to be laid out for building a handsome street, which was called Harmer Street, to commemorate that gentleman's munificence in having so liberally contributed towards its accomplishment. ·

Harmer Street—perhaps the finest, certainly the most uniform, in the town—numbers 51 houses. At the southern extremity is a crescent of nine noble dwellings, adorned with balconies supported on pillars and looking on to neat plantations. The feature of Harmer Street is an elegant edifice on the east side, called the 'Literary Institution,' with a reading-room, billiard-room, and a spacious well-appointed Assembly Room.

This is the fashionable Assembly Room of Gravesend. Concerts, balls, and other genteel entertainments attract the *élite* of visitors and inhabitants. For several seasons it was known as ' Kelner's Bazaar,' a favourite morning promenade and an attractive evening resort for concerts, well rendered at a nominal charge for admission. We regret the discontinuance of these agreeable entertainments, which justly entitled the proprietor to support and commendation.

The first project of a tunnel under the Thames originated at Gravesend, where a meeting was convened on the 18th of July, 1798, to confer on the practicability of a tunnel from Gravesend to Tilbury, which resulted in an Act of Parliament for raising £30.000 in shares, and if expedient to raise a further sum of £20,000. The work was commenced and a shaft sunk upwards of eighty feet, which alone cost £15,000, when the projectors became discouraged, and the scheme was reluctantly abandoned.

The improvements in the town under the operation of the Local Act of 1773 led to the introduction of bathing by machine at Gravesend. CRUDEN states that—' *On the 18th of May,* 1796, *forty-nine inhabitants of Gravesend joined in a subscription of five guineas each, and they purchased a machine at Margate to begin with, which was used for the first time on the 27th of the following month, that they increased the machines to nine, and the establishment is called the Clifton Baths.*'

The water however was turbid, and the old system of machine-bathing is now superseded by a perfection of arrangement, under the able management of Mr. John Lukes, that renders the Clifton Baths worthy to vie with any similar institutions. These baths comprise tepid, cold, vapour, plunging, shower, and swimming baths. The water is received into capacious reservoirs from the high tide, then lifted by steam-power into immense cisterns and filtered; the water being salt, and thus rendered pellucid, possesses the medicinal properties necessary for the invalid.

In front of the Clifton Baths are seats, where the convalescent may enjoy an animated view of the river and the scenery of the opposite coast; while the more robust may luxuriate in an invigorating promenade stretching from the ' Union Yacht Club House ' to the extent of the Clifton Marine Parade.

CHAPTER V.

ALTHOUGH the resident population of Gravesend and Milton had risen in 1833 to nearly ten thousand souls, still there were only two churches; barely sufficient in accommodation for a sixth of that number, exclusive of visitors, who now crowded the town during the summer season. The inhabitants, roused by the emergency, convened a borough meeting at the Town Hall to consider the expediency of building a capacious chapel-of-ease: funds were accordingly raised, and a site of land purchased opposite to Queen Street, upon which an Episcopal Chapel, capable of seating 1,200 persons, was erected.

This noble Gothic structure was commenced the same year, and within little more than twelve months finished. It was dedicated to St. John the Baptist, and opened for public worship the 16th of November, 1834. This chapel was the property of a company of shareholders, and subsequently of the Rev. Wm. John Blew, M.A., the incumbent, who afterwards sold it to His Eminence Cardinal Wiseman, by whom it was converted into a Roman Catholic church, when the side galleries were taken down. A small convent has been added, and schools and presbytery have been erected adjoining it, the whole being enclosed by handsome iron railings.

In 1848 another church was erected near Milton Place. This pleasing Gothic edifice, built of stone, was dedicated to the ' Holy Trinity,' and will seat about 1,200 persons, including a large number of free seats. The organ in the north gallery is an effective instrument. The Rev. C. E. R. Robinson, the present incumbent, succeeded the Rev. Richard Joynes on his preferment.

St. James's Church, on the New Road, opposite Somerset Street, was built in 1850, and is a handsome structure of modern Gothic, with a square battled tower rising in the centre. It stands in a carefully-tended plantation of flowers and shrubs, with ivy luxuriantly climbing the buttresses and surrounding the windows, many of which are filled with memorial glass; the interior is well arranged and fitted with open seats ; the stone pulpit stands on the north side. The Rev. John Joynes, the incumbent, is a faithful and earnest preacher, the friend of the poor, and ever prominent in those Christian graces—love and charity. An old and esteemed inhabitant of Gravesend, R. Blackburn, Esq., since deceased, placed the first organ in this church. He attained the venerable age of ninety years, and was, with his son-in-law, R. E. Morrice, Esq., amongst the most zealous supporters of the church and its excellent institutions. Within a few years, however, a new organ has been erected in the west gallery, which efficiently supports the vocal services of a numerous and devout congregation.

In the upper part of Parrock Street is another stone church, plain and devoid of architectural beauty, but commodious, and capable of seating a large congregation. It was built in 1854, and consecrated as 'Christ Church:' the Rev. Felix A. Marsh is the incumbent.

Distinct of five churches and a Roman Catholic church, there are five chapels belonging to the Dissenters. The 'Independent' chapel in Princes Street was first built in the year 1717, taken down in 1838, and the present capacious building erected on the former site. This handsome chapel, with bold façade, will comfortably seat 1,200 persons. The congregation is numerous and respectable, especially during the visiting season, when temporary residents receive much kindly attention. There are several excellent institutions in connection with this chapel, more especially day-schools, which carefully educate some hundreds of children of both sexes.

The Wesleyan chapel in Milton Road, built in 1812, was enlarged and re-arranged in 1841, and the front wholly rebuilt: during the present year, 1864, it has again been thoroughly repaired and beautified, the original portico, supported on fluted pillars, removed, and new entrances constructed. This is a roomy chapel, with a small organ on the north gallery, and ample seat accommodation for visitors, who are always courteously welcomed. In front is a small burial-ground, with memorial tablets; neat iron railings enclose the whole.

The first Baptist chapel in Gravesend was merely a large room in Stone Street, opened in 1825, which having proved inadequate, funds were raised for the erection of a suitable building in Windmill Street; this structure, called 'Zion Chapel,' was built in 1843, and is a feature of the street, from its commanding appearance. The interior is well pewed, and capable of seating a large congregation.

Zoar Chapel, in Peacock Street, was built by the 'Particular Baptists.' This is a simple plain building, with sittings for about two hundred persons. The schools, however, which adjoin on the west, have a clever contrivance of windows, that open into the chapel, whereby much additional accommodation is gained.

The 'Primitive Methodists,' who for several years worshipped in the original Baptist chapel in Stone Street, have erected a neat and suitable chapel in Darnley Street, with commodious schools beneath.

Our short sketch of Gravesend would be very incomplete were we to omit some notice of charitable bequests, those fruits of Christian love, memories of pious bygones, that live on in youthful freshness.

David Varchell, under his will, dated 15th September, 1703, gave forty shillings to be distributed amongst the poor at his funeral, and three pounds annually in bread and cash to forty poor persons. He further gave a house and four tenements towards the maintenance of the Free School and a brass chandelier for the church.

Richard White gave, by will dated 10th August, 1622, forty shillings annually, to be divided amongst forty poor persons on St. Andrew's Day.

Ann Chapman, by deed dated 11th August, 1709, gave forty shillings yearly, to be distributed in bread to forty poor persons after a sermon to be preached in Gravesend Church on St. John's Day.

James Fry, by will dated 29th April, 1710, gave one hundred pounds for building the east end of St. Thomas's Almshouses, and an annuity of fourteen pounds ten shillings, payable to the master of the Free School, for the instruction of ten poor boys of Gravesend, Milton, and Chalk.

Mary Langworth left twenty pounds, by will dated 26th June, 1699; and Ann Peirce fifty pounds, under her will dated 18th July, 1776. These joint sums, invested in consols, and now producing upwards of three pounds annually, are distributed amongst the poor of Milton.

Dr. Thomas Plume, Archdeacon of Rochester, who died 20th November, 1704, charged Stone Castle (part of his estate) with the annual payment of fees for twenty-six sermons, to be preached alternately at Gravesend and Dartford on Wednesdays during the summer months.

Mrs. Furrell, of London, bequeathed ten pounds to the charity children of Gravesend.

Mrs. Eliza Jewars, from Bengal, in the East Indies, gave to the poor of Gravesend one thousand rupees (£100).

Mr. Henry Pinnock, by his will dated 13th August, 1624, gave three hundred pounds to the parishes of Gravesend and Milton, with certain houses in Milton to be called ' St. Thomas's Houses' for ever, and also two houses and outbuildings with two acres of land at Grays Thurrock, in Essex, for the benefit of the poor of Gravesend and Milton.

CHAPTER VI.

ST. THOMAS's Almshouses were rebuilt in 1837–8. A tablet on the east front in Windmill Street bears this pleasing record:—
' By the Will of Henry Pinnock, dated 13th August, 1624, these houses were left for the better relief and maintenance of poor decayed persons living in the Parishes of Gravesend and Milton;' and on the south front in King Street, another marble slab affords gratifying evidence of local sympathy, although told in few words, as follows:—' The endowment of this Charity was commenced by public subscription A.D. 1862, in grateful remembrance of ALBERT PRINCE CONSORT, and is vested in the Trustees with the hope of future contributions.'

These almshouses, ten in number, built of red brick and stone, present a neat and ornamental appearance, and are carefully adapted for the convenience and comfort of the aged inmates, who fully appreciate the munificence of the founder and the kindness of the trustees ; a brick wall, surmounted by iron railings, encloses the whole. In front of the almshouses is a drinking fountain, appropriately represented by a female figure pouring water from a pitcher; it is, however, to be regretted that this convenience should prove an annoyance to pedestrians, the footpath being generally dirty from scattered water.

The Free School, founded in 1580, stands opposite to the Almshouses in King Street. The present handsome Elizabethan building, of red brick and stone, was erected on the site of the former school (which having become seriously dilapidated was taken down), and the National School united with it, in 1835. The cost of this neat structure was liquidated by donations from the inhabitants,— Earl Darnley,—the Corporation of Gravesend,—and grants from Government and the National Society, in all upwards of £1,300.

Distinct of the Foundation School, there are other good schools for the poor in connexion with the Established Church and the different Dissenters' Chapels ;—Gravesend and Milton can also boast several collegiate and superior proprietary establishments, which deservedly command liberal patronage.

Another important institution is the ' Gravesend Dispensary and Infirmary,' in Bath Street, built on a site of land liberally presented by Earl Darnley, who laid the foundation-stone. Of all charities least open to abuse are those founded to minister to the infirmities of frail nature, while they appeal in mute eloquence to our inmost sympathies from beds of suffering and disease, too often surrounded by want and misery.

This substantial building of brick, approached by a flight of stone steps under a neat portico, is divided into two parts, the front portion being the Dispensary, comprising waiting and con-sulting rooms, the surgery, and the private residence of the indefatigable house-surgeon : here sick poor, not receiving parish relief, have medical aid and medicines for the nominal fee of one penny. The medical staff comprises two consulting and four operating surgeons, who attend in rotation. The Infirmary, which is a distinct building behind the Dispensary, has beds for twenty patients ; on an average there are from six to ten under treatment in the Infirmary, and upwards of one hundred weekly in the Dispensary. This excellent institution is supported by voluntary contributions; each annual subscriber of one guinea is qualified to be a gover-nor. The sphere of usefulness is wide, but we regret to learn that the funds, at present, are very limited ; still we hope that the Samaritan spirit marking our generation will not be wanting in sympathy and benevolence towards the ' Gravesend Dispensary and Infirmary.'

The Parish of Gravesend contains 630 acres, and that of Milton 650—together 1,280 acres. In the first year of the present century (1801), the population of Gravesend was 2,483, and that of Milton 2,056, which united numbered 4,539 persons of both sexes ; the next Government return, in 1811, shows the population of Gravesend to have risen to 3,119, and Milton to 2,470, making a total of 5,589 inhabitants in the borough of Gravesend and Milton at that date. Since then, however, it has increased so remarkably, both in inha-bitants and dwelling-houses, as to render it interesting to trace the progress ; we therefore give *in extenso* the census returns down to April 1861:—

	Inhabitants			Houses
	Male	Female	Total	
1821 Gravesend Milton	1796 1310	2018 1459	3814 2769	671 478
	3106	3477	6583	1149
1831 Gravesend Milton	2555 1939	2542 2409	5097 4348	796 721
	4494	4951	9445	1517
1841 Gravesend Milton	3058 4028	3356 5228	6414 9256	981 1437
	7086	8584	15670	2418
1851 Gravesend Milton	3260 4522	3446 5405	6706 9927	1264 1941
	7782	8851	16633	3205
1861 Gravesend Milton	3988 4754	3897 6143	7885 10897	1385 2096
	8742	10040	*18782	3481

* Population 18,039
On board vessels in the river off Gravesend . 743

Total 18,782

From these statistics we gather many pleasing facts illustrative of
a people who, within half a century, have multiplied their numbers
fivefold, quadrupled their dwellings, and become a corporate body
of considerable status.

Thus the population, which in the year 1801 was returned as 4,539 souls, rose to 5,589 in 1811, and in 1821 to 6,583; being an average increase of one thousand in each ten years of that period. But during the next ten years, ending 1831, we find the population risen to 9,445, an increase of 2,862 persons, occupying 1,517 houses. The most remarkable period, however, was between 1831 and 1841, when the census gives the number of inhabitants of Gravesend and Milton as 15,670, being an increase of 6,225 souls; and of houses 2,418, or 901 additional dwellings.

It is not then surprising that the returns of 1851 should show the excess as only 963 persons, while 787 extra dwellings had been erected, when it is remembered that of the 6,225 increase in population between 1831 and 1841, by far the larger number were imported into the borough either as adventurers in trade, lodging-house keepers, or private residents.

In 1861 the population was 18,782, and houses 3,481, being an increase within forty years of 12,199 inhabitants and 2,332 houses; unexceptional evidence of the capital and importance of the borough, still multiplying in numbers, trade increasing, and building vigorously progressing, with every prospect of returning popularity.

Chapter VII.

We have now reached our last Chapter on Gravesend, for although our inclination might tend to enlarge more fully on this our favourite summer resort, yet in courtesy to a talented lady, whose pen has recently furnished a useful Guide, we refrain from further culling from interesting material before us, in a desire that that lady's interesting work should be patronised to the extent of our best wishes.

That Gravesend has risen in importance as a borough, and increased in population and buildings within the present century to an almost incredible extent, has already been shown. We have only to suggest that a stranger on his first visit might form some approximate idea by commencing with High Street; and if just landed, with gastronomic powers sharpened by a bracing river-breeze, he will be well entertained at any of the abounding restaurants lining the way, among which Tidby's deserves mention, as being capable of dining hundreds, from superior joints, or at pleasure, in courses with fish, poultry, and sweets.

This is a gay though narrow street. Here are the noble Town Hall and extensive Market, the commanding 'Joint Stock Bank,' and superior shops well stocked with every description of articles of food, fancy goods, and all that can be required for wear or ornamentation; so also of the New Road, Windmill Street, King Street,

Parrock Street, not excepting Queen Street, West Street, and other less important localities—all affording ample testimony of the resources and extent of the borough, by the abundance of excellent goods so largely displayed in its numberless establishments.

The great increase of private residences, everywhere skirting the town, is truly surprising; structures of every style, in rows of good houses, semi-detached villas, cottages, and gentlemen's seats, all more or less adorned with flower-gardens in picturesque beauty. Many of these are handsomely furnished as temporary residences, and as a rule may be engaged on moderate terms by visitors.

Parrock Street, on the Milton side, is the longest street in the town: here are many excellent houses, more especially towards the Hill, chiefly the residences of gentlemen and citizens of London. Those known as Brontë Villas, Primrose Terrace, Constitution Crescent, and that neighbourhood, stand on an eminence, with extensive views of beautiful scenery, clothed in rich umbrageous verdure.

Darnley Road, west of the town, is another charming spot: the houses here are mostly semi-detached, standing in gardens sweetly decked in floral beauty, opening upon a fine outspread country. Here again genteel lodgings may be engaged.

Windmill Street is the most popular thoroughfare in Gravesend, from being the direct route to the hill from which it is named. The houses are mostly superior, and inhabited by persons of station and respectability. At the north end are several good shops, and the establishment of Mr. Hall, the esteemed printer and publisher, whose copious library and well-supplied reading-room prove a desideratum to visitors as well as residents. This extensive street is paved throughout with flagstones; the houses have neat front gardens tastefully laid out, enclosed by iron railings, and further embellished by rows of luxuriant trees. At the foot of the Hill is Clarke's extensive nursery-ground, rich and attractive in beauty and botanical variety. Visitors are privileged to promenade in this nucleus of cultivated nature, a boon that claims acknowledgment in the purchase of fruits and flowers.

We have now reached that famed elevation once called Ruggen Hill, then Rouge Hill, and now Windmill Hill, so designated on the erection of a windmill early in the eighteenth century. Beyond the gorgeous panorama of nature here unfolded are other modern attractions for the masses, to us of a far less sublime character. To attempt a description of the scene before us would be no mean difficulty; we therefore reproduce the graphic picture drawn by Pocock, in his interesting 'History of Gravesend':—'*The Hill, consisting of sand and gravel, commands one of the finest views in the Kingdom, as from it may be seen Swanscombe, the place where the Kentishmen opposed William the Conqueror and obtained their privileges; over which appears Shooter's Hill, sixteen miles distant; the town of Grays, in Essex, near which stands the mansion of Mr. Buxton, built in 1791; and to the north, on the summit, is the seat of Lord Petre; Laindon Hill next rises majestically to our distant view, below which we see the villages of Chadwell and Tilbury; to the eastward Leigh and Southend. The shipping lying at the Nore, twenty miles distant, may be seen, and our commerce continually passing and repassing until lost in the distance at Woolwich. In the south-east a long range of stately trees points out Cobham Park, near which is the church of Cobham; to the south we see the mansion of Ifield Court, and in the south-west Knockholt Beeches, at the verge of the County of Kent. This delightful hill takes in not less than a circuitous view of 150 miles.'*

There is now, however, another object to be seen from the Hill, one that commands serious reflection—'*the bourne from whence no traveller returns.*' It is the Gravesend and Milton Cemetery, once a popular tea-gardens for the living, now, alas! the long last home of youth's first bloom as well as of sere old age, where earthly pride decays, and human hopes, like human works, sink into nothingness. We have just lost an old friend of ninety summers, but he has left his mark, for he died as he had lived—'*In hope of a resurrection* TO EVERLASTING LIFE.' His mortal remains are to slumber here, whither we repair to meet them. Winding round by the west side of the hill we cross into a crescent road which shortly brings us to the cemetery, founded in the year 1838. It is entered by a handsome arched gateway supporting the bell-turret, falling back concave, to receive the funeral *cortége* from the road. A neat building rises on both sides of the entrance, serving the several purposes of office, lodge, and dwelling for the custodian; a substantial wall surmounted with iron railings stretches along the front, and a lofty wall encloses the remainder, which covers about six acres, with extensive catacombs at the extremity. There are two chapels, one for the services of the Established Church and the other for those of the Dissenters. We had arrived early, which afforded opportunity for meditation amongst the numerous monumental memorials of dear ones passed away, beautifully decked with flowers, shrubs, and evergreens, more like a carefully-tended garden than a place of sepulture. An occasional mourner, however, would have speedily dissipated the delusion, had such existed,—

Who, stooping as the willows wave,
Bend mourning o'er a hallowed grave.

The first monument that arrests attention is to the memory of four loved children, with a chaplet of everlasting flowers in a glazed case hanging in front, and the following well-known couplet, to complete the inscription:

'Full many a flower is born to blush unseen,
And waste its sweetness in the desert air.'

Some short distance and a tablet tells of another departed child, and appropriately apostrophizes the verse :—

> ' See Israel's gentle Shepherd stands,
> With all engaging charms ;
> See how He calls the tender lambs,
> And folds them in His arms.'

How much to humble human pride meets us at every step! Here we read, inscribed on a simple stone to the memory of a beloved wife, who died at the early age of twenty-seven:—

> ' How loved, how valued once avails thee not,
> To whom related, or by whom begot ;
> A heap of dust alone remains of thee,
> 'Tis all thou art, and all I soon shall be.'

Full of truth as regards the body. But let us rise higher, and cull from the many sweet emblems around us the Christian's hope, graven on stone, as sermons spoken from the tomb :—

> ' On Christ a solid rock I stand,
> All other ground is sinking sand.'

Again—

> ' Far from a world of grief and sin,
> With God eternally shut in.'

Another—

> ' Just as I am—without one plea
> But that Thy blood was shed for me,
> And that Thou bid'st me come to thee,
> O Lamb of God, I come.
>
> ' Just as I am—and waiting not,
> To rid my soul of one dark blot,
> To Thee, whose blood can cleanse each spot,
> O Lamb of God, I come.'

We quote one more, as being the comforting assurance of Scripture, that—

> ' Precious in the sight of the Lord is the death of His saints.'—Psalm cxvi. 15.

Our meditations are ended ; the knell announces the funeral of our departed friend ; we repair to the chapel and hear, in the beautiful language of the Apostle, that ' *this corruptible shall put on incorruption, and that this mortal shall put on immortality : when shall be brought to pass the saying that is written—Death is swallowed up in victory.*'

We now take leave of our friends of Gravesend, so far as relates to this simple sketch of the rise and progress of the borough, and of its resources and people ; proposing to follow with a few desultory observations on neighbouring localities, before passing to those more distant in this interesting county.

NORTHFLEET.

CHAPTER I.

NEXT to Gravesend on the west is Northfleet, containing 3,980 acres, of which about one-tenth is wood and chalk-works. The land, which is marshy on the north-west, undulates towards the south-east, and becomes hilly between Ifield and Nursted.

From a remote date chalk has been quarried here, which gives employment to large numbers of the inhabitants. Out of one of these surprising excavations the '*Botanical*' now '*Rosherville Gardens*' were formed, which are not only a popular resort of excursionists and temporary residents, but also of charitable institutions for the augmentation of their funds.

Rosherville Gardens afford one of the most striking illustrations of romantic grandeur adorning art. When viewed for the first time from the terrace, the beholder may imagine himself transported by the genii of Aladdin's lamp to Fairyland, amidst craggy rocks covered to their summit with trees and shrubs, ornamental fountains, rare birds, groves of perfume, statuary, and lovely flowers, arranged with artistic taste in charming variety. A flight of rude steps leads to the dizzy summit, from which, looking into the gardens beneath, you have a contexture of the whole, and the living masses in their diversified amusements : the sports in the archery ground, Chinese targets, weighing machines, Aunt Sallies, the maze and its intricacies, American bowls, mechanical figures, dancing on the platform and in the Banqueting Hall, the gipsy's tent, and coy maidens stealing to the Sibyl's seclusion; whilst others, seated in retired bowers, listen to the *voice of love* tenderly whispered by the sterner sex.

Along these heights runs a walk of considerable extent, richly decorated with shrubs, odorous flowers, and rustic work. You have here a grand prospect of the noble river and surrounding picturesque scenery. At the western extremity rises a mimic tower of four stories, with battled top; the windows being filled with stained glass, to give the illusive appearance of the seasons when seen through, as directed by the inscription.

Considerable improvements are still in progress, including new banqueting and lecture halls, in addition to the Baronial Hall; an extensive Conservatory for tropical plants, Shrubberies, and a Fernery.

Leaving the gardens for the riverside, we decline sundry invita-

F

tions to ride, and feminine appeals to ' *buy fine shrimps—give you a cotton bag*,' and reach Rosherville Pier, which, being free. forms a morning lounge for visitors. Here ladies prosecute embroidery and fancy-work, or luxuriate in reading, whilst juveniles gambol and refresh themselves with cooling beverages and pastry in the well-stocked restaurant.

Rosherville Pier, although a simple wooden structure, affords equal facilities for passenger traffic with those of the Town or Terrace Piers. It was built about twenty years since by Messrs. Ward Brothers of London, but proved a pecuniary loss to the contractors, and, what was still more serious, the death of the elder brother, from a fatal cold engendered while superintending its construction.

Keeping the river on our right, after glancing at the Rosherville Hotel, of goodly proportions, we pass the ' *Old Sun*,' that quaint little snuggery for picnics and civility, and pause at ' *Crete Hall*,' the neat villa of Miss Rosher, whose widespread munificence so eminently adorns the exemplary Christian lady.

It is high water ; the sun shines brightly on the river and shipping; Essex smiles in verdure and harvest beauty ; the London boat, heavily laden, is rounding the point, as we journey to the romantic wilds amongst the chalk-works on our left. where centuries of labour have formed a waste of natural beauty, in hill and dell. clothed in rich variety of wild herbage extending over many acres. where old and young delight to ramble amongst its intricacies. or scramble to the summit of detached cliffs, like mimic mountains, shaded by trees and wild herbage. Here are unfolded the wonders of creation in the varied strata of earth, gravel, flint, and fossil, in cuttings of great depth : shells, broken and entire, have been found in abundance. In 1828 many parts of a fossil deer were found near the seat of W. Gladdish, Esq. ; which, according to geologists, is by no means surprising. for they consider chalk to be ' *animal remains in various stages of comminution and disintegration while in the ocean, before being deposited on solid foundations*.' A curious old limekiln and portions of a brick wall formerly embedded in chalk are here, which present nothing indicative of great antiquity ; still, from the fact of their being so hidden by a natural formation, they become a subject worthy of investigation.

Perhaps the most interesting time to visit these charming wilds is early morn, when refreshed nature, spangled with the dew of heaven, embraces the first beams of day, and birds, in numberless variety. commingle their matin song: when the cotter's home in the valley, or in ranges on yon high cliff, appear more picturesque. and their gardens in the dell more exuberant in verdure : when the smoke from burning kilns curls gracefully amongst the wild foliage, and the chalk-driver rattles gaily through the echoing glen.

Pursuing our way we reach a massive pile of frowning buildings resembling a fortress, with embattled walls and a castellated gateway. These are the extensive works known as Pitcher's Dockyard for shipbuilding, founded in 1788, and formed out of a large tract of chalk cuttings. Some of the finest merchant ships and men-of-war have floated from these docks, then liberally patronised by Government and the East India Company, and giving employment to many hundreds of shipwrights and labourers, but of late years, unhappily, fallen into comparative disuse. Now, however, the docks have passed into other hands and are in full operation : the hammers of a thousand workmen fall gratefully on the ear, telling of the many happy homes, so lately chilled nearly to despair from want and privation, now rejoicing in the comforts of life.

There are two routes from this point—that diverging to the right leading to the river, and on to Huggens College, flanked by ordinary taverns, engineering and other works, cottages, and the ' India Arms,' once a tavern of some pretensions, when East India shipping had moorings here. Here is also a lighthouse, erected in 1860; next we have the extensive cement works, where dust or mire, according to the weather, begrime the way, with the addition of an odour far from refreshing.

We prefer the sinuous path next the dockyard, by a sort of adit, or cutting through the cliff, which, winding to the summit, opens on to the once village-green. The old town is of irregular form, without streets, and presents a very primitive appearance. There are some shops and snug inns, where visitors and travellers find good accommodation.

CHAPTER II.

ONE of the most interesting institutions in Northfleet is the college founded and endowed by J. Huggens, Esq., of Sittingbourne, situated westward of the town, whither we repair, passing the parsonage on the left, and a line of old-fashioned houses and shops on the right, terminating in a sort of new town, when the college rises before us. It is approached by a handsome entrance formed of three arches with bold iron gates ; the centre arch forms the carriage-way, the others are for pedestrians. A bronze figure of the founder, seated, surmounts the principal arch, under which is a finely-sculptured basso-relievo, beautifully illustrating the parable of the ' Good Samaritan,' followed by the simple inscription, ' HUGGENS COLLEGE, 1844.'

This monument of individual munificence, forming three sides of a quadrangle facing outwards, stands on an eminence in the midst of lovely scenery. It consists of forty superior almshouses with porches to each and double doors for the comfort of the inmates during the winter season. The recipients are decayed persons of respectability, each of whom has four rooms free of rent, and receives £1 per week, paid in person by the venerable founder,

who, although very aged, visits them monthly : about a fourth of
the houses are unoccupied.   In the centre of the west front is a
chapel with an elegant spire, intended for the use of the inmates, but
which from some unexplained cause remains unfinished: this is to
be regretted—an observation induced from remarks by some of the
beneficed, whom age and infirmity had rendered wholly unable to
worship at a distance.   Each house has a back entrance from a grass-
plot in the middle, extending to the outer wall by which the institution is enclosed.   The college, from its elevated position, may be
seen miles distant, a pleasing and striking object—especially from
the Thames.

An elegant silver salver, weighing 30 ounces, was presented to Mr.
Huggens, bearing the following inscription:—'Presented by the
brothers and sisters of Huggens College, Northfleet, to the highly
esteemed founder, John Huggens, Esq., on completing his 88th
year, in token of their grateful sense of his bounty, April 29, 1864.'

We leave this interesting spot in admiration of the founder,
whose munificence and singlemindedness have not waited for death
to supervene, but who still lives to rejoice over his noble work, and
who, when passed away, will still live in grateful remembrance
through many ages.

Retracing our steps to the village, we reach the church of
Northfleet, mantled in ivy.   This venerable fane, dedicated to St.
Botolph, is one of the largest in the county.   Of its precise date
there is much uncertainty, but, from the highest archæological and
architectural authority, the probability is that it dates back to the
twelfth century, and is supposed to have been built on the site of a
former church, as it is known that Northfleet had a church at the
Conquest belonging to Canterbury, which was given to the Priory
of St. Andrew's, Rochester.

Some few years since this grand sanctuary was largely restored,
the gallery removed, a new organ placed on the floor at the west-end,
and open benches, to supersede unsightly pews.   During the past
year (1863) the work was completed by the perfect restoration of the
chancel, upwards of fifty feet in length, which is supposed to date
from the middle (or perhaps rather earlier) of the fourteenth century,
when Peter de Lacy was vicar, who died in 1370, and whose grave
was opened towards the close of the last century, and his remains
discovered wrapped in leather.

This last restoration is very effective.   The chancel floor has been
raised, and laid with highly-glazed encaustic tiles ; the reredos is
massive and tasteful, the arrangement of clergy and choir stalls
perfect ; an excellent choir organ, with diapered pipes, has been
erected by Gray and Davison of London, and the former instrument
removed ; the chancel is effectively lighted by two handsome
candelabra or gaseliers of 25 jets each, the gift of a parishioner ;
the whole, enclosed by the ancient rood-screen, and backed by the

exquisite east window, has a most ecclesiastical and imposing appearance. Amongst the ancient sacerdotal relics is a restored piscina and remains of stone sedilia, of which it is affirmed there were originally four, although three only exist. The church may be described as consisting of a nave and two aisles, with bold octagonal pillars and pointed arches: the south-eastern window, filled with rich memorial glass, was contributed by the family and friends of the late vicar. There are some brasses: one, to the memory of Peter de Lacy, already mentioned, representing the full figure of a priest, is highly ornamental; another, supposed to be that of Sir William Rykeld, or Rickell, represented in armour, with that of his lady, two full-length figures. Sir William lived in the reign of Richard II., and died about 1400. There are also some finely sculptured marble monuments affixed to the walls, amongst which is that of Edward Brown, physician to Charles II., and another that of Richard Davey, Keeper of the Seals to Henry VI.

The exterior is striking and grand: the embattled tower, from which floats a flag on Sundays, was in part rebuilt in 1717, and contains a melodious peal of six bells; on the outside is a flight of twenty-five stone steps, leading to the belfry. The Rev. Frederic Southgate, the present vicar, succeeded to the living in 1858. Amongst the many interesting monuments in the churchyard is a pyramidal mausoleum erected by the founder of 'Huggens College' for his last home when gathered to his fathers; it is of considerable elevation, and elaborate in workmanship, surrounded by an iron railing.

Northfleet has a neat Dissenters' Chapel, built in 1850, and excellent National Schools. In 1801 the line of the London Road was much improved by being carried in a straight line from the 'Leather Bottle' to Gravesend, which still retains the name of the New Road. From the time Gravesend became popular, Northfleet increased rapidly in houses of every description :—here are family mansions, detached villas, rustic cottages and dwellings, scattered profusely over this portion of the parish.

WOMBWELL HALL, commonly called Wimble Hall, is a seat in this parish built on an estate anciently called DUNDALLS. In the reign of Edward III. it was in the possession of the Wangdeford family, but was afterwards alienated to Thomas Wombwell of Yorkshire, who removed into Kent during the reign of Edward IV., and built the seat called by his name, which was rebuilt in 1663. The present mansion, built on the site of the old one, was erected a few years since for Thomas Colyer, Esq., and is certainly one of the finest in the neighbourhood.

IFIELD COURT is a manor at the south west boundary of this parish, originally the property of a family of that name in the reign of Edward I.

HIVE, corruptly for The Hythe, a seat near the banks of the

Thames, northward of the London Road, was many years the property of the family of Chiffinch, who bequeathed it in 1775 to Elizabeth, wife of Francis Wadman, Esq., Gentleman Usher to the Princess Amelia, daughter of George III.

During the reign of Richard II. the *Cistercian Abbey* of St. Mary Graces, London, possessed a valuable manor here called LEUCHES, or MUICHES, which was surrendered to Henry VIII., but where situated is now unknown.

BYCLIFFES, near Rosherville Gardens, the seat of William Gladdish, Esq., J.P., and Colonel of the 1st Kent Artillery Volunteers, is a handsome seat, standing in extensive grounds well laid out, and containing a large fishpond; the Terrace Walk here, by some called the Whispering Walk, has a curious echo. The site of this mansion was formerly the dockyard of Mr. William Cleverley, an eminent shipbuilder, whose granddaughter is the wife of the highly-esteemed proprietor.

We return to Gravesend by the New Road, always a grateful walk, and are charmed by the wild verdure and fantastic formations amongst the extensive chalk excavations on our left, with the ever-living river beyond, and the distant landscape stretching to wooded hills far on the opposite coast; whilst on our right we have a line of sweetly picturesque villas adorned with lovely flower-gardens.

Yon bright fane on the left, in the midst of handsome modern mansions, is St. Mark's Church, Rosherville, built at the sole cost of the Rosher family, and endowed by George Rosher, Esq. This elegant church, in the Transition style of architecture, is a rich specimen of stone-carving and elaborate decoration, and may justly rank amongst the best modern ecclesiastical structures in the county. Entering by the south porch, we find the interior equally beautiful: it consists of a nave and two aisles, neatly paved with tiles, forming diamonds of black, white, and red: a series of clustered columns, carrying five pointed arches in each aisle, support an effective open roof. The chancel, which is exuberant in stone-carving, has also a noble pointed arch, and a good east window filled with richly-stained glass; the memorial windows, on either side of the chancel, are full of character and appropriateness of design; the pulpit and font of carved stone accord with and complete the harmony of the sculptor's art displayed throughout. The church is well filled with substantial oak benches: there is a small organ, elevated at the west end, built by Walker of London; the choir, a small but promising body, sit beneath. The incumbent is the Rev. J. C. Gilling, who was presented to the living by George Rosher, Esq., on the resignation of the Rev. Frederic Southgate, in 1858.

COBHAM.

EVERY visitor to Gravesend has either seen or heard of Cobham; flymen intuitively greet each arrival at pier or station with ' *Cobham, sir?*' whilst Charles Dickens has inimitably pictured a walk to Cobham, and portrayed scenes and characters at the ' *Leather Bottle.*' If, however, any of our readers have not been there, let them take the advice of Captain Cuttle, and ' *make a note of it,*' and remember that they have a treat in store.

The drive or walk to Cobham is amongst the prettiest in the vicinity of Gravesend. If undertaken by a pedestrian, he will enjoy a walk across richly-cropped fields leading to Shinglewell, where mayhap he may incline to refresh with a cup of famous ale at the ' *Halfway House*;' or if, returning by the road, thirsty and fatigued, let him alight at ' *Northumberland Bottom,*' and at the quiet hostelry quaff a glass of ' Barnard's Old '—a sobriquet complimentary of the former kindly host, who supplied this superior ale in the finest perfection.

Cobham is about four miles from Gravesend. It gave the name to a noble house as early as the twelfth century. The first was Henry de Cobham, who was Justice of the Assize during the reign of King John, in 1199; his second son, Reginald, was Justice Itinerant and Sheriff of Kent, Constable of Dover Castle, and Warden of the Cinque Ports. The line of Cobhams were men of mark, and filled high offices amongst the nobles of the land until 1604, when Henry Lord Cobham, his brother George, and others were accused of plotting against the king's life, and found guilty. George was beheaded; Lord Cobham's life was spared, but his estates, said to be worth £7,000 per annum in land and £30,000 in goods and chattels, were all forfeited to the Crown.

The village of Cobham is sweetly pretty. and full of interest. You glance at the quaint inn, perhaps rest in the low-ceiled parlour, surrounded with old pictures, and have a tankard of ' Cobham ale,' which we have satisfactorily proved, and conjure up Mr. Pickwick and his adventures there.

In the year 1362, the thirty-sixth of Edward III., John de Cobham founded a chantry or college annexed to the church of Cobham for five priests, afterwards augmented to seven, for the performance of divine service in it for ever, one of whom was to be master of the chantry, and to preside over the college. The same John de Cobham thoroughly repaired the church at large cost, and liberally supplied it with books, vestments, and other ecclesiastical ornaments. The chantry remained until the reign of Henry VIII., when it was surrendered to the Crown; but, by an Act of

Parliament passed in 1549, it was sold to Lord Cobham. His son, William Brooke, by another Act, passed in 1597, established Cobham College, and erected it on the old foundations. The original chantry was a large quadrangular building, adjoining the south-east part of the churchyard : portions of the east wall overgrown with ivy, the chimneypieces of the refectory, and parts of the north cloister still exist in ruins. The doorway from the chantry to the church is very interesting, standing in ruined grandeur : we are led to meditate on the past, when five centuries since a pageant of priests and brethren passed its portals daily to their stalls in the church, there to celebrate mass for the souls of the founder and his family.

Cobham College is a stone building, partly built out of the chantry, and partly new at the time of its foundation in 1598 : it is, however, difficult to suppose the main building of this date. Some historians aver that, from the figures over the south porchway, where the armorial bearings of the founder are engraved, as well as from the testimony of ancient documents, many parts are much earlier. The visitor to Cobham College must inspect the venerable dining-hall, with its quaint fireplace of carved stone, now used as the chapel, and plunge into the darkness of a cellar of great antiquity, said to have been used as a prison for obstreperous vassals. There are twenty poor persons of both sexes (married and unmarried) located here, of whom one is warden and a second subwarden. Of the remaining eighteen on this foundation, Cobham elects three, Shorne two, Cooling one, Strood two, Hoo three, St. Mary Hoo one, Cliffe one, Chalk one, Gravesend one, Higham one, Cuxton one, and Halling one.

Cobham Church, dedicated to St. Mary Magdalene, stands on an eminence at the entrance of the village. This fine Gothic structure, which dates back to the thirteenth century, has a nave, two aisles, a large chancel, and a square battled tower containing a clock and a peal of bells. It has been recently restored by Earl Darnley, under the superintendence of Mr. Scott, the distinguished ecclesiastical architect. The chancel is magnificent, and contains the grandest collection of sepulchral brasses in the kingdom, memorials of the Cobhams until the transfer of their domains in 1604 to the houses of Lennox and Darnley. These brasses date from the fourteenth century : twelve are of large dimensions and occupy the floor of the chancel, ranged in two rows before the altar; the earliest is that of Lady Joan, *temp.* Edward II. The whole are now, 1864, being restored at the cost of Captain Brooke, a descendant of the former lords of Cobham. Bold columns and pointed arches support an oaken roof, the steps to the communion-table are paved with encaustic tiles ; on the south of the chancel are the usual *sedilia* and *piscina*. There is a splendid tomb of marble in the centre, upon which the light, from a near window, falls with considerable effect ; it supports a recumbent figure with clasped hands (said to be that of Lord Cobham, Governor of Calais during the reign of Edward VI.), with his wife by his side, and his children kneeling.

Cobham Park, which covers about 2,000 acres, formerly extended two miles and a half from east to west, and a mile and a half from north to south. Nature has indeed been lavish here in every variety of verdure and beauty of scenery: towering oaks of immense growth—a sombre walk of a thousand yards between rows of superb lime-trees, and an abundance of large chesnut trees, one of which, called the '*Four Sisters*' from its peculiar growth, measures thirty-two feet in circumference,—lawns of velvet, gay in odorous flowers,—woody dells and gorgeous landscapes in hill and valley rise on every side, animated by the bounding deer, and the singing of birds, forming a magnificent whole, eminently calculated to charm the senses.

On an eminence stands the Darnley Mausoleum, erected in 1783 ; it is built of stone, in the Doric order, octangular in form. The columns at each angle support a sarcophagus terminating with a quadrangular pyramid. Although intended for the family vault, having sixteen compartments, yet it has never been consecrated. The chapel, which is elegant, is ornamented with Brocotello marble, and has a handsome lancet-shaped east window filled with stained glass.

Cobham Hall, a stately mansion of mixed architecture, consists of a centre and wings. The central building was the work of Inigo Jones ; the wings, which were cased with brick, and the windows mullioned during the last century, bear the dates 1582 and 1594. This fine baronial hall may be viewed on Fridays by tickets procurable in Gravesend, when admission is granted to many of the State Apartments, which are superbly furnished. The music-room, measuring 50 feet by 40, is truly magnificent—walls of polished white and sienna marbles ; the roof and upper portions of the walls have bold ornaments on a white ground, richly gilt. The white marble chimneypiece is an elaborate work of art by Sir R. Westmacott. There is a fine organ here presented by George IV.; the floor is of polished oak. The principal dining-room is also beautifully decorated, and the walls covered with pictures by the first masters, and family portraits by Vandyke, Kneller, and Lely. The grand staircase leads to the picture-gallery, 134 feet in length, stored with the finest works of art, including some of Rubens' greatest productions. Without further extending our description the visitor will find exquisite sculpture in every variety—marble statuary, etruscan and other vases, and treasures of art seldom to be witnessed.

Amongst the many curiosities is a gilt chariot, said to have belonged to Queen Elizabeth. Historians, however, are not agreed on this point. It was during this reign (when ladies, and royal ones too, made substantial breakfasts of beefsteaks and ale) that an Act (42 Elizabeth, A.D. 1600) was passed forbidding '*Men riding in coaches, as being effeminate.*'

We cannot take leave of Cobham without an expression of gratitude to the noble Earl Darnley, for the privilege accorded visitors of luxuriating in his park, and feasting in admiration amongst the sumptuous treasures that adorn his gorgeous halls. His Lordship is hereditary High Steward of Gravesend and Milton, a considerable patron of religious and social institutions, and much esteemed throughout the county for courtesy and kindliness of manner.

SPRINGHEAD.

SPRINGHEAD and Watercress are as familiarly associated as Shrimps and Gravesend; it is one of those sunny spots that everybody visits. Let us be companions; the morning is fine, a walk across the fields on a balmy autumn day will prove invigorating.

From a choice of two ways, we select that diverging from the New Road by St. James' Church over the railway bridge, and leaving Darnley Road on our left take an oblique path through an extensive potato-field; on our right is the old mill rapidly revolving to a southern breeze. We leave Perry Street and its slated houses on our left, advancing through golden corn rapidly falling to the reaper's sickle, and waggons bearing away the rich treasure; another potato-plantation, and we reach some fine parkage, adorned with towering oaks casting inviting shadows.

The sun is giving evidence of his power; we seek shelter under their umbrage, and, reclining on a grateful acclivity, read the incidents of a previous day from a London journal. The clock of Gravesend Church booms out the meridian hour; as we reach the road, the elegant seat of T. Colyer, Esq., whose lands spread far and wide, is on our left. We near a farm and, again crossing fields, stand on the brow of Springhead, that charming valley with its meandering stream and dainty cress, an elysium of blushing fruit, of lovely walks, and charming flowers. Yon pale cottage on the other side, nestling in a garden of variegated flowers, is Mrs. Silvester's,— formerly sole proprietress of the whole, but now divided, and in the distinct occupation of Mrs. Silvester and Mr. Arthur. Our first visit is to Mr. Arthur's, on this side of the stream. We descend carefully the steep declivity, as a slip might usher us into the gardens rather unceremoniously; passing a rustic archway we reach the lawn, and an assemblage of visitors vigorously discussing fruit and refreshing beverages cooled in the limpid stream. We prefer ' *Tiffin*,' and enjoy a rasher of unexceptionable quality in the luncheon-room, before basking in this isolated spot of incomparable loveliness. Strawberries of the most luscious quality are largely cultivated, which attract crowds during their season. We have here rustic arbours, velvet lawns, delightful walks,—as well as swings for the juveniles, and superior refreshments, always accompanied with remarkable civility by both the Silvester and Arthur families, in whose joint prosperity we feel interested.

The extensive culture of watercress is truly surprising, not only for country supply, but largely for the London markets, whither it is sent daily. The springs forming this pellucid stream rise in the valley, and flow over a gravelly bottom through the extensive and picturesque grounds. During autumn the beds are wholly cleared of this favourite esculent, the bottom carefully cleansed and levelled, and fresh gravel stones strewed where necessary, over which the stream glides to the depth of a few inches, when the curious process of replanting commences. The young cress is planted, or rather laid, in rows, the leaves of each row covering the roots of its precursor; within a few days the roots strike down amongst the stones and vegetate rapidly, without any covering of soil.

Public gardens would be incomplete without a Sibyl : here, are two, one on each property. ' Old Peggy,' on Mrs. Silvester's side, is aged and infirm from rheumatism ; we had overtaken her a few evenings previous resting by the roadside, and readily gave her a seat in our fly, when she displayed an amount of intelligence superior to her class. On this occasion our gipsy friends on both sides have *silvery* desires of consulting futurity in our behalf, which, as sceptics, we decline, not without remarking the cordiality (although rivals) existing between them in their friendly gossip across the water.

We have an attraction here in the person of Mrs. Clayton, mother of Mrs. Arthur, who entered her 105th year in January 1864, and who still retains her faculties ; she generally rises at 6 A.M. and retires at 9 P.M., arranges her own room (refusing the assistance of a domestic), exercises in the gardens, and still works neatly ; we found her busied preparing vegetables for dinner, from which she rose to acknowledge our enquiries.

When the PRINCESS ALEXANDRA arrived at Gravesend, Mrs. Clayton walked from Springhead, and was present to welcome her on landing. A few evenings subsequently a party of 150 elderly ladies united in a tea-party at the ' Elephant's Head,' Rosherville, to celebrate this national event, when Mrs. Clayton presided, after again walking the entire distance without apparent fatigue.

Taking leave of Mrs. Clayton, we cross to Mrs. Silvester's, and find her, as usual, active, with a kind word for everybody. We well remember a gay day at Springhead—the 14th of August, 1860— when Miss Rosa Silvester was married ; when the sun shone brightly as the bridal party emerged from the house, and ' Old Peggy,' with her best courtesy and, if we mistake not, with a tear, placed a

white rose in the hand of her young mistress; nor do we forget
the profuse wedding-breakfast that awaited their return, so gaily
decked with Springhead's choicest flowers.

We have accidentally met some friends, and, repairing to the
lawn across a rustic bridge, enjoy biscuits and ale in one of the
many picturesque alcoves, whilst our juveniles swing and sport
amidst the many surrounding beauties, and luxuriate in fruit, and
gingerbeer fished out of the stream: here indeed may be found
rural enjoyment, where even the songsters of the wood revel in
harmonious concert.

Our time is gone; we take leave of, and a bouquet from, the
kindly Mrs. Silvester. Boustred, one of the civilest of Gravesend
flymen, is here, and fortunately disengaged; he bears us to the
town, and on the way we retain his services for the morrow.

SWANSCOMBE.

THE morning, fanned by a soft southern breeze, was very beautiful
as we drove through Northfleet on our way to Swanscombe, three
miles distant from Gravesend.

This parish, which takes its name from ' *Sweyne*,' a Danish
monarch, and ' *Combe*,' a camp, contains 438 houses, 2,323 inhabitants, and 2,593 acres of tolerable land, inclined to be gravelly
about the village : of this amount, however, nearly a thousand acres
are marsh and wood, Swanscombe Wood alone covering 600 acres.

The village is healthy and picturesque, from whence, however,
the land rises to the wood, where, according to HASTED, fogs and
vapours concentrate from the marshes, which render it unhealthy.
The old Roman road runs on the south of the wood, said to have
been the vicinity of a Roman station, and favoured by the finding
of coins of NERO and SEVERUS. Here are also several earth-
mounds, some having a hollow at the top, unquestionably of very
remote times.

When the Danes landed at Swanscombe, the Thames flowed
through the valley as high as Southfleet, and shipping found safe
shelter between the hills; but the shipping of those days may now
be compared, in size, to modern Gravesend fishing-boats.

According to tradition, it was here that William the Conqueror—
after the Battle of Hastings—encountered the Kentishmen, who,
appearing with boughs in their hands, resembled a moving forest;
but which, on the approach of the Conqueror, they threw aside,
and stood a large army ready for battle, demanding the confirmation
of their ancient laws and privileges as the only terms of submission.

In 1346 (the 19th year of Edward III.) John Lucas, of Greenhithe, founded a chapel in this hamlet, dedicated to the Virgin Mary. It was suppressed in the reign of Edward VI.; some portions of the walls, however, still exist, but, from being part of a tenement, are not visible. On the banks of the Thames are several wharves for landing and shipping wood, corn, coals, but principally chalk dug from the neighbouring pits.

Swanscombe Church, dedicated to SS. Peter and Paul, is within the diocese of Rochester; it has a nave and two aisles, and a spire steeple, probably of the thirteenth century: some of the windows have been partially restored, but the interior presents that *bane* of all architectural beauty, *whitewash* and *ugly unmeaning pews.* There are some good monuments, principally of the Weldon family, who were distinguished residents during the reigns of Elizabeth and James I.

Anthony Weldon was descended from Bertram de Weldone, one of the retinue of the Earl of Northumberland at the Conquest: his third son was treasurer to Edward VI. Queen Elizabeth, in the second year of her reign (A.D. 1559), granted to Anthony Weldon the manor of Swanscombe: he died in 1574, when his eldest son Ralph inherited the manor and mansion.

On the south side of the church is a handsome mural monument with a finely-sculptured female effigy, intended to represent Dame Eleanor Weldon, near which is that of Anthony Weldon, kneeling at a desk upon which is an open book. The monument of their son Ralph, who died in 1602, is very stately; it represents the recumbent figure of Sir Ralph in armour, his wife by his side, and a son and daughter at their feet: in the front are their three sons and five daughters, figured as kneeling before a desk.

Swanscombe Church, in olden times, was resorted to by large companies of pilgrims, to pray the aid of St. Hilderfirth for the cure of insanity; his portrait, decked in the vestments of a bishop, formed a stained-glass window in the south aisle.

On the banks of the river stands the village of Greenhithe; here luxurious foliage and red brick dwellings, contrasting with the white chalk, have a pleasing effect. A neat pier opens upon the principal street, where steamboats call to embark or land passengers.

Ingress Park is an interesting spot. Formerly Ingress Abbey stood here, which was surrendered to Henry VIII., and ultimately taken down. The late Alderman Harmer purchased the land of Government, and from the stone of old London Bridge built the present elegant Tudor-Gothic mansion, with its charming lawn spreading down to the marge of the river.

This little village was the scene of considerable excitement on the morning of the 11th of August 1863, when the Royal Yacht ' Victoria and Albert,' moored off Ingress Abbey, received on board H.M. the Queen and members of Her august family, when the pier, the park, and the shore were crowded with loving subjects, anxious to testify their loyalty by the waving of hats and handkerchiefs.

———◆◇◆———

STONE,

WHICH is the adjoining parish, takes its name from *Stane*, the Saxon for *stone*, the nature of the soil. It is 17 miles from London, and 4½ from Gravesend, and contains 3,305 acres of gravelly land, inclusive of nearly 600 acres of wood and marsh, with 193 houses and 1,013 inhabitants.

The village, as well as the church, stands on the side of a hill rising from the Thames, and commands an extensive and beautiful landscape, enhanced by the undulating character of the country. Near the south-east boundary of the parish is *Cockleshell Bank*, so called from the immense number of those shells found lying close and thick, a foot in depth; a stratum of these bivalves was disco-vered at Bexley, two feet in thickness, and twenty feet below the surface.

Stone Castle, once the stronghold of the Lords of Stone, is ancient, having been in the possession of the Norwood family early in the fourteenth century, and said to have been built on the site of a former Norman castle; the square battled tower at the east end, covered with ivy, is all that remains of the original, the other por-tions being modern. Sir John Wyllshire (commonly Wiltshire), Comptroller of the Town and Marches of Calais and Lord of the Manor of Cotton, who died in 1526, possessed it in the reign of Henry VII.

Taking a winding lane on the right of the high road, and passing a farm, some neat cottages, the parsonage (a pleasing Gothic structure of flint and red brick), and a handsome house on the right, we reach Stone Church, built of stone and flints early in the four-teenth century, and dedicated to St. Mary. It abounds in fine specimens of Early English, Decorated English, and Perpendicular styles of architecture, and ranks amongst the finest Gothic churches within the diocese of Rochester.

The massive embattled tower at the west-end contains a peal of musical bells, and a clock with two dials painted blue; formerly an octagonal spire of considerable elevation rose from it, but this was destroyed by lightning in 1638, when the bells are said to have been melted from the intense heat. Near the tower, on the north side, is an original doorway full of richness, in elaborated stone-carving, which, although stamped by the wear of centuries, still retains traces of its former beauty; the windows are fine and regular; the chancel, which is large, rises above the roof of the church; on the north side is an ancient chapel built in the Perpendicular style of architecture, having a fine flying buttress reclining against the chancel wall. This chapel—which until recently was in ruins—has a vault in the centre, containing the remains of Sir John Wyllshire and his lady.

The external grandeur of a venerable fane warms desire to enter its portals; an intelligent man is laying grass, and tending the order of the churchyard: he tells us that the rector, the Rev. F. W. Murray, is very kindly to visitors, and would, he thought, comply with our wishes:—this functionary, whose civility deserves mention, was parish clerk and sexton. Profiting by his suggestion, we repair to the parsonage, see the rector, and have to acknowledge with gratitude that rev. gentleman's kindly attention and courtesy.

Upon entering the church by the west door we were much impressed with its beautiful proportions and the grandeur of the restoration. Every vestige of Vandalism had been swept away, with all trace of the obnoxious whitewasher: so light and elegant, the nave and aisles effectively paved with coloured tiles, a sumptuous marble pulpit, handsome open seats, indeed every fitting, whether for use or ornament, exquisitely appropriate. A series of noble pointed arches springing from clustered columns support an open roof. The chancel arch spanning the nave is one of the finest in the county, with a rich stringing of elaborate carving, and other ornamentations of Petworth marble with which the church abounds. There are several memorial and other stained-glass windows. The east window is very fine. One on the south side of the chancel calls for special notice, as being filled with very ancient stained glass, probably of the date of the foundation. There is a *piscina* but no *sedilia*, although a series of arches on the south wall warrant the assumption that they once existed.

The chancel is paved very beautifully with rich encaustic tiles, and the communion-table decked with a superb maroon velvet covering, an elaboration of splendid embroidery, the handiwork of the talented sister of the rector.

The chapel on the north of the chancel has also been restored, and now forms part of the church. Here is the fine altar-tomb of Sir John Wyllshire under a stone arch, and some others. An upper screen of memorial glass, the gift of the parishioners, rises over the entrance from the north aisle. The chapel is fitted with seats for children, where a small organ with diapered pipes has been erected.

There are other good monuments and sepulchral brasses in this church. The most elaborate of the latter is on the south side of the chancel near the communion-table; it represents a cross-flori elevated on four steps. In the centre above the cross is the figure of a priest with inscribed label from the mouth; round the bordure of the flower are other inscriptions, and on the body of the cross, continued on the steps, is an inscription to the memory of ' *John Lambarde, Rector of Stone, obiit Mar.* 12, 1408.' The shield of arms on either side is lost, and portions of the inscription ; an important piece, however, was found during the restoration, amongst rubbish taken from the roof, thanks to the foresight of the rector, who caused all débris to be minutely examined before removed.

We cannot take leave of this magnificent sanctuary, which has afforded us so much pleasure, without recording our high estimate of the rector and his coadjutors, in carrying out so perfectly the restoration—an honour to the parish and a noble example for incumbents of ancient churches to emulate.

SOUTHFLEET.

A BOISTEROUS morning had followed a stormy night when we repaired to the Town Pier for the offices of the shoeblack before starting to Southfleet. A friend, bareheaded, salutes us. He had just arrived from London, and whilst crossing from Tilbury rude Boreas *sans cérémonie* snatched his *chapeau*—a casualty, however, speedily remedied at Mr. Smoker's in the High Street, than whom no better hatter in town or country can be found.

The sun having broken through threatening clouds now evidently dispersing, we start at noon for a five miles' drive through gay and beautiful scenery. Choice fruits temptingly adorn the orchards, stacks of corn are rapidly rising on every side, the thatcher is active, and the ploughman furrows for the next sowing. We pass several luxuriant hop-gardens, and after descending a steep hill alight at the Ship Inn, Southfleet, where a biscuit and ' Old Cheshire,' toned by a cup of good sparkling, proves an acceptable refresher.

Southfleet, which contains 2,340 acres, 160 houses, and 717 inhabitants, and called in Domesday ' *Suthfleta,*' was a place of importance during the Saxon Heptarchy, when one of the Kings of Kent gave the manor and church to the Priory of St. Andrews, Rochester. At the dissolution of the priory the manor reverted to the Crown, which Henry VIII. granted to Sir William Petre, the King's secretary. Sir William afterwards sold it to William Gerrard, who was Lord Mayor of London in 1553, at whose death it reverted to his son John, who was also Lord Mayor of London in 1611. John Gerrard sold the manor to Sir Charles Sedley, descended from an ancient family who had a seat near Southfleet called Scadbury, or Scotbury, as early as the year 1337, of which a farmhouse is pointed out as the only remains.

The parish of Southfleet, once studded with goodly mansions and noble seats, is less known than its historical importance deserves. This may be ascribed to the absence of any public road through the parish, as well as from most of the ancient stately structures having either been removed or converted into farm-houses. There can be no doubt that this locality was invested with interest early in the Christian era. The Roman highway (Watling Street) ran on the northern side of the parish, and a Roman mile-stone dug up near Springhead bore the Roman figure X deeply cut on its side, to denote the distance from some particular station. Here also were turned up by the plough numerous silver and copper coins. Dr. Thorpe, a high authority, assumes that the station *Vagniacæ* was near this spot, which answers to the numerical figure graven on the *Roman milliare*, as being about *ten* Italian miles from the Medway at Rochester.

Some important discoveries were made whilst ploughing at a spot called *Sole field*, when an orbicular vessel made of red pottery was found, capable of holding twenty gallons. This discovery induced further investigation, which unfolded a building of large dimensions, resembling a vault, containing a tomb of stone, the receptacle for two coffins made of lead, enshrining the perfect skeletons of children. In one of the coffins was a superb gold-linked chain adorned with stones and pearls, all more or less decayed. In the same coffin were two curious gold rings for bracelets, ornamented with snakes' heads, and a smaller one set in representation of a hyacinth. Upon removing the pavement of Kentish rag-stone a square sarcophagus, four feet in length, was found containing two glass urns, the largest being fifteen inches high. In these were ashes and a transparent tasteless fluid. Between the urns were two pairs of shoes made of fine leather of a purple tint, elaborately wrought with gold ; the shoes were much decayed, but sufficiently perfect to demonstrate the beauty and richness of workmanship. To trace the history of these remarkable relics would be impossible; still, from the urns containing human ashes, we may fairly infer the period was during the Roman dynasty, which ended early in the fifth century ; and from the jewellery and other costly articles, the remains were those of distinguished personages, probably royalty.

We return to the primitive village called Church Street, of some dozen quaint houses, including that of the blacksmith, the village tailor, a general shop, and the post-office ; the Ship Inn and the endowed school stand on the opposite side, shaded by noble walnut trees.

The school, a substantial structure of red brick, was built in 1637. A grim-looking erection, with iron-barred door and deserted appearance, stands at the east end. It is the village ' Cage,' happily long in disuse. The entrance to the school is by a flight of steps leading to an antiquated porch, over which is a stone tablet notifying that it was founded by Sir John Sedley, or, as the inscription reads,

Sidley, of which we give a literal transcript:—' *The Schoole was founded by ye piety of Sir John Sidley, Baronet,* A.D. 1637, *augmented by Mrs. Elizabeth Sidley his daughter,* A.D. 1639. *Polished and maintained by Sir Charles Sidley, Baronet, his sone, whom God long continue,* A.D. 1657. *Amen.*'

We were invited to inspect the interior, which is light and airy, divided by a sliding partition to form schools for girls and boys, under the careful training of Miss Wiggins and Mr. Baker. A robin was hopping on the beams during our visit, merrily carolling his autumnal song, undisturbed by the chubby urchins beneath.

The little village was all excitement, and everybody lavish of congratulations, even to the kindly hostess of the snug inn, notwithstanding her recent severe loss in the death of her husband. A Miss Martin, the smith's sister, had just married an old Gravesender, in whom we recognised the original vender of *Barnard's Old.*

By the courtesy of the rector, the Rev. G. F. Goddard, we are permitted to inspect the grand old church, standing central in its ancient cemetery. Opening a gate leading to the churchyard we are welcomed by the obliging schoolmaster, who directs attention to a gravestone newly erected by Col. Brasyer, one of India's brave warriors during the late dreadful rebellion, which brought sorrow and desolation to so many British homes. The first name recorded is that of his father, John Brasyer; he died in 1795: the next, his mother, Ann Brasyer, who died in 1837; then follows his brother John, died 1814; a sister Mary, in 1848; and another brother, Thomas, who died in 1851. Colonel Brasyer was born in this parish, of parents in humble life. The acumen of a great mind induced him to leave his home when a boy, with but a solitary sixpence and a mother's blessing to help him in his wanderings. Years – many years—roll away, and he returns to the land of his birth a distinguished hero, revisits his native village, and raises this interesting memorial.

Southfleet Church, dedicated to St. Nicholas, is built of stone and flints, and dates from about the thirteenth century; externally it presents a noble and ecclesiastical appearance, with a massive square-embattled tower, furrowed with age, containing a peal of good bells. The entrance is by a Gothic porch on the south side, over which is a sun-dial resembling that of Milton Church, and bearing the same motto, *Trifle not, your time's but short.* Some of the windows have been restored, and filled with stained glass. The church door is a curiosity of antiquity, several inches in thickness, and studded with bosses of iron; then, again, the lock, morticed in a block of oak, a key nine inches in length, with complex wards, to prove that the locksmith's art was matured even in remote ages. We enter the church and tread its aisles with reverence; for here slumber alike, without mortal distinction, the exalted of the land

and the meanest peasant, where the grandeur of human pomp, long since festered into dust, awaits the resurrection morn.

This interesting church has a nave and aisles, with three noble pointed arches on each side. The windows, of two lights mullioned, are doubtless of the date of the structure; in some of these are fragments of stained glass equally old. From a stone doorway in the tower, and a fine pointed arch opening into the church, there can be little doubt that formerly the principal entrance was from the west end: it is now partitioned off, and the arch boarded up, with a stage of seats for children ranged in front, supporting a small organ. Some of the original rude oak carving may be traced amongst the incongruous pews, as well as encaustic tiles interspersed in the paving, and the outlines of frescoes on the walls, of very early date.

Passing down the nave and under a fine pointed arch, we reach the chancel, some forty feet in length. Here are the ancient oak stalls of the olden priesthood; a triple stone *sedilia* under decorated arches supported by grey marble columns, and the *piscina* in a six-foiled arch. The chancel windows have been restored and filled with memorial glass; the east window is very rich, with figures in ten compartments to illustrate the history of Our Saviour. In the priests' robing room stands a plain oaken chest, containing the registers and other records. This is of great antiquity, and supposed (according to our attendant) to date from the foundation of the church. In this room is another stone niche, which in ages past was a receptacle for either holy water or an image of the Virgin.

There are some good monuments and memorial brasses; the most remarkable are those of the Sedley family in the south aisle, which was formerly a chantry or chapel adjoining the church. Here is an altar tomb to the memory of John and Elizabeth Sedley, dated early in the fifteenth century, supporting two cleverly wrought figures, and two inscriptions in brass, with running inscription on every side. On the pavement in front of this tomb is another large figure in brass. Near the south wall is a curiously small mummy-like figure in brass, evidently very old, but without date; it bears this quaint inscription—*Pray for the soul of Thomas Cobbett, on whose soul Jesu have mercy. Amen, for charity.* The most gorgeous monument is against the south wall, rising nearly to the roof, and erected to the memory of *Joannis Sedley, born 4th January,* 1561, *died 8th July,* 1605, *aged* 44. It represents the full figure of a knight recumbent on an altar tomb surmounted by a rich marble canopy. Behind the effigy rises an ornamental arch, emblazoned with elaborate sculpture forming cherubim, flowers, and other devices, in every variety of marble and decoration. The morion and sword of the knight may be seen on the top of the canopy.

The octagonal font, which is very ancient, has a scriptural

G 2

subject in each compartment; some are palpable whilst others appear
hieroglyphical. We hope the time is not far distant when this time-
honoured pile, like that of Stone Church, shall have been faithfully
restored to the glory of God, and the admiration of every lover of
classical architecture.

MEOPHAM.

It was one of those lovely cloudless mornings peculiar to autumn,
when the air is crisp but not cold, when the spirits become
vigorous and exuberant, that we had selected for visiting Meopham,
famous for health and longevity. A Kentish friend (now of our
house) is to be our companion and whip. We speedily reach
Shinglewell, which takes its name from the shingly bottom of a
deep well, now corrupted to Singlewell. The gardens at the *Half-
way House* are prettily laid out with rustic arbours and swings,
and have deserved popularity for pic-nics and juvenile sports
during the Gravesend season.

Within a short distance, at the extremity of a charming lane,
stands Ifield Church, one of the smallest in the diocese of Rochester. It was built in the year 1596 and dedicated to St. Margaret.
The arms of Sir John Gerrard, Lord Mayor of London in 1611, are
emblazoned on the east window. The living is valued at £120.
The present rector, the Rev. W. Nockells, who succeeded to the
living in 1860, has caused the interior to be repaired and beautified,
and a small organ to be erected. The parish of Ifield is propor-
tionately small, consisting of 312 statute acres of land, twelve houses,
and eighty-eight inhabitants.

Nursted, the next parish, has only nine houses and fifty-seven
inhabitants, with 510 acres of land. The ancient Gothic church
stands on high ground, and forms a pleasing object from several
points. It has a square tower, and contains some good monuments,
principally of the Wentworth family. The rector of Nursted
Church (dedicated to St. Mildred) is the Rev. W. H. Edmeades,
who has held the living since 1828, in his own right, as patron of
this as well as of the adjoining parish of Ifield.

A short drive southward and we near Meopham, pronounced
Mepham, anciently written Meapaham. This large parish has
4,693 acres of land, 220 houses, and 1,123 inhabitants. The air is
remarkably healthy; the parish abounds in small hamlets. King
Athelstane gave Meopham to the Duke Eadulph, who presented it
to Canterbury in 940. Queen Ediva, mother of Kings Edmund
and Edred, gave Meopham to Christ Church, Canterbury, in the

year 961, *for the benefit of her soul.* Henry VI. granted to Meopham an annual fair and a weekly market.

The manor of Dodmore belonged to Sir Peter Huntingfield during the reign of Edward I. Sir Peter was of a noble family, and sheriff of the county. Dean Court, a valuable estate, was in the possession of Alen de Twitham, a favourite of Richard I., whom he attended to the siege of Ascalon in Palestine.

The distinguished scholar and ecclesiastic, Simon Meopham, or rather Mepham, was born in the parish. He was created Archbishop of Canterbury in 1327, and afterwards consecrated by the Pope at Rome. During his primacy he was the subject of much persecution. He died at his palace, Mayfield, February 11, 1333, and was buried in St. Anselm's Chapel, Canterbury Cathedral, where a handsome black marble monument was erected to his memory.

Meopham, five miles from Gravesend, stands high; the village borders the green. The church, dedicated to St. John the Baptist, is large, principally in the decorated style of architecture, with a square-battled tower and a ring of bells. It is entered by a quaint porch, and consists of a nave and two aisles, with noble pointed arches and good windows; although the wear of centuries marks the whole, yet it stands in its original integrity, without modern mutilation. Formerly there were some ancient brasses; the only one however remaining is to the memory of John Follham, who died in 1455; the others were removed during the last century, when the bells were recast, and used to supply additional metal.

Meopham had a church before the Conquest, rebuilt by Archbishop Mepham, between the years 1327–33, on the old foundations. It was repaired by Archbishop Courteney towards the close of the fourteenth century, who built, at the same time, four almshouses near it for poor inhabitants. The sombrous churchyard has few modern gravestones, but some of the more ancient arrest attention, as, having lost every trace of their graven inscriptions from decay, they are again reproduced in living characters of moss rooted in the feeble outlines. Meopham is a vicarage in the gift of the Archbishop of Canterbury; the Rev. John Hooper succeeded to the living in 1854.

Our zealous guide is desirous of extending our drive; his horse is fresh, and so are our spirits; we hail his proposal, and at once start for—

WROTHAM,

Six miles distant from Meopham; the scenery is highly picturesque, especially from the elevated range of chalk hills. We pause on the summit of Wrotham hill in admiration of the gorgeous prospect southward in the vale beneath, outspread on nature's carpet to the

utmost bound of vision; feelings of awe crowd on us as we contemplate this mighty contexture of woods and stately trees—
churches, villages, hamlets, and homesteads—noble mansions and
cottages all alike illumined by the orb of day; whilst the tinkle of
numberless cattle scattered on all sides, the poetry of rural life,
give animation to the whole. We linger on the marge of this
magnificent picture, and then slowly descend to the town.

Wrotham is a parish five miles in length and three in breadth,
covering 8,878 statute acres, with 671 houses and 3,336 inhabitants;
the high road from London to Maidstone runs through the town, in
the centre of which is the market place. During the rebellion of
Sir Thomas Wyatt, Sir Robert Southwell, sheriff of the county,
with a band of gentlemen and yeomen, encountered Sir Henry Isley
and his followers in Blacksole field, whom they defeated with great
slaughter; sixty of the rebels were taken prisoners, and the slain
buried on the battle field.

King Ethelstan gave Wrotham to the monks of Christ Church,
Canterbury, in 964, which they retained until after the Conquest.
The remains of an archiepiscopal palace stand on the east side of
the church, which, very anciently, was the residence of several
archbishops until the primacy of Simon Islip, who pulled down the
larger portion during the reign of Edward III. and sent the materials
to Maidstone for the completion of his new palace. The manor,
with the ruins of the palace, were conveyed to Henry VIII., but
his successor Edward VI. granted the manor and park of Wrotham
to Sir John Mason.

Little Wrotham, a small manor of 130 acres, was in the possession
of Geoffry Talbot in the reign of Henry I., who gave it to Bishop
Gundulph, and the Church of St. Andrew, Rochester. There are
other small manors in this parish, as well as ancient mansions more
or less fallen to decay, and some good seats, to detail which would
exceed our purpose.

Wrotham Church, dedicated to St. George, stands north of the
town, at the base of the hill. It is a noble structure built of stone
and flints, with a nave, aisles, transept, and chancel. According to
the decorated style of architecture which prevailed from Edward I.
to Edward III., it dates from the early part of the fourteenth century.
It has a fine groined archway under the square tower, which contains musical bells and a clock. Some of the decorated windows
have been restored, and filled with memorial glass; the pointed
arches are fine, and, judging from our only opportunity of inspecting
the interior through a grated door, the church has been largely
restored.

We make the circuit of the churchyard, amongst affecting
mementos of departed friends. Time has blotted out many ancient
inscriptions; others tell of the past century; whilst those of the
present speak touchingly of the love of sorrowing survivors:

Accompany us to the east end of the church, and under yon rich chancel window meditate over a simple spot, enclosed by an iron railing with a small open gate—it is the grave of a beloved father!—

> For whom no more the blazing hearth shall burn,
>   Or busy housewife ply her evening care;
> No children run to lisp their sire's return,
>   Or climb his knee the envied kiss to share.

We read that he shook off mortality with the last year; but see the affecting tribute of dear children;—a wreath of jessamine strung on wire graces the head-stone; a cross of fragrant flowers rests midway of the mound, and continues to the base; all around blossom in floral beauty the daily care of loving hearts. Where the rude hand that dare disturb them? Where the heart that can witness such tributes of love, so full of pathos, without emotion?

It is nearing seven, the day wanes, a hilly journey of eleven miles before us, and, but for our cicerone, strangers to the road; we are however in safe hands, speed homeward, and with the curfew hour reach Gravesend in safety.

DENTON.

ON our way to Denton we stop at Milton Church, to read a memorial stone just placed on the south side of the tower entrance. It was erected at the cost of the rector, to the memory of Elizabeth Ribbens, who died at Thames Terrace, Gravesend, in January 1862, at the surprising age of 105 years and seven months. Mrs. Ribbens was a native of Meopham, her husband a servant of the late Mr. Becket, brewer of Gravesend, on whose premises he lost his life many years since, and from whose death the family liberally maintained the widow. We frequently during our annual sojourn visited her. On the last occasion, the September previous to her death, she was evidently failing, her appetite had become bad, and her mind much clouded; this venerable woman lived to have a grand-daughter 50, and a great-grand-daughter 25 years of age.

DENTON, called in Domesday *Danitane,* or Dane town, as having been the habitation of the Danes, contains, including land under cultivation, marsh and water, 1,320 acres, 23 houses, and 101 inhabitants; it is distinguished as Denton near Gravesend from that of Denton near Canterbury, and belonged to the Priory of St. Andrew's, Rochester, in 945; it was confiscated by King Harold, but afterwards restored in 1076; Henry VIII. gave this manor to the Dean and Chapter of Rochester.

The church, dedicated to St. Mary, is described as a small building, with one aisle, a chancel, and bell-tower, standing on a bank close to the road side.   According to Kilburn, service was celebrated here down to the middle of the seventeenth century, when it was principally taken down.   At that time there were only two houses and a farm near the church ; the farm-yard is the supposed site of the cemetery, from human bones having been frequently dug up.

The remains of Denton Church stand in the grounds of a handsome house, nearly hidden from the road by a lofty brick wall.   We were desirous of a near inspection, but the hour was seven in the morning, certainly not the time for visiting, more especially as being strangers to the proprietor.   Still curiosity was awakened ; we boldly rang the bell, a distant foot-fall traverses the long path from the house, anon the gate is opened, we confront a domestic, tell our errand, and are conducted to that gentleman, who unhesitatingly accords our request.   Threading our way through shrubs and trees, we reach the precincts of all that remains of a sanctuary before the Conquest ; the ivy-mantled arches are beautiful even in decay, and the crumbling walls stand, the solitary witnesses of that prayer and praise which in remote ages ascended from this Temple of God on earth to the threshold of that heaven to which every Christian mind aspires.

We had no means for correct measurement, but, judging by pacing within the walls, its dimensions are about 40 feet by 18 feet, closely corresponding to that of Ifield Church.   A pointed arch of stone and flints, in height about 18 feet by 8 feet, divides the chancel from the nave ; this is tolerably perfect ; its wing walls, covered with ivy, rise to an apex above the arch, the elevation of the original roof. Thirteen feet east of the chancel arch are the remains of the east window, a small pointed arch, 6 feet by 3 feet, with parts of its side walls still standing.   Here again that living companion of mouldering ruins clings and clambers to the very summit in solemn grandeur.   Those portions of the north and south walls which still remain extend from the chancel arch to the western extremity, in length about 27 feet.   The south wall is very curious; for, although originally built of stone and flints, it has traces of repairs with brick at a remote period.   In this wall also are the remains of a low stone arch, with short columns and capitals mouldered away and all but obliterated.   Altogether this is a most interesting relic, and we feel grateful for the privilege of minute examination ; still we might express regret that, from being private property, and scarcely visible above the lofty walls that enclose it, much less interest is excited than its sacred character and remote antiquity claim.

A pleasing walk of little more than half a mile from Denton brings us to—

CHALK,

That takes its name from the Saxon word *cealc*, signifying chalk-stone. This parish contains 2,224 acres (including water and marsh land), 78 houses, and 382 inhabitants. The southern side of the parish is hilly and fertile, whilst the north is flat and marshy.

William the Conqueror gave Chalk to his half-brother Odo, Bishop of Bayeux, upon whose disgrace the manor was divided into East and West Chalk. The hamlet of East Chalk lies adjacent to the marshes, and is not considered healthy, especially in autumn, when agues are common. A fair is held here on Whit Monday. The manor of East Chalk belonged to John, son of Herbert de Burgo, Earl of Kent, during the reign of Henry III. ; that of West Chalk was in the possession of John de Cobham in the same reign; but at the dissolution of monasteries, Henry VIII. conferred on George Lord Cobham the manor of East Chalk, in addition to that of West Chalk, which he possessed in his own right.

The church stands on the brow of a hill at the top of a lane on the left of the road; it is dedicated to St. Mary, and is of great antiquity. As early as 1287 (15th Edward I.) it belonged to the Benedictine Priory at Norwich. In 1379 it was exchanged with the Master of Cobham College for the Church of Martham in Norfolk, and remained part of the possessions of that college until the 30th of Henry VIII. (1539), when it was sold to Lord George Cobham.

Chalk Church, isolated from human habitation, peers over some venerable elms, and forms a pleasing object as we diverge from the road on our way to it; the old battled tower, of early English architecture, rises before us, clothed in ivy on the south side, with its three bells and time-stricken walls that may yet brave many ages. Gothic architecture however, which has many licenses in whimsical sculpture, seldom presents such sportive fancy in a sacred edifice as that over the porch door, the only entrance to the church, where a bacchanalian figure is represented clutching with both hands a jug, while grinning at another figure above the centre moulding equally grotesque. Between the figures is a niche, in which formerly stood an image of the virgin saint to whom the church is dedicated. In the south-east corner of the porch are the remains of a receptacle for holy water. The font is very ancient, the proof being its size, which, according to Grose and Warton, are ancient in proportion as they are capacious, being originally used for total immersion, with perforations to let off the consecrated water *that it might not be used by common people for purposes of sorcery.* Some of the windows have been restored, beyond which little has been done in that direction.

An ancient screen divides the nave from the chancel, over which are the royal arms, painted and framed, with the initials C. R. and the date 1600: here are *sedilia* and an odd niche on the north side of the chancel. The north wall excites curiosity, from having the stone heads and tracery of several Gothic windows within six feet of the pavement. Some archæologists who surveyed the church a few years since, and which they considered dated from the eleventh century, were of opinion that some convulsion of nature many cen- turies ago had caused the north side to sink many feet: hence the window-heads in their present position. In the nave is a brass plate to the memory of William Martin, a great benefactor to the church, who died in 1416. Amongst the monuments is that of ' Henry Roy, Vicar of Chalke,' and another for Edward Dering and Elizabeth his wife, obiit 1698.

We have been much interested; and, in taking leave of Chalk Church and the rector, the Rev. William Joynes, who has shown us much attention, beg to thank that gentleman, not only for our- selves, but more especially for his courtesy to our ladies, to whom he kindly gave seats in his carriage on their return to Gravesend—a compliment to strangers we desire thus publicly to acknowledge.

Earl Darnley has given an eligible site of land and £50 to- wards the erection of a National School, to cost £350; the present schools being only two small rooms in a cottage, with an average attendance of forty children, which could be considerably augmented were proper accommodation provided.

SHORNE AND MERSTON.

MERSTON, formerly Merestune, forms part of the parish of Shorne in its civil jurisdiction, and as such assessed to the maintenance of the poor from the time of Queen Elizabeth. In its ecclesiastical state it still remains a separate parish. The church, dedicated to St. Giles, was a chapel to the Church of Shorne, of which only a few ruins remain. The living, value £90, in the gift of the Lord Chancellor, has been conferred on the Rev. William Joynes, Vicar of Chalk.

The parish of Merston (of 150 acres) bounds that of Shorne on three sides, and Higham on the fourth, in which there were no in- habitants in 1455. In a line between the churches of Shorne and Higham is a small wood of some five acres, called Chapel Wood, as being the spot where the ruins of the church stand. In this wood is a deep entrenchment, anciently a fortification, forming a square of about three acres, the sides corresponding to the cardinal points of the compass. The Chapel of St. Giles measured 45 feet by 21, but long before it fell into decay was in comparative disuse, for, according to the *Textus Roffensis*, John Hedon, when licensed chaplain by the Bishop of Rochester, was not obliged *to reside or exercise the cure of souls here till parishioners should resort thither to dwell.* As, however, the church was then standing, the chaplain or his representative was to celebrate mass annually therein on the feast of St. Giles, Confessor and Abbot, and in the meantime *cause it to be decently repaired.*

Shorne and Merston jointly consist of 3,214 acres, 963 inhabitants, and 190 houses. In the *Textus Roffensis* it is written *Scorene*, and in other ancient documents *Soncs* and *Schornes*. The high road from London to Rochester runs through it, southward of which rises the village beyond some orchards and enclosures of sturdy trees. The church stands in the village, gay in rich foliage and abundant fruit trees. The soil of this parish is a fertile loam ; the scenery very picturesque, with pleasing walks between Shorne and the high road, in the direction of the Half-way or Beef-steak House, and on the west by the hamlets of Shorne, Ifield, and Thong : here is Randle Heath and Shorne Wood, and on the west Randle Hall. At the extremity of the parish, on the river bank, stands Shorne Battery. A lovely walk to this spot is at high water by the river-side from Milton, passing the well-known ' Ship and Lobster,' where refreshments and civility abound, to the gratification of many who, after imbibing freely the bracing breeze and feasting on gorgeous landscape, incline to rest and renovate on more substantial viands.

The manor of Shorne belonged to the Crown in the reign of Henry II., afterwards to Henry de Cobham. On the disgrace of Henry Lord Cobham in 1604 it was forfeited to the Crown, and then granted to the Earl of Salisbury by King James ; since then it was sold to Alderman Woodyer of Rochester, and by him conveyed in 1752 to Thomas Gordon. There is a court-leet and court-baron held for this manor under the title of *The Manor of Shorne, with the Hundred of Shamel appendant to the same.* The manor of Randle, formerly Roundale and Rundale, was anciently of some note as one of the seats of the house of Cobham previous to that of Cobham Hall. It was sold in 1793 to Earl Darnley.

On the west side of the London road are some ruins, of which no evidence exists as to their foundation ; but whilst excavating some years since for a building, a stone coffin and human bones were dug up in its vicinity, which circumstance has warranted the supposition that they are the remains of a chantry or oratory. The windmill on the hill at Shorne is a most conspicuous object, and may be seen for many miles distant.

Shorne Church, dedicated to the Apostles SS. Peter and Paul, is another of those battled-tower venerable Gothic fanes with which

Kent abounds. Henry I. gave it to the Monastery of St. Saviour's
at Bermondsey, in whose possession it remained until Henry VIII.,
when that monarch conferred it on the Dean and Chapter of Rochester.   The chancel formerly belonged to the manor of Randle,
but when forfeited to the crown in 1604, with the estates of Henry
Lord Cobham, it devolved to the parish.   The font, made of Bethersden marble, is both ancient and curious, and resembles that of
Southfleet Church, octangular in form, with Scripture subjects carved
in each of the eight compartments round the basin.   The architecture is decorated English, which prevailed in the fourteenth century,
the probable date of the church.

Here are some good monuments and sepulchral brasses. Amongst
the former is that of Sir Henry de Cobham, *le Uncle*, to distinguish
him from his namesake and nephew of Cobham Hall.   Sir Henry
highly distinguished himself at the siege of Caerlaverock, in reward
for which he was knighted by Edward I., and five times filled the
office of Sheriff of Kent.   His altar-monument stands north-east of
the chancel, bearing the recumbent figure of the knight in chain
mail, with an inscription in French, written in ancient capital letters.
Amongst the memorial brasses are those of *John Smyth, who died
in* 1437; *John Smith and Marian his wife*, 1457; *William Pepyr,
vicar*, 1468; *Thomas Ellys, vicar*, 1569; *Edmund Page*, 1550; *and
Elynor Allen*, 1583.   Eastward of these is a stone bearing the arms
of Captain Robert Porten, of the manor of Randle, with an inscription to the memory of his wife Elizabeth, obiit 1704.

William Pepyr, vicar, who died in 1468, gave his dwelling-house
for the repairs of the vicarage; and Thomas Page, an inhabitant,
gave under his will, dated 1495, his house called Normans, in Upper
Shorne, as a dwelling for the vicar and his successors.

Sir John Northwood held large estates in this parish in the reign
of Edward I., the tenure of which he changed from gavelkind to
knight's service, and accompanied the king in his victorious expedition into Scotland.   His grandson, Roger de Northwood, who
succeeded him, held these estates of the king (Edward III.) *in
capite*, by the service, with others of the king's tenants, of carrying
a white standard towards Scotland for forty days during the wars
at his own cost, a custom in England at that time.

Shorne boasted in olden times a celebrity, in the person of ' Mais-
ter John Shorne,' or ' Sir John Shorne,' who was famous not only
for the cure of agues, but as the custodian of the devil, whom he
imprisoned in a boot.   Shrines were erected to his memory.   In
two churches at Norfolk he is figured with a glory round his head
on the rood screen, whilst at Windsor a chapel bore his name.

HIGHAM.

HIGHAM, anciently written *Hercham, Hegham,* and *Heahhum,* contains 3,155 statute acres, 211 houses, and 1,064 inhabitants. The soil is fertile, and produces large quantities of superior vegetables for the surrounding markets; but the air is not considered healthy, from its proximity to the marshes. Higham was part of the possessions of Odo, Bishop of Bayeux, until his disgrace, when it reverted to the crown. King Stephen gave Higham, otherwise Lillechurch, to William de Ipre, Earl of Kent, in exchange for the manor of Faversham. After the death of the king, William de Ipre, with the rest of the Flemish, were expelled the kingdom, when it again came into possession of the crown.

King Stephen founded a nunnery here about the year 1151, over which his daughter the Princess Mary presided, when the community consisted of fifteen nuns of the Benedictine order. The nunnery was afterwards rebuilt near the east end of the church. In 1320, when visited by the Bishop of Rochester, there were only eight nuns, and in 1502, upon the election of a prioress, there remained only three nuns on the foundation: the community was wholly suppressed in 1521. A farmhouse called Abbey Farm has been built on part of the original foundations, of which those portions of stone with Gothic windows are considered remains of the ancient abbey. Contiguous to the farmyard are the ruins of some of the walls, covered with ivy.

Henry VIII. gave to Bishop Fisher the manor of Higham, the site of the nunnery, and the parsonage, for St. John's College, Cambridge; the college to provide *a priest to officiate daily in the chapel of the convent, to celebrate a mass of requiem four times a year, and to distribute twelve pence yearly on Michaelmas day to the poor of the parish.*

Not far from the church, in the flat country, is the hamlet and manor of Higham Ridgeway. Here are considerable remains of a Roman causeway leading to the river, nearly thirty feet wide, the repairs of which were formerly chargeable on the Priory of Higham. It is said that Plautius the Roman general crossed by this way from Essex into Kent when in pursuit of the flying Britons, A.D. 43—an opinion endorsed by Dr. Thorpe and Dr. Plott, two celebrated authorities. This passage is supposed to have formed a causeway across the river from East Tilbury in Essex, which was then fordable. About twenty years since some Roman vessels and a number of coins were exhumed near it.

Great and Little Oakley are two reputed manors in this parish.

Their names come from the Saxon *ac* or *ake*, an oak, and *ly*, a field,
written *Aclea*. meaning ' the place of oaks.' In the reign of Edward I.
both these estates were in the possession of William de Clere.
Great Oakley descended to Nicholas de St. Clere, who, as well as
his successors, were lessees to the Abbey of Higham. In the reign
of Henry VII. it formed part of the possessions of Sir John Sedley,
of Southfleet, whose son, Sir Charles, sold it to Mr. Shales, of Ports-
mouth. Little Oakley was the property of John de St. Clere in the
20th of Edward III. Sir Charles Sedley was in possession of it in
the reign of Charles II., and, after passing from him through several
hands, it was ultimately sold in 1760 to Mr. William Gates, of Rochester, whose son George, town clerk of Rochester, inherited it at
his decease in 1768. George Gates died in 1792, when it became
the property of his sister. There are no courts held for either of
these manors.

In the reign of Edward VI. Sir Anthony St. Ledger held an estate here called ' The Brooks,' consisting of marsh lands in Higham,
which he conveyed to the king; it afterwards came into the
possession of the Stuarts, Dukes of Richmond, from whom it passed
in like manner as Cobham Hall to Earl Darnley. Another estate,
called Mockbeggar, lies at the east end of the parish, on the road
from Frindsbury to Cliffe. South-east, on a hill, stands the ' Hermitage,' an elegant seat, commanding lovely scenery of the Medway
and Thames, stretching to the Nore, and of a vast extent of landscape in Kent and Essex. Sir Francis Head rebuilt this seat, where
he resided; he was also possessed of other goodly estates, including
the manor of Higham Ridgeway. At his death in 1768 the seat
and estates devolved by settlement to his widow, Lady Head, who
died in 1792, when the property was divided amongst descendants
of the family. It is said that this mansion is exuberant in decoration—the ceilings especially—with a superb drawing or ball room
on the west side of unusual dimensions.

Higham extends nearly four miles from south-east to north-west,
and but little more than a mile in breadth. It lies low, next the
marshes, the Thames being the northern boundary. The village
and church stand close to the marshes, which comprise nearly half
the parish. On the eastern side the land is high and the soil
light.

Gad's Hill, in this neighbourhood, claims a passing word from its
association with Shakspere, when gads, or rogues, were wont to way-
lay unwary travellers; where the Danish ambassador was robbed
in 1656, for which he received next day an apology from his marauders, *for the necessity that compelled them to wait on him at Gad's
Hill.* In Shakspere's ' King Henry IV.' (Act I. sc. ii.), Poins, in
addressing Prince Henry, is made to say: *But, my lads, my lads, to-
morrow morning by four o'clock early, at Gadshill: There are pilgrims going to Canterbury with rich offerings, and traders riding to*

London with fat purses : I have visors for you all, you have horses for yourselves. And again, in Act II., after the robbery of the travellers, supposed to have been enacted near the present ' Sir John Falstaff Inn,' when Falstaff and his ' men of buckram ' are about to divide the booty. comes the memorable illustration of ' thief robbing thief,' in the address of Prince Henry to Poins, as —*Now, could thou and I rob the thieves, and go merrily to London, it would be argument for a week, laughter for a month, and a good jest for ever.*

Gad's Hill, however, was notorious for robberies before Shakspere. In 1558 a ballad was published entitled *The Robbers of Gad's Hill.* Sir Roger Manwood, Chief Baron of the Exchequer, writes in 1590 : *Many robberies were done at Gadeshill by horse-thieves, with such fat and lusty horses as were not like hackney horses, nor for journeying horses, and one of them sometimes wearing a vizard grey beard, and no man durst travel that way without great company.*

On the brow of the hill stands the ' Sir John Falstaff Inn,' and swinging on the signpost in front, until lately, a supposed resemblance of the obese gourmand and his libertine prince, which, from long exposure, was nearly obliterated, and is now taken down. We alight here : Shakspere has given interest to the spot, and so does yon elegant structure overlooking magnificent landscape, reposing in delightful grounds of charming flowers sheltered by luxurious trees : it is the country home of CHARLES DICKENS, our great English novelist. We at once call to remembrance the *thousand-and-one* inimitable beauties he has penned ; pictures of real life that reach our inmost sympathies as an impressive reality, clothed in the tenderness of human love, such as alone can emanate from a refined mind and exalted genius that shall long outlive monuments of stone and brass.

Higham Tunnel, a considerable cutting through the chalk cliff, cost £350,000. The Medway Canal ran through it until the formation of the North Kent Railway, when it was filled up, and now forms a tunnel for railway transit.

The parish of Higham had a church before the Conquest. The present structure, dedicated to St. Mary, is of great antiquity ; as early as 1357 it was repaired by the prioress of the Benedictine nunnery. Some historians affirm that Mary, daughter of King Stephen, contributed towards the reparation of this venerable pile. If this be correct, the church dates early in the twelfth century. It consists of a nave, two aisles, a double chancel, and a low tower at the west end containing two bells. Here is a *piscina*, a curious font, some ancient tiles, and several interesting memorials.

The church is undergoing complete restoration, and the vandalisms of the last century removed; the chancel reconstructed and paved with Minton's tiles, and an appropriate railing to enclose the whole. The tower and spire are to be rebuilt, for which designs have been prepared.

Within the inner doorway, behind a primitive iron chest, is the marble tomb of Joan de Hadloe, prioress of the nunnery, who died A D. 1328. Above this altar tomb is a mural monument for Robert Hylton, yeoman to Henry VIII., who died 1529. Amongst other interesting monuments are those of Elizabeth Boteler, 1615, and members of this ancient family; the Rev. W. Inglett, vicar, 1659; the Rev. Richard Pearson, 1710; an altar tomb for Anne Cardwell, 1642; Elizabeth Parker, of Shinglewell, 1670; Sir Francis Head, 1768; and Lady Mary Head, 1792. The living, valued at £518 per annum, is a vicarage, and in the patronage of St. John's College, Cambridge. The Rev. Joseph Hindle, B.D., succeeded to the incumbency in 1829.

A handsome new church in the Gothic style has recently been erected at a cost of upwards of £2,800, near the 'Sir John Falstaff Inn,' a short distance from the high road, in which there is an effective organ built by Willis, of London, the gift of F. Stunt, Esq.

———◆◇◆———

CLIFFE.

Our trip to Cliffe was to have been early in the day, but it rains heavily; we therefore substitute the morning paper, just sent by Mrs. Isern, our obliging news medium, which brings noon as well us fine weather. There is something very beautiful in a country drive after a showery morning, when nature puts forth her loveliest hues in richest foliage, and charming flowers diffuse their sweetest odours. Such was the day that smiled upon us as we journeyed to Cliffe, where we alight at the village inn, bearing the euphonic sign of the 'Six Bells.'

Cliffe, anciently *Clive*, or *Clives-Hoo*, and sometimes *Bishops-Clive*, now called *Cliffe-at-Hoo*, to distinguish it from the parish of the same name near Dover, covers 7,830 statute acres, of which a considerable portion is ,marsh land, with 205 houses and 980 inhabitants. The ancient village called Church Street stands, with its church, on the northern summit of a towering chalk ridge, overhanging extensive marshes on the banks of the Thames. In remote times it was a station for *Watch and Ward* to the river. In the reign of Richard II. beacons were erected here, when the watchmen were commanded, on the approach of hostile vessels, to light them, and *to make all the noise by horn and by cry that they can make, to warn the country around to come with their force to the said river, each to succour the other to withstand their enemies.* At that time the village was of large extent and of considerable importance; but in 1520 a fearful conflagration destroyed the larger portion, from which it never recovered.

During the Saxon heptarchy synods of the clergy and laity were convoked here. These assemblies were remarkable for their splendour and the exalted personages composing them. The king and the Archbishop of Canterbury were joint presidents. The king, with his nobles, represented the laity, and the archbishops, bishops, and abbots the clergy. Between the years 668 and 825 eight synods were holden at Cliffe. The first on record was convoked by Theodorus, who was Archbishop of Canterbury from 668 to 690. He held two, one at Hereford, and the other at ' *Clives-hoo, near Rochester.*' Archbishop Cuthbert held the next synod in 742, when ETHELBALD, King of Mercia, presided, at which a decree was instituted commanding that: ' *Priests should first learn and then teach their parishioners the Lord's Prayer and the Articles of their Belief, in the English tongue.*' In 747 King ETHELBALD, with the same archbishop, assembled the third synod, which was carried out with remarkable pomp and state. The next council was in 798, five years after the translation of Athelard to the see of Canterbury. He convoked other synods in 800 and 803. Cenulph, King of Mercia, presided at both, which happened in troublesome times, when the Danes were harassing the realm. The remaining synods were in 822 and 824, under the presidency of Bernulfe, King of Mercia, and Archbishop Wulfred. These resulted in the restoration to the church of certain lands which had been estranged from it. Archbishop Wulfred, in consequence, is reputed one of its best benefactors.

The manor of Cliffe formed part of the possessions of Christ Church, Canterbury, early in the Saxon rule, which they held down to Henry VIII., when it was conferred on Sir George Brooke, Lord Cobham. Berry, or Perry Court, a manor belonging to Lord Cobham, was forfeited to James I., but afterwards given to Robert Earl of Salisbury, whose wife, Elizabeth, was sister of the fallen Henry Lord Cobham. Mallingden, called Molland, also called Dene, another manor in this parish, was the property of Christ Church until the dissolution of the priory, when, like that of Cliffe, it reverted to Henry VIII. Queen Elizabeth bestowed this manor on William Ewens, who afterwards alienated it to a Mr. Brown. The present owner is Mr. Harvey, of Gravesend Cardons, or Cardans, a manor named after the original proprietor, Robert Cardon, was granted by Edward IV. to the Carthusian Monastery in London (now known as the Charter House), but on the suppression of the brotherhood became the property of the Crown. A small manor at the southern extremity of the parish, called Mortimers, was the estate of a noble family of that name during the reign of Edward I. It was part of the possessions of Sir John Sedley, and was granted a fair by Edward III.

An ancient custom prevails in this parish which imposes on the rector, or his representative, the annual distribution of a loaf of

H

bread and a mutton pie, on St. James's Day (25th July), to as many
poor inhabitants as may demand it.   The origin of the custom is
unknown.   Some little time since attempts were made to substitute
money, but unsuccessfully, and the custom is of necessity perpe-
tuated, although the applicants are few.

Cliffe Church, dedicated to St. Helen, is of remote date, and is a
good example of early English architecture.   The chancel is of the
Decorated order, and the tracery of the windows on either side is
generally considered very fine ; a noble embattled tower at the west
end has a groined roof and three lancet windows, a clock, and a
peal of six bells, cast in the years 1616, 1630, 1670, and 1675.

The extreme length of this interesting church is 216 feet ; the
chancel measuring 50 feet, the nave 150, and the tower 16 feet.
The nave is divided from the aisles by massive circular columns
supporting noble pointed arches.   Against the first column on the
south side is the very ancient font, the antiquity of which is indi-
cated by its magnitude.   The triple *sedilia* and double *piscina* are
richly carved in flowers, figures and grotesque heads.   A finely
carved rood screen of three arches separates the nave from the
chancel.   The ancient stalls of the monks of Christ Church, Canterbury, are still preserved in the chancel.   The east window, originally in five lights, and of the same date as the church, has been
superseded by another, the beauty of which may be questioned.
The carved oak pulpit bears the date 1634, and the rest, which in
olden times supported an hour glass, that of 1636.   There are a
few remains of rich stained glass in a window in the north aisle
representing the Virgin and Child, and an ancient vessel, with
an upper deck lighted by semi-circular windows.

The north and south transepts were formerly chantries ; that on
the north side, now used as the robing-room, has the remains of
two Gothic windows, and a larger one blocked up.   This latter act
is to be regretted, as largely detracting from the general effect of a
finely detailed structure.   The wall of the south chantry was originally covered with fresco-painting, which, from frequent white-
washing, has been hidden.   Some two years since a laudable desire
was evinced to remove an abomination of the seventeenth century,
and to restore, if possible, this early work of art ; but unfortunately,
from using wrong material, the operator nearly obliterated the
whole, save the outline of a fine head encircled in a halo.   Amongst
the Communion plate is a very ancient *paten* of silver gilt, used for
the consecrated wafer by the priesthood in olden times.   It is richly
enamelled in colours of green and blue, and represents the Deity,
our Saviour nailed to the cross, a descending dove, and other detail.
Around this *paten* or salver, measuring six inches in diameter, is the
following inscription—' *Benedicamus Patrem et Filium cum Spiritu
Sancto.*'

Few of the monumental brasses remain that once abounded in

the nave and chancel. There is one to the memory of Bonham Faunce, dated 1652, with the figures of a man and his two wives and two children; another for Thomas Faunce, his wife, and children; a third for Elizabeth Grisome, who died in 1658, and a fourth with the effigies of two children. On one of the pillars, near the tomb of the Baynard family, is an inscription on a brass plate, recording the bequests of John Browne, under his will dated 7th June, 1679—'*For the education of twelve poor children, and a man and woman to teach them.*' Many very ancient stones exhibit the mortices which once held elaborated brasses, two especially in the nave, near the chancel, on one of which may be traced the figure of a bishop, wearing a mitre and bearing a crosier.

In the nave are several coffin-shaped stones, with crosses, of great antiquity. Two of these bear inscriptions in Saxon capitals; that to the memory of John Ram must be of remote date, from the period he held the manor of Cardans. The inscription reads thus — '*Ione la femme Iohan Ram gyt yci Deu de sa alme eit merci;*' the other reads, '*Elienore de Clive gist ici Deu de sa alme eit merci. Amen, par charie.*' In 1857 the exterior of Cliffe Church was thoroughly repaired, and an unsightly buttress, erected some years since against the tower after its injury by lightning, removed.

About a mile from the church is the rectory, an ancient Gothic structure, built in ecclesiastical style, with heavy buttresses, arched doorways, and battled. The Archbishop of Canterbury is patron of this living, worth £1,297 per annum. The rector is the Rev. James Croft, D.D., who was presented to it in 1818. In addition to the living of Cliffe, Dr. Croft is Canon and Archdeacon of Canterbury; he has also been Rector of Saltwood, in this county, since 1812. The latter living alone, according to the Clergy List, is worth £784 per annum.

COWLING.

COWLING, or Cooling, anciently written *Culing*, or *Culinges*, from the Saxon *cu*, a cow, and *ling*, a pasture, signifying '*Cows' pasture,*' lies eastward from Cliffe, and comprises 1,544 acres, 26 houses, and 121 inhabitants. This parish, from its isolated position, is little frequented, although in Saxon times it is supposed to have been one of their early settlements. The soil northward lies low and flat, being a heavy wet clay and unhealthy; the land, however, rises southward to a high hill, upon which is a handsome seat called 'Lodge Hill,' which embraces superb scenery.

In 808, Cenulf, King of Mercia, gave to his faithful servant, Eadulf, '*one plough land and a half, with all its appurtenances in Culinges, according to the bounds mentioned in the Charter.*' In 961,

H 2

Queen Ediva, mother of Kings Edmund and Eadred, gave to the
Priory of Christ Church, Canterbury, all her lands in Culinge, free
of secular service, save the maintaining of castles, repelling inva-
sions, and the repairing of bridges.   King Edward II. in the 10th
of his reign, further granted to the same priory *free warren* in all
their demesne lands in this parish.

During the reign of Edward the Confessor the lordship of Culinges belonged to Leofwyne, a son of Earl Godwin.   Leofwyne was
killed in the battle of Hastings while fighting for his brother King
Harold.   After the Conquest, Culinges (so written in Domesday)
became part of the vast possessions of Odo, Bishop of Bayeux, on
whose disgrace it reverted to the Crown, and was conferred on
Henry de Cobham by Edward I., whose son, John de Cobham,
obtained a charter of *free warren* in 1344, the 17th of Edward III.

The family of Cobhams had a mansion here at the close of the
thirteenth century.   In 1381, Sir John de Cobham obtained license
of Richard II. '*to fortify and embattle his manor house.*' He however pulled it down and erected a formidable castellated castle, since
called *Cowling Castle*, and placed an inscription deeply graven on
brass on the eastern tower, over the principal entrance.   This inscription is still visible, and reads thus:

> Knoweth that beth and shall be,
> That I am made in help of the Contre,
> In knowing of whiche thing
> This is Chartre and witnessing.

This curious record, resembling a deed, or charter, bears the
Cobham arms.   There is some obscurity as to the motive for this
public notification, unless we infer that from the king having strictly
forbidden the erection of *baronial fortresses*, which this really was,
without royal license, it became policy to give it the semblance of
a national defence, and thereby preserve, not only the property, but
perhaps the life of the owner.

Sir John de Cobham died in 1408 (the 9th of Henry IV.), when
his granddaughter Joan inherited it.   She married Sir John Old-
castle, who adopted the title of Lord Cobham, and became possessed of the castle and estates in right of his wife. He commanded
the English army in France, and defeated the Duke of Orleans.
Sir John zealously espoused the doctrines promulgated by Wickliffe,
and was in consequence cited to appear before Archbishop Arundel,
in September 1413, when he was condemned '*as a pernicious and
detestable heretic.*'   He escaped into Wales, where he remained concealed some years; but in 1417 was apprehended by Lord Powys,
brought to London, and on the Christmas Day of that year, '*the
Lord Cobham, with his arms bound, was brought on a hurdle to the
green meadows of St. Giles', and there hung in chains to the cross-
beams of a gallows, his body being sustained in a horizontal position;*

faggots were placed beneath and around him, and in a few minutes all that was mortal of the suffering martyr became a heap of coal-black dust.'

After the execution of Lord Cobham, the Lady Joan, his widow, became owner of the manor, with the advowson of the church, and resided in Cowling Castle. At her death, in 1434, her only daughter Joan inherited the estates, and conveyed them by marriage to Sir Thomas Brooke of Somersetshire, afterwards Lord Cobham, in her right. His descendant, George Lord Cobham, resided here, and nobly defended the castle against the attack of Sir Thomas Wyatt, during the rebellion in the reign of Queen Mary, 1554. Sir Thomas besieged it with six pieces of cannon, but his attempts were defeated; for after battering down the gate, and part of the wall, he marched with his forces during the night to Gravesend.

Cowling Castle is described as a fortress of considerable strength, the walls, of great thickness, forming a solid square building flanked by towers; a deep moat surrounded the whole, which was supplied by the Thames. The principal entrance stood a short distance from the fortress, under an arch, with formidable gates and portcullis, between two embattled towers with flights of steps within each. The gateway and towers still remain in excellent preservation, on one of which is to be seen the brass plate already described. Amongst the ruins are the remains of a circular tower, covered with ivy, and portions of the walls, affording ample evidence of its former strength and grandeur in picturesque ruins that must highly interest every lover of antiquity. Within its walls is a handsome modern mansion, the residence of John Murton, Esq., who, when the members of the Kent Archæological Society visited these antiquities in 1860, entertained them with sumptuous liberality.

Cowling is within the diocese of Rochester. The Church, dedicated to St. James, is an ancient Gothic structure, built of flints and stone; here is a double *piscina*, with *credence* above, and a few monumental brasses. That to the memory of Feyth, daughter of John, Lord Cobham, dated 1508, is in the nave, near the pulpit. In the chancel are brasses for Sybel, wife of Nathaniel Sparks, rector—she died in 1639; and near to it that of Thomas Woodyear, who died in 1611. Shortly after the Conquest, Cowling Church became tributary to the Priory of Rochester. In the reign of King John, the year 1200, Adam Pincerna, or Butler, was patron of the living, which passed into the family of the Cobhams in 1280. The living is a rectory, now in the gift of J. Alliston, Esq., valued at £600 per annum.

Our ride homeward is really beautiful—the air so mild, and the evening so bright and clear—to close a lovely day, as well as our vacation, for we return to London on the morrow. We near Gravesend with the long shadows of evening; the sun is setting in fiery glory before us, and the lady moon just rising in silvery softness as we alight.   Refreshed by a dainty dish of ' *natives*' from old Dame Turrell's, we resolve on a walk through the town, and a parting word with some of the kindly townspeople, who *always* treat us with respect.   That centenarian, old Master Sutherland, is just turning into Bath Street; we greet him, and in an infantile voice he tells us that he has ' *been for a walk, is very deaf, and* 120 *years old.*'   Poor old man, you are very feeble ; your walk has been the length of some dozen houses, occupying as many minutes ; your years on the verge of, but not beyond, a hundred.   He totters on in his blue-striped frock, palsied and curved, leaning on his well-used stick, only to survive a few months, for he died the November following.

We call at Windmill Street for a parting shake with Mr. Hall, who has so kindly ventilated our Kentish sketches in his excellent journal ; and feeling interested in the proposed ' Steam Packet Company,' repair to the High Street, and are told by Mr. Crowhurst, one of the committee (who by the way is our snuff purveyor when here), that there is good hope of the scheme being carried out ; but at the close of the present season (1864) no tangible progress had been made towards a desideratum long felt by visitors.   To tell of the many we met, and of the kind words spoken during this our farewell gossip, would become tedious ; but one thing we must say, that through our lengthy experience we have not yet found the inhabitants of the borough of Gravesend deserving the appellation cast upon them, of being an ' *off-hand people.*'

Our remaining 'JOTTINGS' will emanate from our own fireside, and include a few more of the many notable localities in this ancient county, so full of interest to lovers of history.

AYLESFORD.

SOUTHWARD from Burham, and about thirty-two miles from London, is the parish of Aylesford, called by the Saxons *Episford*, and in Domesday *Elesford*; it contains 4,391 acres of land, 333 houses, and 2,057 inhabitants.   The river Medway flows through it on the north-west, which, from the tide being weak, is a stream of fresh water; it is spanned by a handsome bridge of six arches.

Aylesford town clusters on the northern bank of the river, the back ground rising suddenly high, and upon it stands the venerable church, higher than the roofs of the houses.   In 1240, a Carmelite Friary was founded here, of which a large portion remains.   The Friary was abolished by Henry VIII., and the land and appurtenances conferred on Sir Thomas Wyatt, of Allington, which again lapsed to the Crown on the execution of his son for rebellion.

John Sedley, of Southfleet, possessed the Friars in the reign of Queen Elizabeth, and bequeathed them to his brother, Sir William Sedley, where he resided ; his grandson, Sir Charles, the wit and poet, was born here in 1639. Sir John Banks resided here between 1660-70, and made extensive alterations, incorporating, with good taste, much of the ancient building in the present mansion. Crossing from the town by the noble stone bridge, the land rises in picturesque beauty towards the Elizabethan seat known as ' Preston Hall ;' the grounds, which are laid out with considerable taste, are well clothed by stately elms and varied plantations. The mansion contains a fine collection of paintings by the great masters, both ancient and modern, as well as some good statuary ; it is built on the site of the former house, the seat of the Colepepers, who possessed the manor at an early period.

Aylesford is memorable in ancient history for the great battle fought here between the Britons and Saxons, in 455, when Vortimer, the British king, encountered the Saxons on the banks of the Darent, and pursued them to Aylesford, where a most sanguinary battle was fought on the eastern side of the Medway, in which Horsa, brother of the Saxon General Hengist, and Catigern, brother of King Vortimer, were both killed. Here again, in 1016, Edmund Ironsides, after his victory over the Danes at Otford, pursued them with fearful slaughter, and, but for the treachery of Edric, would in all probability have wholly destroyed the Danish army.

The manor of Aylesford, anciently of the demesnes of the king, was subsequently divided, and held under the tenure of '*ancient demesne*,' a royal franchise, whereby the tenants were only bound to plough the king's lands, or to provide the court with certain provisions ; these immunities were afterwards changed into rents, and gave exemption from toll, with the right of a court to adjudicate on their own property, and release from expenses of knights of the shire, and from serving on juries.

Kits Coty House, one of those remarkable monuments, or cromlechs, frequently found in this country, as well as in Sweden, Norway, and Denmark, stands on a hill north of the town of Aylesford. Tradition asserts that it covers the grave of Catigern, brother of King Vortimer, who was slain in 455 ; but opinions are various on this point. It is composed of four stones, three of which stand upright, forming three sides of a square, and the fourth, eleven feet by eight, weighing nearly eleven tons, laid transversely over. About seventy yards distant was formerly another single stone which stood upright, similar to those of Kits Coty House, since broken and taken away. Towards the south-east, at the distance of a quarter of a mile, was another cromlech of eight or ten stones, now thrown down, lying in a confused heap. In the bottom contiguous to Aylesford is a number of the same kind of stones, some upright with a larger one transversely on the top, once corresponding with that of Kits Coty, and, like it, facing the east; other stones are scattered in a circle around. Still nearer to Aylesford is a remarkable stone, two feet in thickness, fourteen in length, and six in breadth, which, from its peculiar shape, Dr. Stukely has called the *coffin*.

The investigation of the real purpose of cromlechs, literally *stone tables*, has for many ages been an important subject of research with antiquarians. Learnedly, they are ascribed to the Druids, and considered to have been altars, upon which they kept the sacred fire constantly burning. In the woods behind Newydd, near the Menai Straits, are two vast cromlechs; the upper stone of one is nearly thirteen feet, by twelve broad, four feet thick, and thirty tons in weight, supported by five upright stones. The number of supporters to cromlechs is merely accidental, and depends on the size or form of the transverse stone. Cromlech, according to Rowland, is derived from the Hebrew ' *Caremluach*,' signifying a ' *devoted or consecrated stone.*'

That the Druids, or priests of the ancient Celtæ, Britons, and Germans, were the most distinguished scholars amongst the Britons and Gauls cannot be questioned; they were mostly of high birth, wore their hair short and beards long, and when employed in religious ceremonies had white surplices, and chains of gold about their necks. They worshipped the Deity under the symbol of the oak, wore chaplets of oak, and considered the mistletoe as the gift of Heaven, possessing a divine virtue; their temples were woods or groves, fenced round with stones; in the centre of the consecrated groves were altars made of stones of a prodigious size, upon which sacrifices were offered. Cromlechs are pretty generally considered altars used by the Druids; they have also been found in the Neilgherries in the East Indies, which has excited considerable desire to trace the origin of the natives of this part of India, called the Thautawars. Some suppose them derived from an Arab stock; others, from the Romans; and a third, that they were a portion of the lost Hebrew tribes.

Although impossible to determine the origin of this people, yet we have the startling fact before us that many cromlechs have been found in the Neilgherry hills, erected in most remote ages,—yes, many centuries before the Western World had discovered that vast Empire; and that these stone altars consist principally of three upright slabs planted firmly in the ground, supporting a fourth poised horizontally on the top. Of twelve still standing at Achenny, on the Neilgherries, one is an exact representation of Kits Coty House. Distinct of these cromlechs, many upright stones exist in these hills and other parts of India, corresponding with the obelisk or · *'spiral stone'* of the religions of early times, when upright stones were consecrated, the perversion of a custom recorded in

Genesis, chap. xxviii. v. 18—'*And Jacob rose up early in the morning, and took the stone that he had put for his pillow, and set it up for a pillar, and poured oil upon the top of it.*' Ver. 22—'*And this stone which I have set up for a pillar, shall be God's House.*' Whether, therefore, Kits Coty House covers the grave of Catigern, or are the remains of a Druidical altar, we must leave, after thus briefly enunciating the opinions of astute antiquaries : one thing is certain, that they are of very remote antiquity, and wherever found give sparkling interest to the locality.

Aylesford Church is a venerable old Gothic structure, dedicated to St. Peter, with a noble square tower ; it must in part date from the eleventh century, from the Norman architecture abounding. Here are some good brasses and monuments ; the earliest, a brass to John Cosynton, who died 1426 : monuments to the Colepepers, the Sedleys, and Ricauts, including that of Sir Paul Ricaut, the distinguished traveller, who died in 1700: the most stately monument in marble, with recumbent figures, is that of Sir John Banks, who died in 1699. The living is a vicarage, valued at £531 per annum: the Rev. Anthony Grant is the present incumbent.

OTFORD.

OTFORD, in the hundred of Codsheath, claims honour over the whole of this hundred, and formed part of the earliest possessions of the see of Canterbury. It covers 2,852 acres, and contains 177 houses, with 804 inhabitants. This parish, which takes its name from the Saxon word Ottanford, is for the most part low and damp ; here is much meadow land watered by rivulets and springs, which although rendering it moist, and at times marshy, is considered fertile. The chalk ranges rise on the east and west, and the river Darent runs northward, near which is the village, traversed by the old road from Dartford to Sevenoaks. The liberty of the duchy of Lancaster claims over part of this parish, in which is held an annual fair on the 24th of August.

Otford will be ever memorable from two sanguinary battles fought here ; the first, in 773, by Offa, King of Mercia, and Aldric, King of Kent. The slaughter was fearful on both sides, but Offa gained the victory. The other battle was fought in 1016, by Edmund, surnamed Ironside, who marched upon Canute, the Danish King, whom he encountered here, and signally defeated, and, but for treachery, would have wholly annibilated the Danes. The remains of the slain in these battles are continually being dug up in the neighbouring fields. In 1767, many human skeletons were found in the chalk banks on either side.

Otford was given to the Church of Canterbury by Offa, King of Mercia, in 791, but Werhard, a powerful priest, became possessed of it shortly afterwards. Archbishop Wifrid, however, caused it to be restored to the church in 830, part of the possessions of which it remained down to Henry VIII., being styled '*the honour of Otford.*'

In remote times, the Archbishops of Canterbury had a palace at Otford, in which they generally resided, and from whence they issued frequent mandates signed from their '*Manor house at Otford.*' This palace was commodious and retired, having two large parks and extensive woods. Archbishop Becket lived here, and many tales are handed down of the miracles he wrought at Otford; amongst them is one to this effect—the Archbishop desiring a spring of water for the use of the palace, struck his staff into the ground, when water immediately burst forth in great abundance. It is still called St. Thomas's well. King Edward I. was sumptuously entertained here by Archbishop Winchelsea, in the year 1300.   Archbishop Deane re-built some portions, early in the sixteenth century; but his successor, Archbishop War-ham, is said to have rebuilt the whole, with the exception of the hall and the chapel; and here he also entertained Henry VIII. This stately palace was afterwards in the possession of Henry VIII., who enlarged the two parks. Queen Elizabeth, however, made grants of different parts of the estate : to Sir Henry Sidney she granted '*the little Park at Otford*;' and in the 34th year of her reign she conferred on his son, Sir Robert Sidney, '*the site of the honour of Otford, the archbishop's house, commonly called the Castle, and the great Park, containing 700 acres lying in Otford, Seal, and Kemsing.*' The present ruins formed part of the outer court, pro-bably the cloisters, with the remains of a tower. At the close of the last century two towers were standing. This princely archie-piscopal palace must have been of large extent, as the foundations alone may be traced over nearly an acre of land.

Otford Church, dedicated to St. Bartholomew, stands at the east end of the village, near to the ruins of the palace. St. Bartholomew was a highly-reputed personage for the supposed gift of curing bar-renness; his image and a shrine were formerly in this church, to which numberless married ladies resorted to seek his anti-Malthu-sian aid.   The church, which consists of a nave, aisles, chancel, and spire, was rebuilt on the old foundations in the seventeenth century. It has just undergone internal restoration by Mr. G. E. Street, the architect, if we mistake not, who so successfully restored Stone Church. The unsightly wooden pillars, which have been swept away, give place to an arcade of four bays, divided by stone columns ; an arch has been thrown over the nave at the first pillar, and the tower arch opened ; the gallery has been taken down, and ugly pews superseded by open seats; the roof is new, and the chancel neatly paved with Mintons' tiles. The choir of this church, a band of tolerable choristers, have the advantage of the incumbent's kindly sympathies, as well as occasional liberal entertainments at the parsonage. Amongst the monuments is a mural tomb of fine sculpture for David Polhill, son of Thomas Polhill, of Otford, whose grandmother was Bridget, daughter of OLIVER CROMWELL, Lord Protector. Another in the south aisle for Charles Polhill, who died in 1755, is very fine; it represents the statue of a man, life size, leaning on an urn, with a female profile above, and figures in statuary marble of beautiful proportions. There are also other tombs and monuments for the families of Polhill, Bostock, and Brasier, and in the east window the arms of Lennard, emblazoned in stained glass.

The living of Otford is a perpetual curacy in the gift of the Dean and Chapter of Westminster, valued at £179 per annum. The incumbent is the Rev. R. B. Tritton, who was presented to the living in 1845. Two miles eastward from Otford is the parish of—

KEMSING,

Pleasantly situated on the slopes of the chalk ranges, with commanding scenery over the Weald of Kent. It is supposed to have taken its name from some royal camp or fortress anciently situated here. This parish consists of 1,867 acres, with 80 houses and 366 inhabitants; the soil to the south is very fertile, but on the north mostly chalk.

The lordship was remotely the property of a family which derived its surname from this parish, being called Kempsing; subsequently it was in the possession of Lord Saye and Seale. Early in the reign of Edward IV. William Lord Saye sold Kemsing to Sir Geoffry Bulleyn, grandfather of the Earl of Wiltshire, who was father of the ill-fated ANNE BOLEYN, after whose death Henry VIII. claimed the manor in right of his late wife, and ultimately bestowed it, with other estates, on his divorced queen Lady Anne of Cleves.

Just above the village, along the ridge of chalk hills, runs the old ' Pilgrims' Road,' near which is St. Edith's Well. This personage, said to have been born in the parish, bore high repute for the gift of working miracles, and for preserving grain from mildew. After her death a statue was erected in the churchyard, that was held in great reverence, and to which numbers flocked.

The church, dedicated also to St. Edith, stands north of the village. This is a small structure of early English architecture, without aisles, containing few monuments. In the chancel is a gravestone with a brass, and an inscription in black letter, dated early in the fourteenth century, to the memory of Thomas de Hop, and a mural monument for Michael Jermin, D.D., obiit 1659. The living, valued at £396 per annum, is in the gift of the Amherst family. The vicar, the Rev. T. O. Blackall, succeeded to the appointment in 1846.

HEVER.

OUR previous chapter glanced at Anne Boleyn, and the estrangement of the manor of Kemsing from her family by Henry VIII. We may therefore fairly follow with Hever, the once happy home of that unfortunate queen, whose cruel fate darkens the pages of history.

Hever, anciently *Heure* and *Evere*, lies below the sand hills in the Weald, where the oak is most abundant and attains a very large size. The river Eden crosses the parish towards Penshurst, and the Medway flows near the walls of Hever Castle, south of which are the village and the parsonage. This parish extends over 2,608 acres, and has 121 houses and 626 inhabitants.

Hever was originally the seat and manor of a family of that name. William de Hevre was sheriff of the county in 1274, when he obtained a grant from Edward I. of *free warren* over his lands in Hevre, Chidingstone, and Lingefield, and in the reign of Edward III. rebuilt the mansion and embattled it. On his death the estates were divided betwixt his daughters Joan and Margaret. Joan married Reginald Cobham, from which her moiety was distinguished as ' Hever Cobham.' Margaret married Sir Oliver Brocas, when her share was called ' Hever Brocas.'

The ' Hever Brocas ' estate was alienated to Reginald Lord Cobhom of Sterborough in the reign of Henry IV., who died possessed of both manors in 1373. Sir Thomas Cobham, his grandson, sold these manors to Sir Geoffry Bulleyn, a mercer of London, who was Lord Mayor in 1459 ; he died in 1464, when his son, Sir William Bulleyn, inherited the estates. Sir William married Margaret, the daughter of the Earl of Ormond, and had issue a son and heir, Thomas, who was signally distinguished by Henry VIII., for in 1526 the king created him Viscount Rochford, and in 1531 Earl of Wiltshire and Ormond, besides which he was elected a Knight of the Garter. He married Elizabeth, daughter of Thomas Howard, Duke of Norfolk, and by that alliance had a son, George, and two daughters —Anne, the unfortunate wife of Henry VIII., and Mary, the wife of William Carey, from whom descended the Earls of Dover and Monmouth. This earl added greatly to the mansion, afterwards called HEVER CASTLE, which was built of stone, and protected by a moat well supplied from the river. The front was strongly fortified ; two towers, loopholed, supported the boldly machicolated gateway ; massive gates and portcullis were arranged within, and above, furnaces for melting lead and pitch, to welcome enemies who dared enter its portals. Such was Hever Castle during the life of the Earl of Wiltshire and Ormond. He died in the 30th year of the reign of Henry VIII., upon which the king seized the castle and manor in right of his late wife, after having already caused the execution of George, the son and heir. Two years afterwards Henry VIII. granted Hever Castle and Manor, with those of Seal and Kemsing, to his fourth, but repudiated wife, the Lady Anne of Cleves, who held them until her death in 1556, the fourth year of Philip and Mary, when they were sold under royal commission.

Hever Castle is entire, and the interior in tolerable preservation. It is in part a farmhouse, but still the Hever Castle of three centuries since, with the same oak panelling within and the same quadrangular courtyard and lofty gatehouse, even to the quaint gables and lofty roofs without. We fall back in a reverie, and contemplate the heyday of England's Queen Anne, the mother of our Protestant Queen Elizabeth, when shown a room, not luxuriantly furnished, and are told that this was Anne Boleyn's bedroom, even to the bed on which she slept, with the same curtains, tables, chairs, and carved oaken chest.

The great hall has the large oak table of olden times ; the noble staircase leads to a series of chambers, and the long reverberating gallery, wainscotted with dark oak, and ceilings of stucco richly ornamented. On one side of the gallery is a recess approached by two steps, in which you are told Henry VIII. held councils when a visitor at the castle. Next to a window here you are shown a trap door in the floor, leading to dismal dungeons in the deep darkness below. There is a tradition averring that the king cast his queen, Anne Boleyn, into this dungeon to be starved to death, where she remained some days, until her gaoler removed the body for burial, when, to his dismay, the queen revived, and she was sent back to London. This, however, does not accord with the version given generally, which points out a chamber in one of the towers as that in which she was confined, now entered by a small door, then through a secret sliding panel, still called ' *Anne Boleyn's panel.*'

Here is the boudoir of the then happy Anne, and the bay window from which she was wont to watch for her royal lover. How many the boundings of that innocent heart when bugles from yon hills told of the king's approach ; the hopes and joys that beat within her breast as she welcomed him to their favourite seat, when all was sunshine, pointing to a brilliant future ! Her brightest dreams were realised when she became Queen of England in 1532 ; but, alas !

the tragic episode, that ended all her hopes on a scaffold, within four brief years.

Hever is within the diocese of Rochester, and a peculiar of the Archbishop of Canterbury. The village was anciently the property of Sir Stephen de Penchester, whose possessions were most extensive here and at Penshurst. The church, dedicated to St. Peter, stands at the east end of the village. It is an old structure, with a nave, two chancels, and a handsome spire. The architecture is, for the most part, in the Decorated style; the Boleyn Chantry, however, is of the Perpendicular order. In the chancel is the stately altar-tomb, in marble, with a large figure in brass, of Sir Thomas Bulleyn, father of Anne Boleyn : he died in 1538. A gravestone in the nave, bearing a female figure in brass with an inscription in black letter, is to the memory of Margaret Cheyne, obiit 1419. A brass plate, with a figure and inscription, records the death of William Todde in 1585. In the belfrey is a stone bearing a brass plate for John de Cobham, obiit 1399, and an ancient tomb for another of the Cobhams of Sterborough Castle, with a shield of arms graven on a brass plate. The living of Hever is a rectory, with glebe house, in the gift of E. W. M. Waldo, Esq., valued at £372 per annum. The rector is the Rev. W. Wilberforce Battye, who succeeded to the incumbency in 1850.

———•◇•———

TUNBRIDGE.

TUNBRIDGE, in Saxon *Tunbryege* (town of bridges), and in Domesday- written *Tonebrega*, is supposed to take its name from the bridges spanning the five streams of the Medway running through the town, of which that alone to the north is navigable. Near to the principal bridge, built in 1775, is a reputed manufactory for *Tunbridge ware*, founded upwards of a century. This large parish of 15,235 acres, 4,143 houses, and 21,004 inhabitants, presents considerable variety of soil : some portions are low, and subject to inundation. The oak flourishes, and attains a large size. The grass lands are esteemed for fattening cattle; other parts produce excellent corn and hops; but to the south-west the soil becomes sandy.

The town, which is about thirty miles from London by the old coach road, stands nearly in the centre of the parish. The streets, built upon the hill, consist of a main street, of about three-fourths of a mile in length, lying on the old road; it is rather old-fashioned, especially its timber-panelled houses, which are curious. From the main street branch several others, as well as terraces, villas, squares, and pretty modern buildings. An elegant stone church, in the Decorated style of architecture, dedicated to St. Stephen, has recently been erected on the slope.

For upwards of three hundred years Tunbridge has held high repute for its Free Grammar School, founded by Sir Andrew Judd, Alderman of London, a native of Tunbridge. He erected a school-house, with other buildings, purchased lands, and by letters patent of Edward VI. founded this noble institution in 1554, as ' *The Free Grammar School of Sir Andrew Judde, in the town of Tunbridge,*' which he left in trust to the Skinners' Company, who annually examine the scholars, exceeding one hundred and seventy, of whom forty are on the foundation. The revenues, through the careful husbanding of the trustees, exceed £5,000 per annum, and at the expiration of certain leases this institution will rank amongst our richest foundations. The Principal, the Rev. J. T. Welldon, has a handsome salary, with residence and privilege of boarders.

Sixteen annual exhibitions of £100, for either Oxford or Cambridge, emanate from this foundation, distinct of two others of £75 exclusively for Jesus College, Cambridge, a scholarship of £20 at Brasenose, a fellowship at St. John's, Oxford, and ten other exhibitions of less value. Boys resident within a radius of ten miles of Tunbridge are eligible for the charity; others are admissible by payment of a small fee. A neat chapel was erected in 1859 from funds contributed by the scholars and friends of the school.

The Skinners' Company hold their annual examination in May, when the head boy delivers a congratulatory oration in Latin at the gates of the school. After the distribution of bread, money, and clothes to poor persons, according to the will of Thomas Smith, another benefactor, the trustees repair to the school, and proceed with a rigid examination, after which each of the six senior boys is presented with a silver pen, gilt. Tunbridge School has always maintained high reputation for the proficiency of its students and the eminence of the masters, and it stands the principal architectural object of the town. A new school is now, however, in course of erection behind, and the original building is to be largely remodelled. The South-Eastern Railway has a principal station here, which occupies the site of the *Priory*, the ruins being removed for the formation of the line in 1840.

The Priory of Tunbridge was founded in the reign of Henry II. by the Earl of Hertford, Lord of Tunbridge, who, beyond the endowment, gave yearly, ' 120 *hogs in his Forest of Tonebregge, free from pannage; and that the Canons should have two horses every day to carry the dead wood home to them; and one stag yearly to be taken by the Earl's men.*' In 1351, the Priory was destroyed by fire, but speedily rebuilt. Henry VIII., in his 17th year, gave it to Cardinal Wolsey, with other suppressed monasteries, for the endowment of colleges, but on the Cardinal's disgrace it again reverted to the Crown. The buildings of this Priory were very extensive, judging from the outlines of the foundations, which could be clearly traced early in the present century. The great hall and the chapel, used as a barn, were only taken down to give place to the railway. In the grounds was a well, walled round, dedicated to St. Margaret, formerly much resorted to.

Tunbridge Castle is a fine relic of bold Norman architecture, the ruins of which form a conspicuous and interesting object from distant points; the inner gateway, flanked by two massive towers of great strength, still remains, as well as portions of the walls, said to have enclosed six acres of ground. Formerly three moats encircled the castle; the innermost of these was supplied from a stream, now the principal current of the Medway. Over it was a bridge of stone, united by a broad wall to the south-east tower. The other moats enclosed the town of Tunbridge, then little more than the suburbs belonging to the castle. This fortress is full of historical interest. Richard de Fitz-Gilbert possessed it shortly after the Conquest. He was one of the nobles who came over with William the Conqueror, and fought in the battle of Hastings; he afterwards obtained the town and castle of Tunbridge from the Archbishop of Canterbury, where he resided, and was from thence called Richard de Tunbridge. William Rufus besieged the castle, when Richard surrendered, and swore allegiance to that prince. His descendant Richard, son of Gilbert de Tunbridge, assumed the title of Clare, from a lordship he held in Sussex, and became possessed of the castle; he was afterwards created Earl of Hertford and Lord of Tunbridge, and founded the Priory. His brother Roger, Earl of Clare, who succeeded him, was summoned by Archbishop Becket to appear at Westminster, to do him homage, which he refused, on the authority of the king (Henry II.). He died in the 19th year of that reign, leaving a son, Richard, who succeeded to his title and estates. Richard was one of the barons who bore arms against King John, when he was assailed by the king's forces, and Tunbridge Castle taken by storm. It was again besieged by Prince Edward in the reign of Henry III., when the garrison burnt the town. Edward II. held it during his reign, but it afterwards became the property of the Audleys and Staffords, until the execution of Edward Stafford, in 1521. Queen Elizabeth gave the castle to Lord Hunsdon, from whom it passed through many hands, although still belonging to a representative of the noble house of Stafford. It is now used as a military school, and has a range of modern buildings in a line with one of the towers.

Tunbridge is surrounded with picturesque scenery, good seats, and the residences of independent families. It possesses a town hall, joint-stock bank, savings bank, literary and mechanics' institutions, well-stocked shops, and good inns.

The old church, dedicated to the Apostles SS. Peter and Paul, is an ancient Gothic pile, of goodly proportions, with a square tower. The monuments are principally for the inhabitants of the parish, and owners of estates in the vicinity; that with mutilated figures for Sir Anthony Denton and his wife, who died early in the seventeenth century, is interesting, as also a handsome tomb of white marble. At the south-east corner is a sculptured urn, in memory of Ann Elliot, a celebrated actress, a native of Tunbridge; she died in 1796, at the early age of 26 years, and was buried in a vault beneath it. On the north side of the tomb is graven the following elegy:—

O matchless form adorned with wit refined,
A feeling heart and an enlighten'd mind ;
Of softest manners, beauty's rarest bloom,
Here ELLIOT lies, and moulders in her tomb.
O blest with genius ! early snatched away ;
The muse that joyful marked thy op'ning ray,
Now, sad reverse ! attends thy mournful bier,
And o'er thy relics sheds the gushing tear.
Here fancy oft the hallowed mould shall tread,
Recall THEE living, and lament THEE dead :
Here friendship oft shall sigh 'til life be o'er,
And death shall bid thy image charm no more.

Tunbridge is in the diocese of Canterbury. The living is a vicarage, with residence, valued at £763 per annum. The Rev. Sir Charles Hardinge, brother of Viscount Hardinge, held the living from 1809 to 1864, a period of fifty-five years, which, from the infirmities of old age, he resigned, only to survive a few weeks.

SEVENOAKS.

SEVENOAKS, twenty-four miles from London, and six from Tunbridge, is called in the Textus Roffensis *Sequenacca*, from seven large oaks growing on the summit of the hill, whereon is now built the town, with its market, in the line of the old road to Tunbridge. This parish embraces 6,000 statute acres, 1,023 houses, and 4,695 inhabitants, and extends above as well as below the great ridge of sand hills dividing the upland from the Weald. The soil varies; towards the hill, and about the town, it is sandy ; below the hill a stiff clay ; but towards Riverhead it is rich and fertile. The parish is divided into three districts, the town borough, Riverhead, and the Weald,—Riverhead taking the name from its proximity to a source of the Darent.

The town of Sevenoaks stands high, with well-built houses and good inns : it has a market on Saturdays, and a fair in October. Formerly this was a post town of considerable importance and profit to the inhabitants, now absorbed by the railway, much to their discomfiture; still trade flourishes. The many shops are well stocked with the best description of goods, which secures the patronage of

I

numbers of the gentry and wealthy, whose seats and villas are scattered around. Nearly opposite to the *White Hart* Inn are seven trees, commemorative of those from which the town derived its name. Here was a pond, now covered over, formerly in considerable requisition for ducking vixens. The cruel instrument employed was called a *ducking stool*, a sort of chair fixed at the extremity of a long pole, centred on an upright, in which scolding wives were placed, and subjected to immersions according to their oral powers—a barbarism long since exploded.

Sevenoaks has its grammar school, founded and endowed by Sir William Sevenoaks, under his will dated 1432; he also founded almshouses for decayed tradespeople, which were rebuilt in 1737. Sir William was a foundling, said to have been discovered in the hollow of an oak by a wealthy inhabitant, who named him after the town, and carefully educated him. This unknown individual rose to station in the City of London, where he was Lord Mayor in the reign of Henry VI. Dr. John Potkyn was a considerable benefactor to this school during Henry VIII., which in the reign of Elizabeth was incorporated as—*The wardens and assistants of the town and parish of Sevenoak, and of Queen Elizabeth's free school there.* This institution has six exhibitions, without restriction as to college or university, four of which are of £15 per annum.

The manor of Sevenoaks was an appendage to that of Otford, and part of the possessions of the See of Canterbury until the 9th of Henry VIII. It was granted to John Dudley, Earl of Warwick, in the 4th year of Edward VI., upon whose execution for high treason it passed into the hands of Queen Mary, who conferred the manors of Sevenoaks and Knowle upon Reginald Pole, Cardinal Archbishop of Canterbury, who expired in 1558, on the same day as Queen Mary. Bradborne, another manor here, was the property of Sir Thomas Grandison in the reign of Edward III. Sir Ralph Bosville, clerk of the *Queen's Court of Wards*, possessed it in the reign of Elizabeth; his descendant, William Bosville, rebuilt the mansion in 1761.

Amongst the many goodly estates in this parish we have only space for that called Rumpshot, written in old deeds Rumpsted, the surname of an ancient family who possessed it for many generations. Sir William de Rumpstead was an eminent man in the reign of Edward III., and, according to tradition, was the foster-father of William de Sevenoak, whom he found in the hollow body of a tree, as already narrated.

The manor of Knowle was the property of Baldwin de Betum, Earl of Albemarle, in the reign of King John; it descended, by marriage, to the family of Mareschal's Earls of Pembroke, and was afterwards sold to James Fienes, or Fenys, Lord Saye and Seal, in the reign of Henry VI. This eminent statesman was a great favourite of the king, who created him a baron, which excited the jealousy of the House of Commons; they arraigned him, and then hurried him to the Standard in Cheapside, where he was beheaded. His son, Sir William, conveyed the manor of Knowle to Thomas Bourchier, Archbishop of Canterbury, in the 34th year of Henry VI. This archbishop rebuilt the manor house, and died here in 1486. Archbishop Morton resided here, and entertained Henry VIII. Queen Elizabeth granted the manor and mansion to Sir Robert Dudley, Earl of Leicester. In 1603 they were assigned to Thomas Sackville, Earl of Dorset, who resided here, and considerably improved the mansion. It was more or less the residence of the Earls of Dorset down to 1829, when it became the property of the Countess of Plymouth, who subsequently married Earl Amherst.

Knowle Park centres in one of the most superb landscapes England's garden—Kent—can bestow; enormous oaks, venerable elms, and stately beech trees spread over its vast area of 1,600 acres; here is *the old oak*, thirty feet in circumference—there a beech tree twenty-eight. To appreciate this nucleus of loveliness, look from the terrace into the park below and wonder at the gorgeous picture—look beyond, at hamlets and villages, and spires of quaint old churches, peering over intervening trees; woodlands and broad meadows; orchards and rich fields of grain, the pride of the husbandman and the joy of his satellites, those happy sons of toil, whose homes tell of cleanliness and contentment, whose wives, unknown to luxury, heartily welcome to their own fireside the men whose highest ambition is to gain their daily bread by honest labour. We look on yon distant mouldering castles and halls of fame, where once pomp and splendour, state and dazzling equipage, were the things of every-day life, passing through ages from sire to son; a long line of dead-alive, until the living ended, and nought survives save—*storied urn or animated bust*;—tales of the past, that either bloom in sweet remembrance, as fruits of Christian virtues, or memories of ambition unknown in rustic life; where rosy cherubs watch at cottage-doors for father—he who with proud delight kisses each brow, and seeks no higher fame.

Quitting the terrace, we plunge into the endless beauties and fragrance of all that nature can give to charm the senses and elevate the mind; but we must not linger here, for on yon knoll stands the mansion, covering an area exceeding three acres, quadrangular in form, and castellated. Grim square towers and embattled gateways of different periods arrest attention as we near one of them, supported by bold towers, leading to the first quadrangle. Passing under another gateway of much earlier date, we enter an inner quadrangle, which communicates with the attractive portions of the building, and to which visitors are admitted—thanks to the courtesy of Earl Amherst, the noble proprietor.

First is the GREAT HALL, built by Thomas, first Earl of Dorset;

I 2

in the illuminated windows are emblazoned armorial bearings, including those of Queen Elizabeth. This hall, seventy-five feet long, contains some meritorious specimens of sculpture; that of Demosthenes especially, which cost £700 ; some good paintings, and the fire-dogs of Henry VIII. and his queen, Anne Boleyn, brought from Hever Castle.

The BROWN GALLERY measures eighty-eight feet in length, and is of oak, even to the floor; rich stained glass fills the windows, whilst the walls are covered with portraits of illustrious personages ;—here is Henry VIII., Elizabeth, Cromwell, Luther, Wickliffe, Melancthon, Huss, Milton, Dryden, and an array of Reformers. The various articles of furniture, draped and cushioned with velvet and satin, are very interesting as relics of antiquity. On the right of the Brown Gallery is a bed-chamber and dressing-room, containing tapestry and excellent paintings, antique furniture, and a very ancient bedstead of oak.

The SPANGLED BEDROOM is on the left of the gallery. The floor is of oak, and the furniture of Elizabethan date ; here is some tapestry ; the fire-dogs are of silver. The dressing-room contains some excellent paintings by the great masters ; other rare paintings are to be seen in the BILLIARD ROOM and LEICESTER GALLERY.

The VENETIAN BEDROOM and dressing-room, so called as having been that of Nicolo Molino, the Venetian ambassador, while resident here, is again rich in paintings of the great schools.

The KING'S BEDROOM, prepared at a cost of £20,000 for James I., who did not, as was expected, honour Knowle with a visit, is most gorgeous. Here is the identical state-bed, with draperies of velvet and satin, embroidered in gold and silver, and the original costly furniture, relieved by a profusion of silver vases, urns, baskets, and other articles of vertu. The walls are draped with rich tapestry illustrating the life of King Nebuchadnezzar.

We glance at the BALL-ROOM, with its magnificent marble chimneypiece and the fine collection of family portraits; the CRIMSON DRAWING-ROOM, and costly paintings; the DINING-ROOM, adorned with portraits of distinguished literary and scientific men ; the same room where Charles, sixth Earl of Dorset, was wont to entertain the celebrated literati of his day; where Addison, Locke, Garrick, Sedley, and a host of kindred spirits, would cluster round his board, and with merry hearts and jocund smile drink to the noble house of Dorset. In the ORGAN-ROOM are the remains of a very ancient organ, said to have been the second built in England. Next to this room is the chapel gallery; beneath the chapel is a fine vaulted crypt. The walls of the Passage-room, or Chapel, represent, in tapestry, the history of Noah. Here is an antique cabinet, bearing elaborately-carved figures to illustrate subjects from our Saviour's history : *The entry into Jerusalem, Bearing the Cross, Taking down from the Cross,* and the *Entomb-*

ment. Considerable interest attaches to this group of figures, from the fact that Mary Queen of Scots presented them to the second Earl of Dorset within a short period of her execution.

Sevenoaks reposes in beautiful scenery, and the walk from thence to Tunbridge will prove a feast to the pedestrian that loves to luxuriate in the majestic grandeur of nature in her loveliest forms. The church is a noble structure, dedicated to St. Nicholas; the square tower is built in the perpendicular style; it has a nave, chancel, and two aisles. Amongst the monuments are those of William Lambarde, the perambulator, who died in 1601; Earls Whitworth and Amherst; and a brass for Hugh Owen, rector, without date. The living is a vicarage, with a sinecure rectory, valued at £935 per annum; the present incumbent is the Rev. H. F. Sidebottom.

DARTFORD.

DARTFORD, on the river Darent, lies at the north side of the county, fifteen miles from London, and about six miles from Gravesend. It is called in Saxon *Derentford,* and in Domesday *Tarenteford.* This parish has an area of 4,286 acres, 1,318 houses, and 6,597 inhabitants.

The uplands are thin and gravelly, the valleys a rich fertile loam, and on the northern side marsh land stretches down to the Thames. The town of Dartford is seated in a valley between two hills, one of chalk and the other of a sandy loam. The railway crosses the Darent and the marshes by a long viaduct, from which this really important town is seen to advantage. The principal street, which flanks the old road from London to Dover, is a scene of bustle and excitement on market day; here are plenty of well-stocked shops, and numerous inns; the latter, however, we fear, suffer in some degree since steam has superseded the good old coaching times, when numerous post travellers would alight at one or other of these inns and partake of the good fare awaiting them, while postillions, less pretentious, luxuriated under the auspices of buxom cooks by their blazing hearths, when muffled guards were wont to wind their horn, the precursor of the dashing stage-coach, with its blowing horses and semi-frozen passengers. We well remember those days, and the delight with which we have plunged into the creature-comforts placed before us.

A bridge spans the river, built at the expense of the county. In the reign of Edward III. there was no bridge, but a ferry, valued among the rents of the manor. The first bridge (both narrow and steep) was built during the reign of Henry VI.

There was formerly a considerable fishery here, even as late as

James I. ; for, according to the records, *The royal manor of Dartford received for the fishery six salmon annually* ; and the *manor of
Dartford Priory received a yearly rent of £50 for a fishery.*

Dartford must have been a place of some note early in the
Christian era. The Watling Street of the Romans is very conspicuous between Dartford and the Brent, on its way to Shinglewell
and Rochester, near which are three small barrows plundered of
their contents. Barrows are very ancient repositories for the dead ;
they are of different kinds and sizes. Those formed of stones
heaped up are mostly found in Scotland, and are supposed to be of
Roman origin ; whilst those of earth, in the form of a mound, are
attributed to the ancient Britons or Danes. Many of the latter
have been discovered in Kent. On digging into these barrows or
tumuli, many curious relics have been found, such as urns of burnt
pottery, containing calcined bones and ashes ; skeletons, with the
knees pressed to the chest ; bones entire enclosed in stone coffins ;
other bones merely buried ; trinkets ; and, in one instance, large
numbers of beetles, indicating that the same superstition governed
the people deposited in these barrows as belonged to the ancient
Pharaohs, when the Egyptians enclosed with the sacred ibis similar
insects.

In the reign of Henry II. the manor of Dartford was conferred
on St. Paul, a Norman lord, which Henry III. gave to the Earl of
Albemarle ; it afterwards reverted to the crown. Edward II., however, gave it to his half-brother, Edmund de Woodstock, Earl of
Kent. It was in the possession of Lord Stanley during the reign
of Richard III.

Frederic, Emperor of Germany, sent the Archbishop of Cologne
with a suite of noblemen to Dartford, in the reign of Henry III., to
demand in marriage Isabella, sister of the King, where the nuptials
were solemnised by proxy previous to her departure for Germany.

Edward III. celebrated a famous tournament here in 1331, after
his return from France, at which the élite of the English nobility
were present. It was here also that Wat Tyler, an inhabitant,
raised the revolt in the 5th of Richard II., when his daughter
received the insult, and who marched hence to London as the leader
of 100,000 men.

Dartford heath was anciently famed as the rendezvous of Tox-
ophilites—dexterous bowmen. They bore the appellation of the
Royal Kentish Bowmen, and had a noble house called the Lodge
on the western side of the heath, fitted expressly for their use. Half
a mile eastward is another heath, called Dartford Brent, memorable
as the spot where Richard Plantagenet, Duke of York, encamped
his army in 1452, and where, also, in 1648, General Fairfax con-
centrated his forces.

In remote times the Knights Templars held lands at Dartford,
which were called the *Manor of Dartford Temple*, but after

Edward II. had seized them and imprisoned the Templars, the lands were called the *Manor of Temple*. This manor was given by Act of Parliament, in the 17th of the same reign, to the prior and brethren called the *Knights Hospitallers*. It reverted to the crown in the reign of James I., who gave the estates to the Earl of Salisbury.

Edward III. founded and endowed a nunnery at Dartford about the year 1355, which was dedicated to St. Mary and St. Margaret. This priory was richly endowed and of large extent. The nuns were of the order of St. Augustine, and mostly ladies of high birth. According to Kilburn, Bridget, daughter of Edward IV., was prioress here, as were also the daughters of the Lords Scope and Beaumont, with other noble ladies, most of whom were buried within its walls. At the dissolution of this religious house, the annual revenues, as estimated by Speed, exceeded £400— a considerable sum in those days. It afterwards formed a temporary royal residence for Henry VIII. and Queen Elizabeth. Edward VI. gave the manor and priory of Dartford to the Lady Anne of Cleves for her natural life, of which she died possessed in the 4th year of Queen Mary. The remains of the priory are built of brick, of the date of Henry VII. (fifteenth century), and comprise a large embattled gate-house, and a wing on the south. The orchards and gardens spread over an area of twelve acres, surrounded by a stone wall, of which portions remain.

The first paper mill in England was erected here in the reign of Elizabeth by Sir John Spillman. He was jeweller to the Queen, and, with her license, had the sole privilege of collecting rags for ten years for the manufacture of writing-paper. Since then Dartford has been noted for its paper mills, an illustration of which is afforded in the colossal works of Mr. Saunders, known as the *Phœnix Paper Mills.* It was here also that iron was first prepared for wire drawing, as early as 1590, by Godfrey Box. Beyond oil and corn mills, driven by the water-power of the river, there is an extensive gunpowder manufactory, which, although valuable for purposes of national defence, is withal a fearful neighbour in the event of accident.

There were formerly two chantries in this parish. That of St. Edmund the Martyr stood in the upper burial-ground of the parish, and had a charnel-house beneath it; the other was founded by Att Stampitt, vicar, in 1338, for *one chaplain to celebrate divine offices daily for the health of his soul.*

The church, dedicated to the Holy Trinity, stands at the east end of the town, and is an ancient early English gothic structure of large proportions. It has a bold embattled tower at the north-west, a nave and chancel, with aisles, and two other aisles on the north and south sides. The screen, in the decorated style, although not in good preservation, is interesting. The recent restoration of this

noble church, at a cost of £1,700, has been very solidly and faithfully carried out by Mr. A. W. Blomfield, the architect. It was
reopened December 23, 1862.   There are some good brasses and
monuments ; amongst them the altar tomb of Sir John Spillman,
with figures kneeling before a desk ; he died in 1607: another altar
tomb for Clement Petit, and brasses for Richard Martin and his
wife, 1402 ; Agnes Molyngton, 1454 ; William Rothele, 1464 ; with
numerous others of later date.   The living is a vicarage in the gift
of the Bishop of Winchester, valued at £534 per annum.   The Rev.
G. J. Blomfield, M.A., succeeded to the incumbency in 1856.

ERITH.

ERITH, from the Saxon *Ærre-hythe*, meaning old haven, is an
ancient village and parish bounded by the Thames, five miles from
Woolwich, and fourteen miles from London Bridge, by the North
Kent Railway, with an area of 4,585 acres, including water, 763
houses, and a population of 4,143 persons.   The view of Erith from
the Thames is the most picturesque on its banks : bold rising
woodlands, and magnificent scenery full of animation, arrest the
attention of every steamboat tourist, whilst the venerable spire of St.
John's, peering through rich foliage, stands—the monitor of departed
glory—the living witness of nearly six centuries, pointing to the
hope and home of every believer.

Robert Bloomfield, whose poetical effusions will always be
esteemed for their beautiful simplicity, bequeaths us a grateful
tribute to Erith, on his recovery from illness, which he prefaces
thus :—*I esteem the following lines, because they remind me of past
feelings which I would not willingly forget* :

> I seek thee where, with all his might,
>   The joyous bird his rapture tells ;
> Amidst the half-excluded light
>   That gilds the foxglove's pendent bells ;
> Where cheerly up the bold hill's side
>   The deep'ning groves triumphant climb,
> In groves delight and peace abide,
>   And Wisdom marks the lapse of time.
>
> O'er eastward uplands, gay or rude,
>   Along to Erith's ivied spire,
> I start, with strength and hope renew'd,
>   And cherish life's rekind'ling fire.
> Now measure vales with straining eyes,
>   Now trace the churchyard's humble names,
> Or climb brown heaths, abrupt that rise,
>   And overlook the winding Thames.

The village of Erith, once a corporate town of some importance,
formed an irregular line of street leading to the river.   Since the

census of 1851, however, it has nearly doubled in population and dwellings, which may be attributed to railway communication and the construction of a pier. There are two railway stations in this parish—Abbey Wood and Erith—distinct of the pier, where Gravesend steamers land visitors during the season. These facilities have led to the erection of handsome villa residences and seats, and numerous family houses. Here is a good hotel, with pleasure gardens fronting the Thames, animated materially by numerous gay yachts generally anchored off the pier, which, added to salubrity of air, charming scenery, and lodgings at moderate charges, have of late years brought Erith into notice as a resort for visitors. Let us hope that the unfortunate proximity of the great southern outfall of the metropolitan sewer, with its consequent exhalations, may not prove damaging to its rising interests.

Half a mile west of Erith Church is Belvedere House, built on the site of the mansion of Lord Baltimore, who died in 1751. It was afterwards sold to Sampson Gideon, Esq., at whose death in 1762 it reverted to his son, Sir Sampson, who was created Lord Eardley in 1769. He rebuilt the mansion, and principally resided there. The late proprietor, Sir Culling Eardley, whose death brought sorrow to so many at Belvedere, materially improved this property by leasing his lands for building purposes. Here are handsome villas and semi-detached residences rapidly rising to a town, where many citizens of London reside, now that railway transit has brought a twelve-mile journey within a short half hour of the metropolis. Here is also a chapel, dedicated to ' All Saints,' under the governance of trustees, valued at £100 per annum. The Rev. J. H. Bernan was appointed minister in 1856. The Baptists have also a neat little chapel, which was opened on September 29, 1863.

Belvedere House is a noble brick structure, standing on the brow of a hill, with a fine prospect over the Thames far into Essex. The grounds are most extensive, laid out with considerable taste in beautiful walks and choice plantations. The house, replete with every luxury in furniture and fittings, may be viewed by tickets, and will well repay a visit, the paintings especially, most of which are by the great masters; for although a number of the best were sold in 1860, there still remain fine specimens of Rubens, Teniers, Vandyck, Murillo, and others.

Azor de Lesneie, in the time of the Saxons, was possessor of Erith, when it was called *Lesnes*, otherwise Erith. In the reign of Henry II. it was granted to Richard de Lucy, Chief Justice of England, who founded the Abbey of Westwood, which he liberally endowed. In 1179 he retired from office, and became a monk in his own monastery, where he died and was buried within a year.

This monastery, of the St. Augustine order, was founded in 1178, and retained its name as the Abbey of Westwood until 1291,

when Edward I. changed it to *Lesnes Abbey*, and conferred on the Abbot of Lesnes and his successors free warren of all the lands. Godfrey de Lucy, a near relation of the founder, was a munificent benefactor during this reign, when the Abbey Chapel was consecrated to the Virgin Mary and St. Thomas the Martyr. After its suppression in 1524 it became private property, and was in the possession of Sir John Hippesly in 1630. Weever (vicar of Erith in the reign of James I.) in his *Funeral Monuments* tells us that the chapel having laid long in ruins, Sir John Hippesly appointed workmen to dig out the rubbish, when they discovered a monument of the Lucy family, in the form of a stone coffin, covered with a marble slab, bearing the recumbent figure of a knight in full armour. Within the tomb was a coffin of lead, which he thus describes:—
In a sheet of lead, fit for the dimensions of a body, were the remains of an ashie dry carcase, whole and undisjointed, and upon the head some hair. They also found other statues of men, and one of a woman in her attire and habiliments.

Dr. Stukeley further enlightens us as to the original structure, which he represents as *standing on a pleasing prominence half-way down the hill towards the marsh; above is a very large and beautiful wood of oak. Part of the original house or seat of the founder is now a farm-house. Of the monastery, towards the south, little remains; there were two grand gateways, long since destroyed. South of the dwelling is the church, built of stone, of which only the north wall remains. The outward wall of the cloisters, on the south side of the church, are still standing; there are also ruins of the refectory, hall of the canons, and sub-prior's apartments. Coffins of stone and monuments have frequently been dug up; these were of the canons, who were always buried along the cloisters.* Little now remains beyond the garden wall, and that of the refectory on the north side, although critical eyes describe the site of the cloister court. Abbey farm, however, covers a portion of the original monastery. Several ancient seals of Lesnes' Abbey are still extant, five of which are figured in *Measom's Railway Guide.*

The parish of Erith is in the diocese of Rochester and deanery of Dartford. The old ivied church, dedicated to St. John the Baptist, is of early date, probably of the thirteenth century, from the early English architecture abounding, although portions exhibit the decorated and perpendicular styles, additions subsequent to the foundation; it has a nave, north and south aisles, and a double chancel. The most ancient brass is dated 1405, being for John Aylmer; an altar tomb for the Countess of Shrewsbury, 1568; a monument for Francis Vanacker, Lord of the Manor of Erith; an ancient brass for *Ellin Atte Coke*; and a goodly monument by Chantrey to the memory of Lord Eardley, with many other memorials. It is an interesting fact that in the reign of King John, the year following that of the Magna Charta, the royal commissioners met the opposing barons in Erith Church to negotiate peace. The living of Erith is a vicarage, in the gift of Lord Wynford, valued at £600 per annum. The Rev. C. J. Smith, M.A., was presented to the incumbency in 1852.

Little did we anticipate, when writing of Dartford, and glancing at the fearful proximity of powder mills, that our present chapter would close by noticing an appalling reality, the explosion of two magazines of gunpowder at Erith, dealing death and destruction far and near, unprecedented in this country for the area over which its effects were felt, even to the bounds of a radius of fifty miles, involving the loss of life and an enormous amount of property. Scarcely a home in the vicinity escaped without shattered windows, even to the venerable ivy-mantled church of Erith. To form an approximate estimate of the damage, one estate alone at Belvedere required upwards of a ton of glass to repair. We mingle sympathies with the sufferers, whose serious calamity was told simultaneously to millions of British subjects on the memorable birth-morn of October 1864.

GILLINGHAM.

GILLINGHAM, written in Domesday *Gelingeham*, adjoins Chatham on the north-east. The soil is poor, principally an unfertile red earth, intermixed with rotten flints; the parish southward is hilly and dreary, with coppice woods of oak, and covers 6,683 acres, including water. Gillingham has several small hamlets among the woods, which are miles distant from the parish church; the population number 14,608, and the houses 2,072.

The manor- of Gillingham was the property of Canterbury Cathedral ages before the Norman Conquest; an archiepiscopal palace adjoined the churchyard, the remains of which are a stone building, now converted into a barn 110 feet by 30, supposed to have been the great hall of the palace.

A great battle was fought here between Edmund Ironside and King Canute; William, surnamed Gillingham, the learned monk who wrote a history of the nation, was born in this parish in the reign of Richard II.

In the last century a large urn was dug up in the salt marshes, containing burnt bones and ashes. A fort was erected on the shore in the reign of Charles I., but was not very formidable, for, during the Dutch expedition of 1667, only four guns were capable of service; it is now called Gillingham Castle, a mere ruin.

There are several manors in this parish; the largest are East and West Court, Twidall, with a sub-estate called Dane Court, and the Grange (anciently Grench). The manor of Grench in the reign of

Edward III. was bound to find one ship and two able and well-armed men for the service of the King for forty days.

John Beaufitz, of Twidall, founded and endowed a chantry in 1433, which he dedicated to St. John the Baptist, *for one priest to celebrate mass for the souls of himself, his wife, and ancestors*. According to Philipott, the chapel was in the north wing of the main building, handsomely wainscoted, and, from the seats and other remains, must have been a neat and elegant piece of architecture; it was taken down, with part of the old house, in the year 1756.

Near the manor house of Grange are the remains of a chapel and prison, with two entrances under stone arches; the walls are of great thickness. In the principal arch the iron stanchions once supporting a massive door are still remaining. Within a short distance is another large building of remote date, the walls equally thick, and in which the outlines of large arched windows may be traced. One writer gives the date 1385, the 8th of Richard II., with the builder, John Philpot. Seymour endorses this opinion so far as naming Sir John Philpot as the founder, but without giving any date.

Hume records an historical fact that renders Gillingham interesting to antiquarians, although it is less known, or rather less considered, than others of less importance. In the eleventh century Godwin, or Goodwyne, Earl of Kent, having allied his daughter Editha to Edward the Confessor, summoned a general council at Gillingham to establish the succession of the throne to the heirs of that prince. The Danes opposed his views, but Godwin's adherents outnumbered them, when Edward was declared King in 1042 and the Saxon line restored. Upon the death of Edward, Harold, son of Godwin, assumed the throne, under the pretence that the late King had named him as his successor. William of Normandy, however, making the like claim, invaded England, and killed Harold at the battle of Hastings, in 1066, when he ascended the throne as William the Conqueror.

The county convict prison stands near the coast-guard station in this parish; it was built in 1856 for 1,200 prisoners, besides officers, warders, and servants. Opposite to the convict prison is St. Mary's Barracks, an invalid depôt for sick and wounded persons returning from abroad.

On the summit of a hill, at the east end of the village, stands the ancient parish church, dedicated to St. Mary Magdalene, overlooking the Royal Dockyard, the River Medway, and diversified scenery, as well as being itself a picturesque object from distant points. This noble church, partly Norman, though mainly in the perpendicular style of architecture, bespeaks sad neglect. Entering by the west, and descending a flight of four steps, we witness much bad taste in ugly, unmeaning pews, and the absence of reverence for a time-honoured pile in the decay that surrounds us. Passing down the nave between handsome columns and fine pointed arches, we reach the chancel, with its double stone *sedilia*, near which is an ancient monument. On the south side is a chantry or chapel, recently cleansed, but bearing a miserable appearance, without a vestige of its former paving, or any monumental records beyond a raised stone to the memory of William Hayward and his wife Alice, dated 1610–1612. Near the chancel are two ancient memorial stones, once bearing brasses. According to Phippen, *there have been tombs here to the families of Boys, Hulme, and Drawbridge*, of which none remain. There were brasses also of the Beaufitz family (fifteenth century), several of whom were buried here.

The font is very ancient, and of large dimensions, octagon in form and Norman in execution. There are north and south aisles, and a bold stately tower at the west end, with an early English porch, over which is a niche, said to have been once tenanted by a statuette of *Our Lady of Gillingham,* and held in great sanctity— so much so that in olden times pilgrimages were made to Gillingham to worship at her shrine.

The *Registrum Roffensis* contains an account of the painted glass in the windows of Gillingham Church in 1621, which are described as being filled with subjects of Scripture history, and the portraits of Robert and John Beaufitz, with their arms and names.

The living is a vicarage, valued at £643 per annum. The Rev. John Page, D.D., has been the incumbent since 1822.

UPCHURCH.

UPCHURCH, once the property of the Leybournes, lies close to the marshes; of 5,138 acres of land, nearly 1,200 are fresh and salt marshes. The village stands on high ground nearly in the centre of the parish, near which is the church. The land is considered thin and poor, which favours the growth of broom and fern, whilst towards the south there is much woodland, principally oak coppice; the elm flourishes here, and abounds in the hedgerows. There are 468 inhabitants, occupying 113 houses. The exhalations of humidity from the marshes subject the residents to intermittent fevers ; hence the limited population.

The interesting feature, however, of Upchurch is the remains of an extensive Roman pottery, which, from the examinations of distinguished antiquarians, is supposed to have been a principal manufactory during the Roman epoch, ending in the fifth century, when the coast line, now partially submerged at high water, was dry land, and covered with the houses of workmen, pottery works, and kilns. In the beds of the creeks many fragments of large pottery have been got out of the mud, and on the banks of the creeks, after digging below the surface, the remains of several kilns were discovered, and excellent specimens of Roman art, many of which are in the possession of the vicar; they are in various colours, some of beautiful design and classical in form.   Similar potteries have been traced for miles on the banks of the Medway. The clay in this neighbourhood being very superior and most abundant, explains the reason why the Romans made this locality the important seat of large pottery works.

The parish church, dedicated to St. Mary, is an ancient structure in the decorated style, once the property of the Order of Lisle Dieu in Normandy, but now that of All Saints College, Oxford, to whom it was given by Henry VI. in 1439.   It has a nave, north and south aisles, chancel, and transept.   In the chancel are stone *sedilia* and painted glas ┐indows. A winding staircase from the chancel leads into a vault ..⁰d with human bones, the history of which is unknown.   The Rev. John Woodruff was appointed vicar in 1834; the living is valued at £243 per annum.

THE ISLE OF SHEPPEY.

CHAPTER I.

THIS island, of about thirty miles in circumference, is bounded on the north by the Thames, and on the west by the Medway, whilst on the east and south an arm of the sea called the Swale ow spanned by the railway bridge, completes its insulation. T. Swale will be long memorable as the waters wherein St. Augustine baptized 10,000 converts to Christianity on the morning of Christmas-day 597.

The Isle of Sheppey was known to Ptolemy. The Saxons called it *Sceapige*, the *island of sheep*, from the large numbers fed there. The land rises from the shores on the south-east and west; on the north runs a range of clay cliffs six miles in length, rising to an elevation approaching 100 feet, but gradually declining towards the extremities. The sea has washed away and undermined these cliffs in many places. Ireland tells us that, *so great is the loss of land at the more elevated parts, that sometimes near an acre has sunk in one mass from that height upon the beach below, with the corn remaining entire on the surface, which has subsequently grown, increased to maturity, and been reaped in that state, with very trifling loss to the owner.*

There is much pasture land on the southern side, famous for the fattening of cattle, of which large numbers are sent to the leading markets. Fresh water is scarce, excepting between Eastchurch and Minster; here the land, surrounded by hedgerows of elm, produces good corn, and the general aspect wears a rich Kentish charm when clothed in nature's verdant garb, beyond which we of the middle seasons cannot dilate.

Whilst the Saxons generally resorted to the Isle of Thanet, the Danes selected that of Sheppey as their landing-point, where they frequently wintered. Their first visit was in the year 832; they then ravaged and plundered the island. On their next appearance, in 849, they remained through the winter. These incursions were frequent until 1016, when King Edmund gained a great victory over Canute and his army; many *tumuli* or barrows, the supposed graves of the Danish commanders, have been found on the southern side.

Pyrites (copperas stones) abound on the beach, but less so than when, in the fifteenth century, the neighbouring poor were employed to collect them in heaps by ship-loads. The continuous wear of the cliff tends to dislodge fossils, of which large numbers have been gathered. The late distinguished naturalist of Faversham, Mr. Jacob, published an interesting account of vegetable and animal fossils collected by himself on this island in 1757, hardly to be paralleled for variety and amount in the like area. The same writer has also published an interesting catalogue of the many curious plants he observed growing over the whole surface whilst prosecuting his scientific researches.

King's Ferry was formerly the principal passage for carriages, cattle, and passengers, maintained at the charge of the landowners and inhabitants by an assessment made annually. The staff of officers comprised a ferry warden, constable, two ferrymen, and a ferry keeper, the latter having the privilege of dredging for oysters within prescribed bounds. King's Ferry is now a thing of the past, the fine railway bridge being adapted for carriage and passenger traffic, distinct of its especial purpose.

There are seven parishes on this island—Minster, Queenborough, Eastchurch, Warden, Leysdown, Elmley, and Harty.

———◇———

MINSTER

OCCUPIES high ground on the north side of the island, and is the principal parish, taking its name from the Saxon word *minstre*, 'a monastery,' of which a few fragments remain near the church in the village.

Sexburga, wife of Ercombert, King of Kent, founded a monastery for seventy-seven nuns, of which she was principal until about 675, when her daughter Ermenilda became lady abbess. The Danes, however, cruelly persecuted this sisterhood, and ultimately dispersed them. The monastery was afterwards abandoned, until William the Conqueror, who, on the murder of the prioress of Newington, removed the nuns to this ruined house, which was ill maintained until 1130, when Archbishop Corboil dedicated it to SS. Mary and Sexburga; he restored the structure, and re-established the institution with Benedictine nuns. The revenues of the monastery were valued at £139 per annum in 1384, but at the suppression of religious houses in the reign of Henry VIII. an abbess and ten nuns were all that remained on the foundation.

The manor of Minster, with the site of the monastery, belonged to Sir John Haywood in 1623; at his death in 1636 he bequeathed them for charitable uses. In 1651 £50 per annum was settled on the parish of St. Nicholas, Rochester, for the relief of the poor ; these estates, however, increasing in value, the trustees were enabled to purchase, from the savings, £636 South Sea stock, which sum was transferred to the Mayor and Corporation of Rochester, in 1718, for the maintenance of charity schools.

The manor of *Newhall*, once *Borstal*, was the property of Fulk Peyforer in the reign of Edward II. Sir William Cromer, Lord Mayor of London, died possessed of it in 1433 ; towards the close of the seventeenth century it was enjoyed by John Swift, Esq., who rebuilt the mansion, where he resided. *Rushingdon* is another manor, given by Henry II. to Christ Church, Canterbury. Philippa, Queen of Edward III., purchased this manor, and conferred it, with the farm of *Dandely*, on the Hospital of St. Katherine, London. This monastery, to quote from Ireland, consisted of *a master, three sisters, and ten beadswomen, with officers and servants.*

The parish of Minster, which includes the town of Sheerness, has an area of 11,035 acres, including water ; 2,305 houses, and a population of 13,964 souls, of which number 1,352 persons are on board vessels.

The church of Minster, dedicated to the SS. Mary and Sexburga, is a fine old gothic structure, with nave, aisles, and double chancel ; the square tower is surmounted by a turret, with a clock and musical bells. In the north chancel is the tomb of Sir Thomas Cheney, whose son, Lord Cheney, caused his father's remains, with those of his ancestors, to be removed from a chapel where they were buried, and re-interred in this chancel. Here are some good monuments ; that of a man in full armour reposes under an arch on the north side ; on the south side is an ancient tomb, bearing the recumbent figure of a knight, with a horse's head sculptured in marble above, to the memory of Sir Robert de Shurland, both dating from the thirteenth century. Here is also a good brass, representing a-knight in full armour, with sword and spurs, and a female figure by his side, supposed to be commemorative of Sir John Northwood and his lady, but beyond the word *hic* nothing is legible. The living is a perpetual curacy, in the diocese of Canterbury, valued at £169 per annum ; the Rev. R. C. Willis succeeded to the appointment in the year 1847. There is a chapel of ease at Sheerness, dedicated to the Holy Trinity, in the gift of the incumbent of Minster Church, which is also a perpetual curacy ; this living is valued at £200, but the cure is sixfold that of the mother church. The Rev. George Bryant, M.A., has been incumbent since 1845.

—•◇•—

K

CHAPTER II.

SHEERNESS.

THE glory of Sheerness is the dockyard, covering an area of sixty acres, enclosed by a brick wall. Although a chapelry to the parish of Minster, and within its ecclesiastical jurisdiction, it is now separated in its civil government.

In the reign of Charles I. the site now called Sheerness was a watery swamp; but after the Restoration a fort mounting twelve guns was erected to defend the passage of the Medway. When the Dutch war was proclaimed shortly afterwards, it was determined to erect a royal fort. The King, Charles II., made two journeys in the winter of 1667 to inaugurate the work; it would, however, appear with little success, for when the Dutch made an attack on the navy in the same year, they destroyed the whole. and landed a large force. This daring act led to the construction of formidable fortifications at different points on either side of the river, improved and multiplied from time to time until the present; now presenting a magnificent coast-line of heavy cannon, to sweep from our waters any hostile power that dares invade them. After the erection of the fort, a royal dock was made, principally for the building of small ships of war, and the repairing of others; old ships of war, called breakwaters, were formerly stationed here, intended to check the force of the tides: these were the homes of sixty or seventy families, when the numerous *brick* chimneys rising from the gun-decks gave the appearance of a floating town.

In 1809 the dockyard was reconstructed for first-rate line of battle ships; year by year, from that time, stupendous works were prosecuted with indefatigable zeal. In 1822 a basin was opened sufficient to dock twelve of these colossal vessels; within a few years additional docks were completed, as well as immense storehouses, factories, and other buildings; a wall of stone 800 feet in length, collateral with the town pier; a basin, 520 feet by 300; three docks, 245 by 90 feet, with iron gates, each pair weighing 160 tons. Without, however, following up to the present the magnitude of operations that have raised the dockyard of Sheerness to prominence amongst the many skirting our coast, we may merely mention that, distinct of the numerous works affording employment for large numbers of artisans and labourers, the establishment, a few years since, of an extensive steam-engine factory alone employs several hundreds. The dockyard was formed on a complete morass, the excavations from which furnished soil sufficient to raise the level of the swamp twelve feet. During these operations many interesting antiquities were dug up, amongst them a remarkably fine carving in oak of our Saviour, of large size. The well that supplies water for the houses of the Admiralty and its vicinity is 365 feet deep, and 8 in diameter.

The town of Sheerness may be described as *Blue Town* and *Mile Town*, and the suburbs *Banks Town* and *Marina*. *Blue Town* is within the garrison limits, and has a pier.   In 1827 some sixty houses were destroyed by fire, and in 1830 fifty more shared a like calamity.   *Mile Town*, without the limits of the garrison, has a line of fortification on the outside, with a ditch to a fleet running to the sea-wall towards the Medway, which forms the outer side of the moat that surrounds the works. *Banks Town* and *Marina* lie on the coast, with good modern houses, inns, and public gardens. Here is an excellent beach, and fine bracing sea air; the water is transparently clear, and invigorating to bathers : those dainty little bivalves, *native oysters*, are abundant here.

Besides the chapel of ease to Minster Church is a new Roman Catholic Church, erected near the sea, and opened by Bishop Grant on September 14, 1864.   It is a good specimen of gothic architecture, designed by Pugin, built by Smith of Ramsgate, and capable of seating 500 persons.

During the season Gravesend steamboats make daily excursions to Southend and Sheerness, whilst the ordinary route is by railway.

QUEENBOROUGH.

THIS is a small parish of 500 acres, 172 houses, and 973 inhabitants.   Here was an extensive manufactory of copperas in the fifteenth century, which is still continued, but on a small scale, owing to the dearth of material.   During the Saxon kings it was named *Cyningborgh.*   They had a castle adjacent to the Swale, afterwards called the Castle of Sheppey.   Edward III. erected a noble structure on the site of the Saxon castle, and, in honour of his queen, Philippa, gave the parish its present name, *Queenborough,* and constituted it a free borough by charter in 1366, with a Mayor, the townsmen being the burgesses, two markets weekly, and two fairs. This Edwardian castle, six years in building, was finished the year following the incorporation, being intended for a defence of the island and a refuge for the people ; King Edward was occasionally resident here.   This fortress was maintained and repaired by the State down to Queen Elizabeth.   After the death of the first Charles it was condemned as useless, sold, and pulled down.   The

K 2

constables of this castle were men of high rank, John of Gaun
amongst them, in the 50th year of Edward III.

Lime-burning and the manufacture of Roman cement giv
employment to many of the inhabitants, as do also the oyste
fisheries, established some centuries since.

Queenborough is within the ecclesiastical diocese of Canterbury
the church, dedicated to the Holy Trinity, was formerly a chape
to Minster Church, but now a donative in the gift of the Mayo
and Corporation, ranking as a perpetual curacy, with a pitiabl
stipend of £85 per annum. The Rev. Richard Bingham, M.A.
succeeded to the incumbency in 1856.

---•◇•---

CHAPTER III.

EASTCHURCH.

EASTCHURCH stands on high grounds in the middle of the island
lying eastward of Minster; hence its name. The parish extend
over 8,621 acres, with 206 dwelling-houses and 996 inhabitant
the village being nearly in the centre, and the pretty little churc
adjacent. The manor of Milton claims over this parish.

The manor of Shurland takes its name from Sir Jeffrey d
Shurland, who was a man of note in the reign of Henry III., an
governor of Dover Castle in the year 1225. His son, Sir Robert
was Lord Warden in the reign of Edward I., and attended the Kin
to the siege of Caerlaverock, in Scotland; he had free warren of al
his lands, and the right of the *wreck of the sea*. He died toward
the close of the thirteenth century, and was buried in Minste
Church, with the head of a horse projecting from above his tomb
A legend, current for centuries, tells us that Sir Robert, passin
Minster Church on a certain day, saw around an open grave
crowd disputing with a priest who had refused his offices withou
pre-payment; the priest was known to him, and, in disgust, h
drew his sword and struck off his head; fearful of the power of th
Church, he retired to his mansion. Shortly afterwards Kin
Edward was sailing by the island, when, with great daring, th
knight spurred his horse into the sea, and swam to the King'
vessel, two miles from the coast, to sue for pardon, which wa
granted conditionally that he swam back again; on landing he wa
met by a witch, who prophesied that the horse would ultimatel
prove his death; this he determined to defeat by at once killing th
animal. A year after, being of a hunting party, he dismounted o
the beach, and whilst walking struck his foot against what appeare

a stone, which proved to be the skull of his horse; a sharp fragment of bone pierced it, and he shortly died, after directing that a horse's head should be affixed to his monument. This legend, however, may be ascribed to the privilege of Sir Robert de Shurland, who, possessing the right of wrecks on the coast of his manor, was entitled to claim all remains scattered on the shore, to the extent of a lance, pointed towards the sea at low water, from the saddle of his steed.

Northwood, another manor of some repute, was remotely the property of Jordan de Sheppey, whose son, Stephen, adopted the surname of Northwood, having possessed a manor in the parish of Milton, on this island, of that name; these manors, in olden times, were distinguished as *the manor of Northwood within Sheppey* and *the manor of Northwood without Sheppey.*

The manor of Kingsborough stands near the centre of the island; this, as its name imports, was Crown property, where *general court and law day* was held annually in the King's name, and homage sworn, for faithful choice of a proper officer, as constable over the island.

At the west end of the village rises the gothic church, dedicated to All Saints, with its battled roof, and tower containing five bells, a nave, two aisles, and triple chancel: it was probably built towards the close of the fifteenth century, for a patent of the 9th of Henry VI. secured to the abbot and convent of Boxley certain lands in the parish for the building of a new church. This is a sumptuous living, valued at £1,724 per annum. The rector and vicar is the Rev. T. B. Dickson, B.D., who succeeded to the living in 1858.

WARDEN

Is the next parish, north of Eastchurch, with an area of 796 acres, 10 houses, and 47 residents. The village stands high; the uplands are mostly arable, those in the vale pasture, but towards Eastchurch it abounds in furze and broom; the side towards Leysdown is marshy, and submerged at high water.

The manor of Warden was the property of John de Savage, of Bobbing, in 1295, in which year Edward I. granted a charter of *free warren* for all his lands. John Sawbridge, of Ollantigh, purchased the manor of a descendant of Lord Delawar. He was an alderman and Lord Mayor of London; on his death, in 1795, it descended to his eldest son. According to *Ireland*, the whole parish, with the exception of a tenement and six acres of land, was his property.

This parish is in the diocese of Canterbury; the church, dedicated to St. James, was rebuilt of stone about the year 1830; the living is a rectory, valued at £70 per annum.

LEYSDOWN,

FORMERLY *Leysdon*, a compound of two Saxon words—*lesive* a pasture, and *dune* high. This parish consists of 4,302 acres, 53 houses, and 215 inhabitants; it is bounded on the north by the cliffs, and on the south by the Isle of Harty.

Mr. Jacob, already referred to, discovered, in 1750, embedded in the clay washed from the cliff, the remains of an elephant; these comprised a spinal vertebræ, a tusk measuring eight feet, a thigh bone four feet, pieces of grinders, and other fragments, but all so impregnated with pyritical matter as to prevent their removal without falling to pieces.

The old church, dedicated to St. Clement, was a very ancient gothic structure of goodly proportions; the battled tower, like that of Pisa, was a leaning one, and for many ages was seven feet out of the perpendicular. After the body of the church had fallen in, the tower was taken down to within some ten feet of its base, sufficient, however, remaining to mark its fearful posture, and the beauty of its very early architecture.

The present church is a very small structure, having an unpretentious wooden turret. The living is a vicarage, in the gift of the Archbishop of Canterbury; it is united with the perpetual curacy of Harty, the joint value being £300 per annum. The Rev. L. W. Lewis, M.A., has held the appointment since 1862.

ELMLEY

Is a parish of 2,341 acres, with 35 houses and 140 inhabitants. Although accounted part of the Isle of Sheppey, it is separated from it by a small stream on the north side, called the Dray. Goodly numbers of sheep are fed here: tiles and bricks are also made on a rather extensive scale; indeed, the parish generally wears a healthy and prosperous aspect.

The church, dedicated to St. James, has been rebuilt. The old church was for many years sadly dilapidated, without door or windows, merely four bare walls. The living is a rectory, in the gift of All Souls' College, Oxford, valued at £340 per annum. The Rev. J. O. Ryder, M.A., Canon of Lichfield, is the present incumbent.

HARTY.

Harty, like Elmley, is a little island, separated from Sheppey by a small stream; its name comes from the Saxon *heordtu*, meaning herds of cattle, for which the island was famous in those times, and even now feeds large numbers, being mostly agricultural, the property of large farmers. It embraces 3,488 acres of land, including water, 26 houses, and 159 inhabitants.

The abbey of Faversham held an estate here, called *Le Long House*, in the reign of Edward I., and a second, *Abbats Court*, in the time of Henry VII. The nunnery of Davington also had 140 acres of pasturage in the reign of Edward III., whilst the chapel of St. Stephen's, Westminster, held another estate, called *Pery Marsh*, down to the 1st of Edward VI.

The church, which anciently belonged to the Benedictine nunnery of Davington, is small, with a nave and chancel, and formerly north and south chantries; it is dedicated to St. Thomas the Apostle. The living, which is annexed to that of Leysdown, is valued at £50 per annum.

SITTINGBOURNE

Takes its name from the Saxon word *Sædingburna*, i.e. *the hamlet by the bourñe*, afterwards written *Sedingbourne*. This parish, 42 miles from London, extends over an area of 1,008 acres, with a population of 4,301 persons, occupying 800 houses. The land rises from the marshes to the town, which is cheerful and populous; the soil is mostly a fertile loam. Formerly the village was environed by orchards of apples and cherries; most of these, however, have given place to hop plantations.

The town flanks the London road, and forms a long wide street of substantial brick houses, with inns and good accommodation for travellers. It was at the 'Red Lion' inn that Sir John Northwood entertained Henry V. on his triumphal return from France; the banquet, although splendid and worthy of the royal guest, cost only 9s. 9d.; but at that time wine was only 2d. per pint, and other charges in the same ratio.

A noble family mansion stood about the centre of the town, the residence of the Tomlyns; afterwards that of the Lushington family, by whom their Majesties George I. and George II. were sumptuously entertained on their way through the town, to or from the Continent. Subsequently the mansion became the 'George

Inn,' and enjoyed considerable popularity from its royal associations; now, however, it has degenerated into an ordinary tradesman's shop.

The population has doubled since the census of 1851, which may be attributed in part to the formation of a railway station, the erection of cottages on Snip's Hill for brickmakers, and to freehold land having been sold for building purposes.

In 893, the Danes, after landing at Milton, built a castle at a place called Kemsleydown, near Milton Church. This fortress, from being overgrown with brushwood, was in after ages called Castle Rough. King Alfred marched a large army into Kent, and raised a stronghold about a mile from the Danish entrenchments, portions of the massive stone-work of which were remaining at Bayford Castle early in the present century.

Bayford Castle was the residence of Robert de Nottingham in the reign of Edward I., from whence he dated several deeds, still extant. His successor, Robert, possessed also the manor of Goodneston, once the property of Goodwyne, Earl of Kent, who, having rebelled against Edward the Confessor in 1052, repaired for safety to Bayford Castle. In the reign of Henry VI. Humphrey Cheney disposed of this castle to Mr. Richard Lovelace, of Queenhithe, London; it was afterwards sold with the manor to Mr. Ralph Finch, of Kingsdown, whose son Thomas passed it away to Sir William Garrard, Lord Mayor of London, A.D. 1555. In the seventeenth century it was converted into a farm-house, and called Bayford Farm.

Chilton, formerly a reputable manor in this parish, was the property of William de Chilton in the reign of Edward I.; Philip, Earl of Chesterfield, possessed it in 1725. At a short distance from Chilton stood the noble mansion of Fulston, anciently called Foggleton, the early residence of the family of Garrards, from whom Sir William Garrard, the purchaser of Bayford Castle, descended. The south-east chancel of Sittingbourne Church belongs to the Chilton manor, and the south chancel to the Fulston estate.

Queen Elizabeth in her sixteenth year incorporated the town of Sittingbourne under the title of a *Guardian and free tenants thereof*, with a weekly market and two annual fairs; this charter was enlarged in the 41st year of her reign to a *Mayor and Jurats*. According to a survey of the parish made in the year 1567, there were eighty-eight houses, two quays, one vessel of twenty-four tons, and two of one ton.

The church, dedicated to St. Michael, stands at the east end of the town, near which rises a spring of good water; it was burnt out on the 17th July, 1762, the tower and bare walls alone remaining. A brief which was granted the following year for its restoration was delayed by the owners of the three chancels belonging to Bayford, Chilton, and Fulston refusing to contribute.

During the next year, however, it was completely refitted. This church, conferred on the Benedictine nunnery of Clerkenwell by Richard II., but given up to the Crown during Henry VIII., now forms part of the ecclesiastical possessions of Canterbury. It is a noble structure, consisting of nave, two aisles, two east chancels, and two transept chancels. The tower is early English, with a steeple containing a clock and six bells. The archdeacon holds his visitations here in the archbishop's chancel. The octagon font is interesting, and bears the arms of Archbishop Arundel. Most of the windows anterior to the fire were filled with coats of arms in stained glass, of which little remains.

The Fulston chancel contains a monument to the memory of Thomas Bannister, obiit 1750, and two loose funeral brasses, one for Robert Rokell, who died in 1421, and the other for John Cromer and his two wives.

In the chancel belonging to the Chilton estate are ledger-stones for the family of the Lushingtons. The fine monument of Dr. Lushington, however, was wholly destroyed during the fire. In the large vault is but one coffin, enclosing the remains of Mr. Harvey, who died in 1751.

The Archbishop's chancel, now belonging to the incumbent, has a memorial for Matthew, grandson of Archbishop Parker, obiit 1645.

The chancel belonging to the Bayford estate has a monument of great antiquity on the north wall, supposed to have been erected about the time of Edward IV., for a female member of the family of Lovelaces; it represents a woman recumbent in a recess under a handsome decorated arch. *Black* describes the figure as dressed in grave-clothes, with the shroud turned aside, *so as to bare her neck and bosom, across which nestles an infant, also shrouded.* No inscription remains to tell the sad story of this mother, said to have died in childbirth at Bayford Castle.

The living, valued at £212 per annum, is in the patronage of the Archbishop of Canterbury. The Rev. H. T. Walford, M.A., the vicar (who is also perpetual curate of Iwade, in this county), was appointed in 1846. The vicarage is on the north side of the church-yard, adjoining which is the only piece of glebe land belonging to the living.

FAVERSHAM.

FAVERSHAM, by the road forty-seven miles from London, or by railway forty-nine, has an area of 2,469 acres; the inhabitants, numbering 6,383 persons, occupy 1,204 houses. Many Roman antiquities have been found in the parish, proving that it must have been known to the Romans during their occupation of this island. Cenulph, King of Mercia, in a charter dated 812, named it *the King's little town of Fefresham*. King Alfred conferred its name upon the hundred of which it forms part; and King Athelstane held a national council or parliament here about 930.

The lands are fertile and well cultivated, and mostly unencumbered by trees or hedgerows. Hops flourish in the upper parts of the down, where there are several orchards. A large tract of marshes bound the parish on the north, whilst on the south-east are some remarkable pillared excavations in the chalk; the most notable is called *Hegdale Pit*. Various opinions have been formed as to their former purpose; some believe that the Saxons dug these caverns as places of refuge for their families and property from the attacks of the enemy; others that from hence was dug the chalk for the building of King Stephen's Abbey in 1147.

Many persons of note were natives of Faversham. *Hamo de Faversham*, a famous Franciscan friar, first provincial of his order in England, was born here; he died in 1244. *Adam de Faversham* was archdeacon of Essex in 1271. *William de Faversham*, a commissioner of Edward I., *Simon de Faversham*, chancellor of the University of Oxford in 1304, *Thomas de Faversham*, honourably mentioned in a charter of Edward II., *Richard de Faversham*, Lord of Graveney in the thirteenth century, and *Stephen de Faversham*, first monk of Christ Church, Canterbury, in 1324. *Henry Page*, of Faversham, was commander-in-chief of the navy in the reign of Henry IV. He took 120 French ships laden with treasure, died in the 13th year of Henry IV., and was buried in Faversham Church.

Sir George Sondes was created Earl of Faversham in 1676. He died in 1678, and was succeeded by Lord Duras, his son-in-law, who was a knight of the garter, and general of the King's army; from his death in 1709 until 1719 the title was in abeyance, in which year Erengard Melusina Schuylenberg, Duchess of Munster, was created Countess of Faversham; Anthony Duncombe succeeded to the title of Earl of Faversham in 1763, but, dying without an heir, the earldom became extinct.

The manor of Faversham was the property of the Crown until the reign of Stephen, who conferred it on William de Ipre, Earl of

Kent in 1141, in reward for his eminent services. In 1147 the King exchanged this manor for that of Lillechurch, having resolved with his queen, Matilda, to found an abbey here; this monastery was built at a short distance from the town, and dedicated to St. Saviour, when they appointed Clarembald, prior of Bermondsey, abbot, and gave the manor of Faversham in perpetuity for its maintenance. Clarembald received his benediction as Abbot of Faversham from Archbishop Theobald at the high altar of Canterbury, November 11, 1147, in the presence of Queen Matilda and the Bishops of Worcester, Bath, Exeter, and Chichester. Queen Matilda died in 1151, and was buried in the church attached to the abbey; her eldest son, Eustace, was buried near his mother, and King Stephen also in 1154. The only vestige of the abbey remaining is the boundary wall, now enclosing the orchard of Abbey Farm. When the church of the monastery was taken down, it is asserted that the bodies of King Stephen, his queen, and their son, were taken out of their coffins for the value of the lead and thrown into the creek; this, however, the inhabitants deny, believing that the bodies were re-interred in the parish church, although without any record of the particular spot.

Many crowned heads have visited Faversham; Mary, widow of Louis XII. of France, sister of Henry VIII., sojourned here in 1515, when the expense of entertainment, according to the chamberlain's account, was 7s. 4d. Henry VIII. and Queen Catherine visited Faversham in 1519, and the King twice afterwards; on the last occasion he was presented with *two dozen capons, two dozen chickens, and a sieve of cherries*, which cost £1 15s. 4d. King Philip and Queen Mary passed through the town in 1557. Queen Elizabeth slept two nights at Faversham in 1573, and King Charles II. dined with the Mayor on his restoration in 1660. The visit of James II. in 1688 was far less gratifying; the King having attempted to escape in a vessel lying at Shellness, after the landing of the Prince of Orange, was captured by Faversham boatmen, who, after taking away his cash and watch, imprisoned him at the 'Queen's Arms' inn, from whence he was removed to the residence of the Mayor.

The town of Faversham, within the limits of the Cinque Ports, is situated close to the creek which runs to the Swale. The principal streets form an irregular cross. Court or Abbey Street, which is broad and handsome, leads to the site of St. Saviour's Abbey. The leading inns are the 'Ship' and 'Railway Arms.' In East Street, near the 'Ship,' are some curious old wooden houses.

Queen Elizabeth founded a grammar school, which she ordered to be called *The Free Grammar School of Elizabeth, Queen of England, in Faversham*. It contains a good library, and has been enriched by sundry gifts. Two charity schools for clothing and instructing boys and girls were established here in 1716.

The oyster fishery is an important means of support, and general benefit to the town, as affording employment to large numbers. *Hasted* states that in his time upwards of one hundred families were maintained from this source alone.

The church, dedicated to the 'Assumption of our Lady of Faversham,' is a large early English structure, built cruciform, of flints, with quoins of stone. Previous to 1755, it had a large square castellated tower rising from the centre, since taken down. The tower at the west end, which is low, is now surmounted by a steeple some seventy feet high, erected in 1794 out of a bequest of £1,000 from a wealthy inhabitant, and £500 given by the Corporation. As early as 1440 there were five bells in the tower, augmented to six in 1459 : in 1749 they were re-cast into a peal of eight bells. Behind the tower is a strong timbered chamber, formerly called the *tresory* (treasury), the depository for sacramental plate and other treasures. In 1533 an inhabitant left, under his will, a bequest for the building of a new *jewel-house*, at the discretion of the Mayor for the time being. Judging from the architecture and other existing details, the church was probably erected towards the close of the reign of Edward I.: this is further established by the finding of a silver penny of that reign under the base of one of the piers that supported the centre tower.

In 1745 Mr. George Dance, an eminent architect of London, restored the interior, when an organ was erected at a cost of £400 ; within a few years, however, it has been wholly restored by our famous ecclesiastical architect, Mr. G. Scott, and now stands a grand monumental witness of the architectural taste of the early fathers. The transepts are separated into three aisles by double rows of fine columns ; the frescoes, early English, on the first pillar, east side, which for many ages had been hidden by whitewash, have been brought out with surprising effect ; they illustrate a series of chronological events in the life of our Saviour. The old font has been superseded by one of alabaster, of beautiful design. There are three *sedilia* and a *piscina* in the chancel, and the original stalls of the brethren of the abbey, on one of which is carved a fox with three stolen chickens ; the east window is filled with stained glass. The oldest brass, dated 1448, is to the memory of William Thornbury, vicar of Faversham ; another for Henry Hatch, who died in 1533 ; a monument, with a figure kneeling, dated 1614, for Thomas Mendfield ; another for Thomas Southouse, 1558 ; and a memento to the memory of John Fagg, 1508 ; besides numerous others recorded in *Weever's Monuments* ; a tomb under a decorated canopy is pointed out as that of King Stephen, but there is nothing identical. Anciently there were two chapels in the principal chancel, dedicated to the 'Holy Trinity' and 'St. Thomas the Apostle,' distinct of several altars in the aisles, as well as in the chancels.

The living is a vicarage, valued at £342 per annum, belonging to the Dean and Chapter of Canterbury. The Rev. C. Collins, M.A., succeeded to the incumbency in 1847.

RECULVER.

RECULVER is full of interest to every lover of early English history. The Romans called it *Regulbium*, the Saxons *Raculf*, and afterwards *Raculf-cester*. The Romans erected a fort and a watchtower, which were said to have been built by the Emperor Severus A.D. 205, where the first cohort of the Vestasians was garrisoned in the fifth century. Of this famous old fort much of the mouldering east and south walls remain, overgrown with ivy and wild herbage in luxurious profusion.

We gather from *Hasted* that the fort covered an area of eight acres, forming a square rounded at the corners; that the north wall, from the inroads of the sea, had fallen on the shore with quantities of coin released from its foundation. These Roman coins included the consular Denarii, and others of nearly all the emperors from Julius Cæsar to Honorius, which are proofs that the Romans had very early a settlement here. Some of the brass coins of Tiberius and Nero were as fresh as if just struck. British coin had also been found, made of *electrum* (three parts of brass to one of gold), as well as small silver pieces of the size of an English twopence, stamped with rude heads, Christian crosses, and strange characters, and Saxon coins with the names of *Edperd*, *Eadlard*, *Edelbred*, and *Ludred*.

Leland, who wrote in the reign of Henry VIII., tells us that the fort was then full a quarter of a mile from the sea, whereas now the sea has reached it, and continues to gain upon the land between this and the North Foreland. The falling of the cliff from these inroads has at various times exposed the foundations of Roman buildings, water-cisterns, fragments of urns, pottery, brass and silver utensils, and from the frequent discovery at low tides of pieces of domestic articles, the assumption is warranted that the ancient town of Roman times has been submerged for ages, and probably extended, as *Hasted* intimates, some distance into the sea, even as far as the *Black Rock*.

Pursuing these reflections, we are carried back *nineteen hundred and eighteen years*, to the landing of Julius Cæsar, who could not have failed, as an experienced general, of seeing the necessity for fortifying this arm of the sea, leading to the mouths of the Thames and Medway, navigable for the largest vessels of those days; and as the eminences at each extremity of that estuary were specially adapted for such purposes, camps would be marked out, afterwards secured by walls, the first grand works of the Romans in Britain; to be followed by those mighty strongholds, Reculver and Richborough, whose walls, measuring from nine to twelve feet in thickness, are so remarkable for firmness of cohesion, that huge masses of those at Reculver, weighing many tons, having fallen on the beach, long defied the powers of ocean to detach the materials from their adhesion to each other.

After King Ethelbert's conversion to Christianity in 597 he gave his palace at Canterbury to Augustine as a residence for himself and the priesthood, and built another at Reculver, within the area of the Roman walls, where he resided until his death in 616.

An Augustine monastery was established here early in the seventh century; the precise date, however, is unknown. A manuscript in the Bodleian library records a grant of lands from Lothair, King of Kent, to the monastery at Reculver, A.D. 679. Egbert II. in 747 bestowed certain tolls, and subsequent kings of Kent enriched it with benefactions of land. The monastery and manor, with its church, were given to Christ Church, Canterbury, A.D. 949. Bishop Tanner supposed the abbots and monks were removed on the annexation, from which cause, and the termination of the regal dignity of Kent, Reculver appears to have gradually diminished in importance. In the eleventh century the sea began rapidly to encroach, and about the same time the water of the estuary to decline, thereby destroying its navigability, and with it a source of considerable profit.

Considering the extent of the fortress of Reculver, covering eight acres, the massiveness of its walls, and that, after the Romans, a royal palace, a monastery, and an abbey church have severally been built within its area, Mr. Boys, the learned topographer, is at a loss to account for the absence of the ruined materials, which at Richborough, though thrown down, remain in huge masses on the spot. *Hasted*, however, very fairly assumes that, after the Romans had left, the inhabitants applied the materials to building in their town, which must have been of considerable extent, although subsequently covered by the sea.

Reculver Minster continued a church of considerable importance, under the governance of a Dean, down to the fourteenth century, and stood in the centre of the fortress walls. We cull from reliable authorities the following description of this time-honoured temple, afterwards called *The Church of the Two Sisters*. From whichever point of view contemplated, whether land or sea, near or distant, it was a beautiful object of vision, imposing and picturesque in the highest degree from its peculiarity of structure, twin spires, and elevated proximity to the sea ; its extreme length from west to east was 120 feet, breadth of west front 64 feet, height of the towers 63 feet, and total height to the summit of the spires 106 feet; the principal entrance was from the west, through a highly ornamented doorway of Caen stone, with Saxon mouldings; the wall rising between the towers to an apex had a rose window and two others beneath.

The quoins were of squared stones; the rest of the walls were of flints and pebbles, mixed with Roman bricks; the towers square and broad, with a spiral staircase in the southern tower leading to the balconies. In one of the spires were four bells, and on the top of the other a representation of the Crucifixion, to which passing vessels lowered their colours. The north entrance was under a circular Saxon arch ornamented; the arches of the windows, passages, and doors were of mixed architecture, some rounded in the Saxon style, others pointed Norman, and a few had the trefoil form. In every part of the structure these two styles prevailed; the Saxon known by its round arches, round or square pillars, zigzag mouldings, and the absence of buttresses; the Norman by pointed arches, slender and clustered columns, and strong buttresses. Thus the nave pillars were square (Saxon), supporting pointed arches (Norman), whilst three Saxon circular arches, supported by round pillars, formed the entrance to the chancel. The floor of the church was of cement, four inches thick, of beautiful smooth red surface and extreme hardness, mixed with figured tiles. There were a nave and aisles, but no transept; at the extremity of each aisle was a chapel or chantry; that on the south side was said to contain the sepulchre of King Ethelbert. *Weever states that he saw a monument of antique form, mounted with two spires, in which, as tradition says, the royal corpse was deposited.*

This church must have retained some of its former magnificence as late as *Leland,* for he tells us that *at the entrance to the chancel was one of the fairest and most stately crosses, nine feet in height, standing like a fair column; its base was a large unwrought stone, above which the column was round and richly carved, terminating with a cross.* He further describes a very ancient copy of the Gospels being in the church, written in large Roman letters, upon the boarded cover of which was a large crystal stone engraved CLAUDIA AREPICCUS.

To the two towers, called *The Sisters,* which for centuries have been a land-mark for mariners, a traditional tale attaches: Frances Saint Clair, lady-abbess of a convent near Faversham, while suffering from illness supposed to be mortal, vowed that in the event of her recovery she would visit the shrine of the Blessed Virgin at Bradstow (Broadstairs), with a costly offering for the Virgin's intercession: on her recovery, in fulfilment of that vow, she, with her sister Isabel, embarked on a Faversham passenger vessel the 3rd of May (about the year 1499), when a violent storm arose, which wrecked the vessel on a sand-bank called the 'Horse,' near Reculver. The abbess, with some of the passengers, crowded the boat, which bore them safely to the shore. Her sister Isabel

remained on the wreck, which could not be approached for fou
hours, when the remainder were rescued, after great suffering fror
cold; but Isabel died the following day, to the overwhelming grie
of the abbess, who, to perpetuate her memory, as well as to consti
tute a sea-mark for mariners, caused the decayed towers of th
ancient church to be repaired, and two lofty spires to be added
which she directed to be called *The Sisters.* The towers are a
that now remain of this ancient monastic church; and the church
yard, which was entire within walls in 1805, having a broa
carriage-way between it and the cliff, is now bared to the sea, th
outer wall being washed down with the cliff, exposing huma
remains embedded in the earth, many of which are strewed upo
the beach.

The present parish church, dedicated to St. Mary, was built i
1811 on rising ground not far from the castle, with materials fro
the Abbey Church of the *Two Sisters.* During the removal (
those materials, the workmen were instructed to search in a cer
tain spot for the remains of King Ethelbert. Leaving their worl
as was customary, for a short time, the wall gave way in th
interval, and from some unknown recess had fallen antique ston
figures of the twelve Apostles, and a lion, the whole being richl
ornamented with thin plates of gold. The old church abounde
with monuments, some of which were removed to the new church
one of these, all but illegible, bears the following curious inscrip
tion :—

Here, as Historiographers have saide,
St. Ethelbert of Kent whilome King was laid;
Whom St. Augustine with the Gospel entertained,
And in this land has ever since remained.
Who, though by cruel Pagans he was slain,
The crown of Martyrdom he did obtain.
Who died February 24th in the year 616.

Amongst the relics preserved in the new church are three ex
ceedingly ancient carvings in stone—one especially, representin
three human figures performing some religious rite; they presen
very much the appearance of Roman remains, but, being unfortu
nately placed high on the wall, are too far removed to allow c
minute examination. The living is a vicarage, in the gift of th
Archbishop of Canterbury, valued at £198 per annum. The Rev
G. W. D. Evans has held the incumbency since the year 1832.

THE ISLE OF THANET.

———◦◦———

This historic island, situated at the north-east point of the county of Kent, takes it name from the Saxon word *Tenet*, and was in remote times insulated by the Stour, then called the *Wantsume*, a bold and navigable channel of some eighteen feet broad, but now a puny stream scarcely dividing the rich pasture land through which it meanders.

Augustine and his forty monks debarked at Ebbe's Fleet on this island, A.D. 507; the rock on which the former landed was preserved through ages with superstitious veneration, from being supposed to bear his foot-print.

The island forms an elongated oval, nine miles from east to west, and five from north to south, computed to contain about forty-one square miles, or a little less than 27,000 acres of fertile land; anciently there was much woodland, long since grubbed up and converted into tillage. During the Danish incursions the natives retired to the woods to secure themselves and families. A small intrenchment may be traced at Chesmunds, and several caves have been discovered under ground, where, doubtless, the harassed inhabitants sought shelter. Some of these caves or caverns are extensive and deep; one especially, discovered in 1780, consisted of seven rooms varying from twelve to thirty-six feet square, each communicating by arched avenues; some of the larger rooms have conical domes thirty feet high, supported by immense chalk columns. The descent to these caves is by rude steps, leading to a passage fifty feet in length, opening on to the apartments, which extend one hundred and ten feet in a direct line; the bottom is of a fine dry sand, whilst the sides and roof are rocks of chalk. Here is a well of excellent water, twenty-seven feet deep, and one hundred and seventy feet beneath the surface of the earth. The date of these excavations cannot be known, but history records the fact that in the reign of King Sigeburt, who came to the throne in the year 648, the Danes used to visit the island almost every year, during which they committed horrid depredations; it is therefore probable that, within the seventh century, these caverns were excavated as hiding places from these marauders.

The ancient Britons inhabited this island, of which many

L

evidences have been found in cash, amulets of gold, electrum, and brass, and in digging of wells, varieties of primitive tools. Then succeeded the Roman dynasty. Numbers of their coins were found under the cliffs near Broadstairs (the ancient Bradstow), amongst them one of the Emperor Constantine, and another in silver of Domitian, exclusive of large quantities in parcels. It does not appear that any Saxon coins were found here, although Hengist and Horsa landed at *Hepesflete* (Ebbe's Fleet) with fifteen hundred men in the year 449, and was possessed of the Isle of Thanet in return for his assistance to King Vortigern.

The chalk cliffs are rather elevated on the north and east, and between Margate and Pegwell Bay, firm and durable, although after stormy weather masses have fallen, in which have been found large pieces of amber. Amongst the causes that render the Isle of Thanet a popular resort in the season are, the salubrity of the air and the dryness of soil. With the exception of the marshes, the face of the country is very beautiful in hill and vale. Luxuriant corn stretches on every side, interspersed with hamlets, and cottages mostly built of chalk, which give a charming diversity, whilst the broad sands and grand expanse of sea completes a gorgeous whole.

The agriculturists of this island have been long famous for good farming; their products generally are remarkable for quality and weight, wheat and barley especially, which command superior prices. London seedsmen deal largely with them for seeds of all the esculent plants, as having a preference in the market.

The sea has made considerable inroads since the Conquest. Thousands of acres to the north and east, now submerged, were anciently dry land. At low water mark rocks or footings of the chalk cliffs are visible nearly three quarters of a mile from the existing shore, once high and dry on the coast; then again, on the south and west sides of the island, hundreds of acres now dry and under cultivation were in remote times covered by the sea, and formed a navigable stream, on the marge of which, at Ebbe's Fleet and Stonar, stood the water-mills of the Abbot of St. Augustine.

The surface of the country is level, with but few pastures. Household herbs of superior flavour grow luxuriously, fennel grows naturally in the hedges, rosemary attains several feet in height. Mr. Lewis observes that in 1723 he had two hedges seventeen yards long and five feet high. The honey collected on the Isle of Thanet is remarkable for excellence of quality, and has a high value in the markets of the metropolis. This superiority is attributable to the quantities of thyme, marjoram, and that class of herbs growing on the island of which bees are extremely fond.

As population increased forests diminished, until very little woodland remains. There are some tolerable elms about Minster, and sycamores nearer to the sea. The oak does not thrive, the soil and situation being inimical to its habits. The roads throughout the island are excellent, which renders excursions exceedingly pleasant. From the scarcity of enclosures, however, there is but little game for the amusement of sportsmen beyond a few hares, rabbits, and partridges, but no pheasants, although wild fowl surround its shores during the winter.

It has been frequently remarked that the humbler inhabitants were equally skilled in holding the helm and the plough. *Camden* described them as both fisher and husbandmen. According to the season of the year they catch fish, perform voyages, export merchandise, manure the land, plough, harrow, reap, and store the corn.

With respect to the existing state of the middle classes, those of Margate, St. Peter's, Broadstairs, and Ramsgate depend largely on the resort of company thither during the summer months; the rest are for the most part farmers, who, being persons in easy circumstances, live in a free and hospitable manner, and have the credit of being very courteous to strangers.

———◆◇◆———

BIRCHINGTON.

BIRCHINGTON adjoins the sea. It was formerly called *Birchington in Gorend*, and at other times *Gorend in Birchington*, from a place so called, where the parish church is said to have anciently stood. It contains 2,070 acres, including water, 188 houses, and 813 inhabitants, and is bounded by lofty chalk cliffs. This parish is within the jurisdiction of the Cinque Ports, and is a member of the Port of Dover. The village, which is lighted with gas, stands towards the centre, and the church contiguous, sheltered by some lofty elms. The houses being on a gentle acclivity command beautiful scenery, and a superb view of the vale of Canterbury; and, though twelve miles distant, the tower of the cathedral stands out most conspicuously. The main road from Sarre to Margate is on the southern side of the parish, and next the shore *Hemming's Bay*, so named from the Danish commander who was supposed to have landed at that point in 1009.

The manor of Quekes (or Quex, as sometimes written in ancient deeds,) stands south-east, about three quarters of a mile from the church. In 1650 this manor was in the possession of Henry Crispe, sheriff of the county, who was forcibly carried prisoner to France, and there detained until he paid £3,000 as his ransom. William III. was an occasional visitor at the manor house, which was a noble timber and brick edifice; it has however been largely rebuilt, having two towers, one containing a good peal of bells.

L 2

These towers have a picturesque effect, and may be seen at a considerable distance.   The room, or rather the bedchamber, of William III. is still shown.

The ancient church, dedicated to All .Saints, which is now undergoing thorough restoration, stands on high ground, with a nave of six bays, two aisles, and three chancels.   The north chancel belongs to the manor of Quekes, and contains many family monuments and the remains of a fresco painting.   The south chancel has been converted into a vestry.   Formerly the windows were filled with stained glass, of which few vestiges remain.   There were also, anterior to the Reformation, several altars dedicated to different saints distinct of the high altar.   Amongst the monumental brasses are those of Richard Juex (perhaps another spelling for Quex), 1449, Richard Juex, 1459, Margaret Crispe, 1508, and John Heynes, 1523. ·   The tower stands at the north-east corner, surmounted by a spire covered with shingle.   Birchington is a chapelry to the church of Monkton, in the gift of the Archbishop of Canterbury.

ST. NICHOLAS-AT-WADE.

This parish has an area of 5,660 acres, 133 houses, and 590 inhabitants.   It is so called from its situation, *ad vandum*, near a wading place or ford across the ancient *Wantsume*.

The village and church stand high.   Westward it presents a level marsh, bounded by the *Nethergong*, whilst northward it is washed by the sea.   Shoart is an estate about a mile north-east of the village, near which is the little borough of All Saints, where once stood a church, of which no vestige remains, it being now united to St. Nicholas.

The church of St. Nicholas is ancient, probably built towards the close of the thirteenth century.   It is a noble structure of flint and Roman bricks ; the windows, doorways, and quoins are of stone; a square tower rises at the west end.   There is a nave, two aisles, transepts, and double chancels, the north chancel being lay property.   Formerly the south transept was a chapel dedicated to St. Thomas the Martyr, wherein was his effigy.   Two early English arches lead to the north chancel : the font is also early English, the windows and tower Decorated.   Three beautiful Norman arches divide the nave from the south aisle.   This church has been faithfully preserved, with little departure from its original integrity.   It is a small living of £161 per annum, in the patronage of the Archbishop of Canterbury.   The Rev. H. Bennet, vicar, was appointed in 1859.

SARRE,

ANCIENTLY written *Serre* and *St. Giles at Serre*, is a small village containing 43 houses, 169 inhabitants, and 653 acres of land. It appears formerly to have been more populous when the passage between Northmouth and Richborough was navigable, with a commodious haven for vessels. Then it was considered healthful as well as pleasant, but on the decrease of the waters, the marsh lands, before covered by the sea, generated fogs and vapours, and soon rendered this district unhealthful, which accounts for the diminished population.

The parish church of Sarre, dedicated to St. Giles, stood on a hill, but from the loss of the inhabitants the parish was united to St. Nicholas, when the church was abandoned, and rapidly decayed.

MONKTON.

MONKTON, the next parish to St Nicholas, although covering 2,364 acres, has but 374 inhabitants, and 87 dwelling houses. Its name has been variously written. *Domesday* gives it *Monocstune*, meaning Monks-town, as belonging to the monks of Christ Church, Canterbury, granted them by Queen Ediva in 961. The village stands low, with the church by the side.

Monkton Church, dedicated to St. Mary Magdalene, is ancient, but small, with a nave, chancel, and a square tower, four bells, and a very primitive wooden staircase. Formerly there were two aisles, the arches of which still exist in the outer walls : some remains of stained glass with antique armorial bearings, and the heads of early priors, adorn the windows. There are few monumental remains. A brass dated 1450, to the memory of a priest, is interesting. The living, a vicarage in the gift of the Archbishop of Canterbury, is valued at £672 per annum, to which, however, must be added the chapelries of Birchington and Acol, as included in the stipend. The Rev. R. P. Whish, M.A., prebend of Wells, has held the living since 1832.

DANDELION,

ANCIENTLY written *Daundeleon* and *Daundolyonn*, is a large estate in the parish of St. John's, in the possession of a noble family of that name as early as Edward I. John Daundeleon, who resided here in the reign of Henry IV., gave a Flemish bell to St. John's Church, thus inscribed '*Daundeleon* I.H.S. *Trinitati sacra, sit hac campana beata.*'

Although the old baronial hall has been swept away, still the gateway remains in tolerable preservation, and is an interesting relic of the days of bows and arrows. It is built of brick and flints in alternate rows, loop-holed, with a spiral staircase leading to the embattled summit. Over the gate, on the centre of the cornice, are the family arms. An interesting discovery was made in 1703 under the side of the gate entrance, when a small room was exposed containing funeral urns of pottery and glass, supposed to be Roman, and on the opposite side a sort of well prison.

MARGATE.

MARGATE, 19 miles by rail from Canterbury, and 101 from London, extends over 4,572 acres of land. and has 2,194 houses, and 10,019 inhabitants. In the reign of Elizabeth, Margate, then *Mereyate*, was a poor fishing village, consisting of 107 mean old houses irre- gularly built. It, however, had some reputation in the coasting trade, for according to the maritime survey made at that time (8th year of Elizabeth), they had fifteen vessels, ranging from one to eighteen tons burthen, with sixty seamen, largely employed in the carrying of grain.

The bay is famous for bathing, with a fine clean sand of gentle descent, from which the sea ebbs nearly half a mile at low water. The east and west sides being defended by rocks, the swell and surf seem to slumber between them, although directly open to the northern sea, with a run of 1,380 miles, north half east before land could again be reached, which would be the coast of Greenland.

The passage from England to Holland being the shortest from Margate, many distinguished personages have landed and embarked here. William III. on his way to and from Holland; George I. twice landed here; Caroline, Queen of George II.; the great Duke of Marlborough after his campaigns : the late Duke of York sailed from and disembarked here in 1793; and the famous Admiral Duncan landed here after his great victory in 1798.

The stone pier, designed in part by Rennie, and built between the years 1810-15, at a cost of £60,000, is about 900 feet in length and 60 broad, with an elevated promenade 18 feet in width, lighted with gas, much frequented in the season. The lighthouse which stands at the extremity was built from a design by Mr. Edmunds in 1829, at a cost of £800. The old wooden jetty has been superseded by an iron landing-place above 1,200 feet in length.

The Town Hall, of Tuscan architecture, built in 1820, is a handsome building of goodly proportions. The interior arrangements are well suited for their purpose. A few portraits of Margate celebrities adorn the walls. There is also a good bust of Sir Thomas Staines : this structure cost £4,000.

The Royal Sea Bathing Infirmary, supported by voluntary contributions, commends itself to all classes of visitors. The first stone of this institution was laid in 1792, at Westbrook, in that part of the town called *Buenos Ayres*, and opened in 1795. The reports of revolving seasons abundantly testify of its value. It has been enlarged to the extent of two hundred beds, and it is further contemplated to make a large addition to the building for the reception of one hundred children.

Michael Yorkley, a Quaker, founded in 1709 ten almshouses now called ' *Draper's Hospital*,' one to be the residence of a Quaker as overseer, the others for aged widows, who are supplied with warm clothing, firing, and a weekly allowance according to the funds, which being scarcely sufficient for their maintenance, the recipients sell trifling fancy articles to visitors, and are permitted to receive tea parties during the season. To the honour of the philanthropic Quaker, he humanely willed that the deserving of *any* sect were eligible for election.

In the year 1787 the Charity Schools were founded, when a suitable building was erected near Hawley Square. The children, then sixty in number of both sexes, since considerably augmented, are clothed and educated at the voluntary cost of the inhabitants, aided by the contributions of visitors. A curious discovery was made in 1791 by some workmen, while digging the foundations for three houses behind these premises. Deep in the chalk they reached several graves containing human remains, which, although perfect skeletons, speedily crumbled to dust on exposure. In one grave was a coin of the *Emperor Probus*, and in another one of *Maximianus*. Near the same spot a Roman urn, containing ashes, was dug up the following year.

The theatre in Princes Street, Hawley Square, is a neat brick building, erected in 1787 at a cost of £4,000 ; during the season good performers from the metropolitan theatres give excellent entertainments to crowded audiences. The assembly rooms in Cecil Square command considerable patronage from the superiority of entertainments during the season. The evening concerts are

supported by good talent, and the balls conducted with due regard
to the respectability of visitors.   The building presents a noble appearance, with a bold façade, supported by pillars; the principal
room is lofty, and measures one hundred feet by fifty feet, the
orchestra being placed at the western end.   There is no dearth of
amusement at Margate to suit every taste in bazaars, libraries, and
news-rooms; the Tivoli gardens, which are laid out effectively, are
much frequented for dancing, with the adjuncts of singing and fire-
works; then, again, the lovely rides and walks for the health
seeker, the unrivalled facilities for bathing in the sea or at any of
the well-appointed establishments, with a superb sand and bracing
saline air, so delectable for the convalescent.   Marine Terrace and
the Fort, furnished with plenty of seats, are the popular promenades, enlivened on the upper pier with good instrumental music
every evening.   Cecil Square was built to meet the necessity for
handsome houses, at a cost of £8,000; these dwellings are large and
commodious.   Since then, however, building has progressed to a
surprising extent; first-class houses are numerous, even for families
of distinction, of which fact the Royal Crescent is a good illustration.   Lodging houses are abundant, and generally speaking well
suited for temporary residents; visitors, however, preferring an
hotel have a good variety to select from.   The town is well lighted
and paved under an Act granted in 1813, maintained by a rate
chargeable on the householders.   The municipal authorities consist
of a mayor, four aldermen, and a council of twelve.

Distinct of the churches of St. John and Trinity, which we shall
describe anon, and St. John's Hall, in Cecil Street, licensed by the
Archbishop of Canterbury as a chapel of ease to the mother church,
are several chapels belonging to Dissenters.   The Wesleyan Metho-
dists have a chapel in Hawley Square; Ebenezer Chapel (Baptist),
New Cross Street; Zion Chapel (Lady Huntingdon's), Addington
Square; New Congregational Church, a handsome modern building,
Union Street; Roman Catholic Church, Prince's Crescent; Friends'
Meeting House, on the road to St. Peters; Plymouth Brethren,
Hawley Square.

The cemetery, near to Marsh Court, on the road leading from
Margate to Minster, comprises eight acres of land, very beautifully
laid out by the late Mr. Cormack, a man of great botanical skill;
Sir Joseph Paxton was one of his earliest pupils.

The venerable parish church, dedicated to St. John the Baptist,
stands on a knoll, about half a mile from the pier; though low, it
is of considerable length, built of flint, with ashlar stone quoins,
windows, and doorways.   It has a nave, north and south aisles, and
three chancels; the aisles are separated from the nave by pillars and
arches of mixed architecture; one of the chancels is dedicated to
St. James.   The square tower, surmounted by a short spire, stands
at the north-west corner, and contains a peal of eight bells, with a

good clock. The church underwent considerable repairs in 1808, but in the year 1845 it was restored and beautified, when the east and west windows were renovated, some being filled with painted glass, a new altar-piece erected, and (worst of all) the centre aisle refitted with *pews*. The richly carved font, which is very interesting, dates from the time of Henry VII. The organ was the gift of the late Francis Cobb, Esq.

There are some very ancient brasses and monuments in this church : amongst the brasses is one to the memory of Thomas Smith, dated 1433; others for Nicholas Canteys, 1431; Richard Notfield, 1446; Thomas Cardiff, 1515; Luke Spraklyn, 1591; a brass, graven to represent a ship in full sail, for Roger Morris, 1615; and in the chancel another, beautifully portraying a knight in plate armour, for Sir John Dandelion, obiit 1445. Most of the ancient families resident in the parish were buried in the church, evidenced by the numerous monuments and tablets still existing bearing the names of Crisp, Cleve, Cleybrooke, Norwood, and others.

St. John's Church is supposed to date from the middle of the eleventh century, and was until 1200 one of three chapels on this island belonging to Minster, when it was made the parish church. The living is a vicarage in the patronage of the Archbishop of Canterbury, with a stipend valued at £681 per annum ; the Rev. C. S. Astley, M.A., has been the incumbent since 1854.

Trinity Church, which was erected between the years 1825 and 1829, is built of brick, cased with stone. The elegant tower is 135 feet high, and from its elevation may be seen at very distant points; the exterior is effective in decoration and carved stone, forming buttresses, pinnacles, and finials; not less so, however, is the interior, with a lofty nave, and north and south aisles elaborately groined. The windows are filled with stained glass; the east window, some thirty feet in height, is especially effective from the varied hues permeating. A vaulted arch, covered with beautiful tracery, forms a recess for the communion table. The organ, which represents a shrine, stands in a recess at the west end, where is an elaborately carved stone screen, with pierced arches, buttresses, and pinnacles. The living is a perpetual curacy, in the gift of the vicar of St. John's, valued at £221 per annum, to which the Rev. S. Prosser was presented in the year 1846.

KINGSGATE.

THIS is a romantic spot in a valley near the northern shore of the
sea, formerly called *Bartholomew's Gate*, but after the landing of
Charles II., with his brother the Duke of York, in the year 1683, it
was changed to *Kingsgate*, in commemoration of that event. The
embattled gate, with frowning portcullis, of which little remains,
was built in a breach of the cliff, on the eastern side of which was
graven, ' *God bless Barth'lems Gate*.' In remote times there was a
strong fortress, with massive towers, supposed to be Roman, from
the discovery of an earthen vessel under one of the foundations
filled with Roman coins.

Tradition points to Kingsgate as the spot where the great battle
between the Danes and Saxons was fought in 853. Tumuli were
opened here in 1745 and 1765, discovering numerous graves dug
out of the chalk, covered with flat stones ; these contained human
remains, the bones large and perfectly sound, but speedily crumbling
to dust after exposure to the air ; some urns, made of coarse pottery,
were found at the same time. Over the largest of these tumuli a
rude gothic building was erected by Lord Holland.

Kingsgate Castle, a mimic fortress, stands on the summit of a
perpendicular cliff, which from the sea has a peculiar effect ; this
castellated structure, overgrown with ivy, is of considerable elevation, which renders it a picturesque object. It was built by Lord
Holland for stables, in imitation of the style of castles erected in
Wales, during the reign of Edward I. ; since then it has been converted into a residence.

Whitfield Tower stands a short distance from the cliff, with a
shaft of lofty altitude as a landmark ; it was built on the estate of
a former proprietor, whose name it bears. Lord Holland bought
this estate, and erected a mansion, on the model of *Tully's Formian
Villa*, facing the sea, but sheltered by the cliff. The centre is of
the Doric order, the wings of flint ; over the doorways are white
marble slabs, sculptured. The saloon has an elegant ceiling,
artistically painted by Bartoli and Richter, and supported by
scagliola columns.

Lord Holland displayed much freakish fancy in the erection of
chalk and flint structures round this seat. Amongst others is a convent, in imitation of a Kentish nunnery, with the remains of a
chapel and five cells, now forming residences for poor families ;
also a mock fort, consisting of a round tower with a flag-staff,
fortified out-work, and ditch ; this structure, called the *Countess'
Fort*, designed for an ice-house, was never completed. At the

upper end of the grounds is a column of Kilkenny marble, called the *Countess' Pillar*, with an inscription to the memory of the Countess of Hillsborough, who died in 1767.

———◦◦———

THE NORTH FORELAND,

So written to distinguish it from the *South Foreland*, between Deal and Dover, is a promontory at the north-eastern extremity of the county, and the supposed *Cantium* of Ptolemy; Roman seamen knew it as the *Cantium Promontorium*.

A striking object here is the lighthouse, one of the most important on the British coasts, from its close proximity to the Goodwin sands. Sailors designate the North and South Foreland lights *the long mark for going clear off the South and off the Goodwin*. Although there is every reason to suppose that from a very early date there was a light of some sort here, yet we have no particular record until the reign of Charles I., when, in 1636, Sir John Meldrum was licensed to erect and maintain lighthouses on the North and South Foreland, and empowered to receive from all English vessels passing one penny per ton, and from foreign ships two pence, out of which the state was to be paid £20 annually. This grant, which remained in private hands until early in the eighteenth century, was then conferred on Greenwich Hospital. In 1832, the Trinity brethren, in consideration of £8,300 paid by them to the Hospital, took possession of the Lighthouses, and effected a reduction in the dues, and a re-arrangement of the entire system.

The lighthouse erected on the North Foreland by Sir John Meldrum, built of timber, lath, and plaster, with a large glass lantern on the top, was destroyed by fire in 1683, after which a beacon was substituted; but before the close of the same century a massive octagonal edifice of flint, two stories high, was constructed; on the summit was placed a capacious iron grate, exposed to the air, which, after sunset, exhibited a blazing coal fire. In 1732 it was enclosed, forming a lantern, the flame being maintained by bellows perpetually in motion during the night; this expedient, said to be for the economising of coal, appears to have proved a failure, as numerous craft foundered on the Goodwin Sands through the light not being perceptible at sea. This fact led to the removal of the lantern, and the restoration of the former arrangement, whereby many like casualties were escaped.

In the year 1793 the structure was thoroughly repaired and raised by two stories of substantial brick-work, making its present elevation to the top of the lantern nearly one hundred feet. Patent lamps, with magnifying lenses, superseded coal fires ; these are placed in a room lined with copper, about ten feet diameter, around which is a gallery commanding sea and landscape of marvellous magnificence.   The present arrangement of light is considered perfect, and so brilliant as to be seen in clear weather thirty miles distant.   Visitors to the island are permitted to inspect this interesting object, and are kindly welcomed by the attendant, who explains the method of lighting, and obligingly affords any information required.

Admiral Monk fought his great battle off the North Foreland in 1666 ; the engagement lasted four days, the English with fifty-four sail, against a Dutch fleet of eighty.

ST. PETER'S.

THE sweetly pretty village of St. Peter's stands on a pleasing eminence, and boasts many reputable inhabitants.   The houses are neat ; many elegant seats and gay gardens adorn the vicinity, and the order everywhere displayed elicits admiration.   Distinct of the village are several small hamlets scattered over the parish ; on the north is Sackett's Hill, so named after an ancient family, most of whom were buried in St. Peter's Church.   Hackenden Down and the hamlet of Stone belonged to the Pawlyns, another ancient family.   Near this spot stood in olden times a beacon *to alarm the surrounding country upon occasions of invasion.*

The parish extends over 3,312 acres, with 686 houses, and 2,855 inhabitants.   The church, dedicated to St. Peter, stands upon rising ground, and although not large, has a very picturesque appearance ; this is a fine specimen of Gothic architecture, said to date from the twelfth century.   Like most ancient churches, it is built of flint, with stone facings to the windows and doorways, the porch being more decorated, and the entrance under a mitred arch of wrought stone.   The battled tower, with stone quoins and buttresses, is remarkable on account of a fissure on the east, and another on the west sides ; tradition asserts that the shock of an earthquake in 1580 caused these rents, which extend from the top nearly to the bottom, and although subsequently filled up, may still be traced.   St. Peter's has a nave, two aisles, and three chancels ; the middle chancel is spacious, indeed beautiful, the roof being in compartments, enriched with carved work.   Formerly, exclusive of the high altar, were others dedicated to *St. James, St. Mary of Pity,* and *St. Margaret.* The font is of white marble.   The interior has been restored through the exertions of the late vicar, the Rev. Sanderson Robins.   In the nave and chancels are several monuments, and in the church-yard tombs and memorials for many who once figured in this parish. The father of the great orator, Richard Brinsley Sheridan, was buried here; a tablet to his memory was erected a few years since by a stranger to the neighbourhood, who caused an inscription to be graven on it, ending thus :—

> He who builds a church to God, and not to fame,
> Never inscribes the marble with his name.

The church cemetery is supposed to be even of an earlier date than the church, for in 1831, whilst digging round an ancient tomb, an inscription was discovered to the memory of ' WILLIAM NORWOOD, DDCXXII.' (A.D. 1122.)

The living is a vicarage in the gift of the Archbishop of Canterbury, valued at £560 per annum. The Rev. C. F. Tarver, M.A., chaplain to the Queen and the Prince of Wales, succeeded to the incumbency in 1863.

BROADSTAIRS.

THIS town derives its name from the Saxon words *Brad, stow*, broad place, and although formerly a small village, has increased into a fashionable watering-place. There can be little doubt that the Romans resided in this neighbourhood, from the number of coins found after the falling of portions of the cliff, and that, at a later period, it was well fortified, of which evidences exist east and west of YORK GATE. An interesting relic of York Gate remains in good preservation, thanks to Lord Henniker, who repaired it at his own cost in 1795. According to the inscription over the arch, it was built by George Culmer, A.D. 1540, and although now merely a massive flint arch, was once defended by a portcullis and strong gates. There was a wooden pier at Broadstairs during the reign of Henry VIII., built by members of the Culmer family for the convenience of the fishing trade, then forming the larger portion of the inhabitants. In 1667 it was nearly destroyed by a terrific storm, but restored at the national expense, and again repaired in 1791 under an Act of Parliament. The present pier, which has no architectural beauties, was built in 1809, after the total destruction of its precursor by tempest.

We are told by Kilburne, an authority, however incredulous it may appear, that on a sand bank near this spot, called Fishness, a monstrous fish ran itself ashore in 1574, and died; its roarings were heard a mile distant as the tide receded. ' *The length of this leviathan was sixty feet, the nether jaw opening twelve feet, allowing three men to stand in the opening. A man stood upright in the socket of the eye, and another crept into the nostril. The ribs measured fourteen, and the tongue fifteen feet: from the top of the back through was fourteen feet, while the liver loaded two carts.'* Hasted also states that four monstrous whales were landed on this island in his time, one of which was sixty feet long and thirty-eight feet in circumference, with teeth two inches in length.

East Cliff Lodge, between Broadstairs and Ramsgate, was the favourite marine residence of Caroline, Queen of George IV., when Princess of Wales; it was built by Benjamin Hopkins, Esq., having extensive grounds very tastefully laid out.

The remains of an ancient chapel dedicated to *Our Lady of Bradstow* still exists, where in olden times offerings of considerable value were made; indeed, this chapel was held in such reverence by mariners that they saluted it on passing, and after storms would land and make costly presents to propitiate their patron saint. Some of the walls and windows of this chantry now form portions of a Baptist Chapel, as well as a dwelling house.

Broadstairs is patronised by visitors preferring calm and quiet to noise and excitement, for here we meet the illustrious and titled, as well as the choicest of our literary celebrities, all alike enjoying the delightful seclusion it affords. The town, which wears an aristocratic appearance, has considerably increased within a few years in superior dwellings, good hotel accommodation, and convenient lodgings for temporary residents; the lovely walks and quiet promenade on the cliff, embracing the beauties of nature, breathe calmness and serenity, the food of meditative minds. An elegant villa at the entrance of Broadstairs, the seat of the late T. Forsyth, Esq., commands one of the most superb views on the island; it was a favourite residence of Her Majesty, when a child, and her beloved mother the late Duchess of Kent.

There are three chapels: the Wesleyan, in Harbour Street; Providence Chapel, in High Street; and the Baptists', in Albion Street, formerly the chapel of *Our Lady of Bradstow*, already referred to.

Trinity Church was erected in 1829, by public subscription, as a chapel of ease to St. Peter's; it was assigned an ecclesiastical district in 1850. This neat Gothic structure is built of flint, and contains sittings for about 1,000 persons. The living is a perpetual curacy, in the gift of the vicar of St. Peter's, valued at £180 per annum. The Rev. C. F. Newell, M.A., has held the incumbency since 1850.

————◦◇◦————

RAMSGATE.

In making Ramsgate our present theme, early associations rise
vividly before us; for here our first impressions of the beauties of
Kent were developed some thirty-five years since in the companionship of the friend of our youth,—the unswerving, cherished
friend of after life, now, alas! resting peacefully in his quiet grave
in the ancient cemetery of St. John's, Hackney. In him, exemplary piety adorned a noble nature, full of sympathy for suffering
humanity: his walk through life was worthy of his Christian
profession; his end was peace; and his memory will long live in
the affections of many loving hearts.

Ramsgate, or *Riums-gate*, as anciently written, is ninety-seven
miles from London by railway, and faces the sea on the south side
of the island. It was formerly, like its neighbour Margate, a
simple fishing village of huts built of wood and thatched, and stood
near the coast, until the encroaching sea drove the inhabitants
more inland. In the year 1565 there were only twenty-five inhabited houses, and fourteen vessels, ranging from three to sixteen
tons each, which employed seventy seamen in fishing and carrying
grain to the several markets. Towards the close of the seventeenth century (after the revolution of 1688) Ramsgate rapidly
rose to an important town ; the extension of trade with Russia and
the East proved of the greatest advantage to the inhabitants, who,
having vigorously embarked in the adventure, were successful, and
not only improved their houses, but considerably multiplied their
numbers.

This charming town stands on the declivity of two hills, opening
on to the sea. In clear weather (looking across the ocean) the cliffs
between Calais and Boulogne may be seen without telescopic aid ;
then again, from any eminence we may view the whole island, and
read the past, rich in memories of the Romans and of the Saxons,
and call to remembrance the fact that the first inklings of
Christianity were brought to the ancient Britons through this
island, where Augustine preached the Gospel to Kentish men, and
by his instrumentality their pagan king, Ethelbert, became a
convert, and was baptized ; and on the Christmas day of the same
year, A.D. 597, ten thousand of his subjects dedicated themselves
by immersion to the same faith. Surely then THANET must be
dear to every believer in that Sacred Writ which England has not
only translated into every language and tongue, but sent her
missionaries through every land to propound the truths therein
proclaimed.

According to Leland, there was a pier at Ramsgate in the reign of Henry VIII. which afforded little security in stormy weather. The loss of many ships on this coast during a violent gale in 1748 having brought public attention to the necessity for a suitable harbour, an Act of Parliament was granted the following year, and in 1750 a new harbour was commenced from the designs of William Ackenden, Esq.: the work progressed with spirit for four years, when disagreements arose, and the whole was stopped until 1761; it was finished towards 1790, at a cost of from six to seven hundred thousand pounds,—a high-sounding sum, 'tis true, but bearing a very small proportion to the property and valuable lives thereby saved. This royal harbour has an area of fifty acres, capable of giving refuge to from four to five hundred vessels; it is nearly circular, and built of purbeck and portland stone; the water area forms two harbours, the inner of which has immense flood gates, with an elegant iron bridge across: on the east and west sides are splendid piers, some twenty-six feet wide: the length of the east pier is two thousand feet, and that of the west fifteen hundred feet, both of which are invigorating promenades. The Lighthouse, which stands at the extremity of the western pier, is a neat structure of stone, with argand lamps and reflectors, only lighted during nights when the tide is sufficient for the safe riding of vessels.

Ramsgate pier, forming the boundary of the harbour, extends nearly a thousand feet into the sea, and has a deserved pre-eminence as a promenade for beauty and fashion, seen advantageously on the arrival of the steamboat, when the loving smiles and beaming eyes of Albion's fair daughters greet the treasured ones they had awaited. From the west pier, on the face of the cliff, rises a novel staircase of steps called *Jacob's Ladder*, leading to Nelson's Crescent, West Cliff, and the Paragon: a similar flight, known as *Augusta Stairs*, runs from the sands to the Mount Albion estate, a pleasant spot amongst villas and elegant houses.

The Pier House is a handsome structure, used occasionally as a temporary residence by the trustees. It was on this spot George IV., on his visit to and return from Hanover, in 1821, addressed his subjects present, and commanded that the haven should be designated the "*Royal Harbour of Ramsgate.*" An obelisk of massive granite, Egyptian in design, was shortly afterwards erected at the cost of the inhabitants and harbour authorities in commemoration of the event: on the north and south sides are inscriptions in English and Latin, somewhat excessive in adulatory phraseology.

The sands are most beautiful, and extend a mile outwards at low water. The bathing rooms on Kent Terrace, which face the sea are replete with every appliance, whilst those who prefer a plunge into the briny deep have every facility in bathing machines numbers of which are perpetually traversing the sands according to the tide. Perhaps one of the most gratifying illustrations o:

"LONDON OUT OF TOWN" is to be found here on a fine summer morning, where the formalities of society are wholly ignored;— where the senator, the merchant, the scholar, even to the artizan, mingle, without distinction, in friendly converse; where loving mothers enjoy the sports of their darling treasures, and superannuated grandsires forget their infirmities in the ecstacies of *little toddles* digging in the sand, or dancing with joy at the sportive waves. Then, again, who can enumerate the many hearts won on Ramsgate Sands, the many who have met here as strangers, but returned to town ardent lovers, and whose names, within a brief period, have graced an important column of the *Times* newspaper.

Ramsgate, patronized by the aristocracy, as well as by the upper and middle classes, wears a superior appearance in excellent houses, squares, terraces, and every description of building to constitute a first-rate town. The Market in York Street is a neat covered building, erected in 1839. Over the vegetable market is the Town Hall, having a bold façade, supported by noble columns. It contains an original portrait of Her Majesty, painted by Fowler in 1840, pronounced to be one of the best likenesses ever executed. The Music Hall in George Place is spacious and handsome, and in considerable requisition during the season for lectures, balls, and concerts. Here are numerous charities and schools, and a Seaman's Infirmary in Trafalgar Place, built by subscription, and supported by voluntary contributions, but principally by the neighbouring gentry. The Ramsgate and St. Lawrence Dispensary was established in 1820, since which time it has admitted 42,029 cases. According to the last report, from the death of many old subscribers, the funds are much impoverished, and the trustees are compelled to make an earnest appeal for increased aid, which we hope will call forth all the sympathy this excellent institution demands. The libraries are well supplied with modern publications, as well as classical and historical literature. The Marine Library is a fashionable lounge in summer.

Sir Moses Montefiore has a charming seat about a mile from the town, known as East Cliff Lodge, communicating with some remarkable caverns, excavated in the cliff descending to the shore.

The parish of Ramsgate includes the ecclesiastical district of Christ Church and part of Ellington hamlet, the remainder being in St. Lawrence. A chapel of ease to St. Lawrence was built at Ramsgate in 1791, under an Act of Parliament, but from the increasing population a new church, dedicated to ST. GEORGE, was erected in 1829 at an outlay of £24,000. This elegant Gothic structure has an area of 148 feet by 68 feet, and will seat 2,000 persons, of which 1,200 sittings are free. The living is a vicarage in the gift of the Archbishop of Canterbury, valued at £400 per annum. The present incumbent is the Rev. J. M. Nisbett, M.A., Rural Dean of Ramsgate.

M

CHRIST CHURCH, in the vale near Queen Street, was built by private subscription in 1847. This is a neat edifice of Kentish ragstone, with a pretty spire. The living, a perpetual curacy, is vested in trustees. The Rev. T. H. Davis, M.A., was appointed incumbent in 1853.

HOLY TRINITY is another perpetual curacy, in the patronage of the vicar of St. Lawrence. It was built in 1849 on the Mount Albion Estate. The Rev. J. Gilmore, M.A., succeeded to the curacy in 1858.

St. Augustine's Roman Catholic Church is an effective specimen of *Early Decorated*, designed by the late A. Welby Pugin, the founder of the church. The walls are of flint dressed with Whitby stone, a revival of the style of one of our early English churches, with richly carved screens, noble chancel, a Lady Chapel, and the Founder's Chapel, St. Ethelbert's aisle, a south transept, and an altar dedicated to St. Lawrence. The church measures 90 feet by 60 feet, and the windows are filled with rich coloured glass.

The Dissenters have eight chapels, and the Jews a Synagogue at Hereson, built by Sir Moses Montefiore.

ST. LAWRENCE.

ST. LAWRENCE, the venerable Mother Church of Ramsgate, and little more than a quarter of a mile from that fashionable town, is very pleasantly situated on a knoll, with the pretty little village of its own name adjoining. This is an interesting church, partly built by the Saxons, having three chancels, a nave, and two aisles. The tower, supported by four pillars, rises from the centre, on the capitals of which are some very curious sculptures, and on the outside of the battled tower a range of small octagonal SAXON pillars supporting semi-circular arches. The church is built of field stones, rough cast over, and has the appearance of having been erected at different periods. In the middle chancel are monumental brasses, and a very ancient slab for one Umfry. The north chancel is said to have been built by the Manstons many centuries since. when there was a high altar, as well as others in chapels, dedicated to St. James, St. Catherine, St. Thomas, and the Holy Trinity. Here are several monuments for ancient families, including those of the *Nicholas'*, the *Spracklings*, and the *Thatchers*. A mausoleum of Caen stone of fine workmanship has been erected in the churchyard for the Countess of Dunmore and her son Colonel D'Este, brother of the present Lady Truro. In 1857 the church was largely restored by Smith and Son, of Ramsgate.

St. Lawrence Church was a Chapelry to Minster Church until

about the year 1200, when it was made parochial. In 1275 the then Primate ROBERT consecrated the churchyard, stipulating that none of the inhabitants should be buried there without the express permission of the vicar of Minster. It appears, however, that a composition was subsequently made and confirmed by the Archbishop. The living is a vicarage in the patronage of the Archbishop of Canterbury, with a stipend of £162 per annum, to which the Rev. G. W. Sicklemore, M.A., succeeded in 1836.

This parish abounds in small, well populated hamlets, with some goodly estates; the lands, which are more enclosed than the northern parishes, extend nearly three miles from east to west, and about two miles from north to south. Nether Court, the residence of the vicar of St. Lawrence, is an elegant gentleman's seat near the church, which belonged to the family of Goshall until the reign of Henry IV., after which it passed through many hands.

Manston is a pretty little village of a few cottages between Ramsgate and Minster, inhabited by cotters, whose rustic simplicity and primitive amusements interest many visitors unaccustomed to rural artlessness. Manston Court, near the village, is an estate of some importance, the property of a family of that name in the reign of King John, whose descendant, William Manston, was Sheriff of Kent in 1436; it was here that Henry VI. held his Court in the same century. The mansion has been converted into a farm house, but there are some remains of the ancient picturesque chapel at the north end, where the only parasite that clings to ruins clothes its mouldering walls with rich foliage. Garrows Villa is a pleasing mansion, formerly the residence of Sir William Garrow, who built it for his summer seat; it was recently in the occupation of T. N. Harris, Esq.

PEGWELL BAY.

EVERY sojourner at Ramsgate or Margate is attracted to Pegwell Bay, the scenery near it being very beautiful, and the sands expansive at low water; it is reputed for lobsters and shrimps of superior quality. Paley gives us a pleasing description of what he had frequently remarked here in a calm evening at ebbing tide. We give a transcript, which reads thus:—'*I have frequently observed the appearance of a dark cloud, or rather very thick mist, hanging over the edge of the water to the height of, perhaps, half a yard, and of the breadth of two or three yards, stretching along the coast as far as the eye could reach, and always retiring with the water. When this cloud came to be examined, it proved to be nothing else than so much space*

*filled with young shrimps in the act of bounding into the air from the
shallow margin of the water, or from the wet sand.'* The *Belle Vue
Inn*, from its contiguity, and the good catering of the proprietor,
enjoys liberal patronage.

MINSTER.

MINSTER, five miles west of Ramsgate, derives its name from the
Saxon word *Minstre*, a monastery, has an area of 6,170 statute
acres including water, 261 houses, and 1,588 inhabitants. The
village lies at the base of the island, nearly central of the parish,
from whence the land rises northward. The cottages are particu-
larly neat and clean, with gay well-tended gardens, and pretty
climbing plants carefully trained round doors and windows; here
roses and honeysuckle, jasmine and woodbine, grow luxuriously in
odorous beauty and variety, the fascinating charm of our English
villages, and the delight of metropolitan visitors. The farms in
this parish are amongst the largest in the county, and the proprie-
tors are mostly wealthy.

The Manor of Minster, called in Domesday *Tanet Manor*, was
part of the possessions of Egbert, King of Kent, A.D. 670, who,
having been accessory to the murder of his cousins Ethelred and
Ethelbright, gavé this manor, in extenuation of his crime, to
Domneva, their sister, for the erection and maintenance of a
monastery to the memory of the princes, wherein she and her
nuns might pray for the king's absolution. This monastery,
afterwards called *St. Mildred's Abbey*, was built near the spot
where Minster Church now stands, when Domneva was appointed
first abbess by Archbishop Theodore. She was the wife of a
Prince of Mercia, by whom she had a daughter, Mildred, who
with herself had taken the veil. Domneva's sister was also a nun,
and became an inmate of this monastery of seventy nuns. Mildred, who was much revered, succeeded her mother. After the
death of Mildred, Edburga became abbess, but finding the building
inconveniently small, erected a more stately fabric and built
chapels, one of which she dedicated to SS. Peter and Paul. About
the year 750, the body of St. Mildred, who had been canonized, was
moved to it, when, according to tradition, many miracles were
wrought. Edburga herself was also buried here, and afterwards
sainted. The Danes repeatedly ravaged the convent, laid waste the
lands, reduced the sisterhood to grief and poverty, and finally
destroyed it by fire, in the flames of which many of the nuns
perished; the chapels, however, remained uninjured, for in one of
them service was afterwards celebrated for the inhabitants of the

parish. In 1027 King Canute gave the site of the monastery, the manor, and all the lands to the Abbott and Convent of St. Augustine—a gift subsequently confirmed by Edward the Confessor. The remains of the monastery were converted into a Court Lodge, afterwards called Minster Court. The manor, with its rents, was valued at £232 4s. 3d. in the reign of Richard II., and the land appertaining thereto estimated at 2,149 acres.

Minster Church, dedicated to St. Mary, was partly built by the monks of St. Augustine, and is considered one of the oldest in the kingdom. Some historians believe the nave to be part of the church built by the Abbess Edburga in the eighth century; the pillars being thick and short, and the arches circular, fully according with the architecture of that period. This noble edifice consists of a nave, north and south aisles, chancel, transept, and a battled tower, from which rises a spire; on the spire was formerly a globe, surmounted by a cross covered with lead bearing a vane, and above that a smaller cross of iron; these were removed in 1647 by the famous fanatic Richard Culmer, who termed them *monuments of superstition and idolatry.* The tower contains a clock and a peal of five bells. The pillars and arches are Saxon, the transept and chancel early English, the latter being vaulted with stone, but not the transept, although the footings left indicate such to have been the original intention. The church was closed in 1862 for partial restoration and thorough repair, when all the ugly pews were swept away and some painted glass windows introduced; it was re-opened in May of 1863. Formerly there were altars dedicated to the Holy Trinity, St. James, and St. Anne, and a rood loft; the collegiate stalls in the chancel are still preserved. In the north transept is an ancient tomb beneath an arch of Saxon sculpture, with an inscription in early French for *Edile de Morne;* in the porch and nave are numerous flat gravestones of great antiquity, the inscriptions being wholly worn away. The monuments are numerous and interesting; two are black marble altar-tombs elaborately sculptured. For several centuries a large bible secured by a chain was to be seen—all that now remains is a portion of the brass-bound cover chained, as originally, to the side of the *Bible pew.*

The living is a vicarage in the gift of the Archbishop of Canterbury, valued at £733 per annum. The Rev. R. F. Wheeler, M.A., has been incumbent since 1851.

RICHBOROUGH.

RICHBOROUGH, the Roman *Rutupiæ*, and the Saxon *Reptacester*, was a city of considerable importance early in the Christian era, whence ran the great Roman military road—*Watling Street*—in one continuous line through the county to London, and onwards to North Wales; when its stupendous castle commanded the entrance of an extensive port at the mouth of a bold channel, by which the maritime commerce of ancient England passed to and from the Thames, down to the seventh century. These waters formed an extensive bay, supposed to have commenced near Ramsgate Cliffs, stretching beyond Sandwich, five miles in width, and covering the present sites of Stonar and Sandwich, now fertile lands and populous neighbourhoods.

According to ancient history, this port (*Portus Rupinus*) was celebrated during the dominion of the Romans in Britain as a safe and commodious harbour—(*stationem ex adverso tranquillam*), as termed by Ammianus,—and even after the Romans it continued the favourite port of the Saxons until the sea had receded to the destruction of its navigability. Large quantities of Anglo-Saxon coins have been found, commencing with *Sceattas*, the earliest, and others down to the ninth century, warranting the assumption that Richborough retained some of its importance to that period. We have already remarked that the fort of Richborough on the east, and that of Reculver on the north, defended the mouths of a great maritime pass eight miles in length, and from the resemblance of their existing remains, were most probably built at the same time, under the Emperor Severus, about the year 205.

Richborough Castle stands on a high hill overlooking a deep precipice, and at the foot was the haven. Upon the south-west slope stood a city or large town, of which not a vestige remains. Historians, however, differ as to the precise site. *Ptolemy, Orosius*, and the *Venerable Bede* are agreed as to the existence of a Roman city or large town, whilst *Leland* and *Camden* are unanimous in asserting that the ancient town surrounded the castle on the slope of the hill, the foot being washed by the strait which formerly bounded the Isle of Thanet.

That there was a town, and an important one too, is fully demonstrated by the numberless graves and barrows spread over the flat lands, enshrining many Romans and Saxons, and perhaps, as *Black* gives it—' *the bones of some distinguished Roman soldier, slain in a struggle with the fierce Celtic aborigines of Kent.*' Some early writers tell us that the cemetery of this Roman station was two miles distant, probably at Osengall, where lines of graves dug out of the chalk have been discovered which contained numerous skeletons, as well as relics in knives, swords, shields, early Saxon coins, and jewellery, important links in the chain of ancient English history—reminiscences of the Romans and of the Saxons, those forefathers of our race—the progenitors of a mighty people whose voice has penetrated every land, and whose laws, literature, and language command the respect and admiration of every civilised nation throughout the world.

Near the castle are still some remains of an amphitheatre called by *Leland*, *Littleborough*, and *Stukeley*, a Castrensian amphitheatre. The circumference is about 220 yards, rising twelve feet above the arena.

The ruins of Richborough Castle are in remarkable preservation considering their remote antiquity, for with the exception of the *Vindonum* of the Romans at Silchester, in Hampshire, they are the most perfect throughout the kingdom, standing in massive grandeur, an enduring monument of Roman art in the third century, whilst most of our castles of the middle ages have crumbled into ruin.

The magnificent remains of this Roman fortress may be described as a parallelogram nearly north and south, east and west, containing an area of five acres. The north wall is far the grandest portion of the ruin, without aperture or loop-hole, richly spread over with broad masses of luxuriant ivy. This wall measured originally 560 feet in length, of which about 440 still exist, varying in height from 10 to 30 feet, and from 11 to 12 feet in thickness, the whole being built with flints faced with white stones and tiles, an imposing example of Roman workmanship in the beautiful regularity of the courses of tiles and stones ; thus—the squared stones, at five feet from the base, are separated by a double layer of yellow and red Roman tiles, each tile being about an inch and a half in thickness, then a course of stone work, and again coloured tiles, repeated at intervals of from three to four feet continuously to the summit. In this wall is a postern or entrance to the fortress, called by the Romans the *Porta Principalis*, afterwards the Postern Gate. We pass this entrance and find ourselves in a corn field once the area of the fortress. Towards the centre of this field was a barren part in the form of a cross, which for ages was the subject of superstitious legend, until some massive foundations were discovered, thus described by Black:—' *This cruciform structure rested on a foundation of masonry 5 feet thick, 145 feet long, and 104 feet wide. Its ' shaft' ran north and south to a length of 87 feet, and 7 feet 5 inches broad. The arms extended 46 feet, and their breadth was 22. Beneath it was discovered in 1822 a remarkable subterranean building (132 feet by 94) whose use it is impossible to conjecture, and which has never yet been fully examined.*' Here also were found brass and lead and broken vessels, and a bronze figure of a Roman soldier, playing on an instrument resembling the *bagpipes*.

The south wall measured 540 feet, of which 250 feet still remain, but more ruined than that on the north. The west wall was 484 feet long, with an opening in the centre, and near it the remains of a tower. This entrance was the Decuman Gate of the Romans. Other square towers may be traced in the walls, supposed to have been watch towers rather than for purposes of defence.

There can be no doubt of the early importance of this citadel of the Romans, for the Venerable Bede, who wrote eleven hundred years since, pronounced it the '*chief thing of note on the southern coast*,' and that the Isle of Thanet was divided from the other land by '*the River Wantsum, which is about three furlongs over, and fordable only in two places, for both ends of it run into the sea*,' proving that the noble estuary which had formed the direct course for shipping from Gaul to London was, even in his day, a respectable river. *Leland*, again, gives the following quaint description of the castle and city :—'*Richboro' was, or ever the River Stour did turn his bottom or old canal within the Isle of Thanet, and by likelihood the main sea came to the very foot of the castle. The walls, which remain there yet, be in compass almost as much as the Tower of London. They have been very high, thick, strong, and well embattled. The matter of them is flint and stone, marvellous and long bricks, white and red, after the Britons' fashion. There is great likelihood that the goodly hill about the castle hath been well inhabited. Towards Sandwich is a great dyke, cast in round compass, as it had been for fence of men of war; and there is more antiquities of Roman money found at this place of Richboro' than any place else in England. Within the castle is a little parish church of St. Augustine and an hermitage. I had antiquities of the hermit, the which is an industrious man. Not far from the hermitage is a cave where men have sought and digged for treasure. I saw it by candle within, and there were conies—rabbits. It was so straight that I had no mind to creep far in. In the north side of the castle is a head in the wall, now sore defaced with weather : they call it Queen Bertha's Head. Near to that place, hard by the wall, was a pot of Roman money found.*'

Antiquarians are much indebted to Mr. C. Roach Smith and Mr. Thomas Wright for publishing the results of their successful researches amongst the antiquities of Richborough, Reculver, and Thanet. Through them we learn that the citadel of Richborough was once splendidly ornamented with white Italian marble, in cornices, mouldings, and other decorations, of which, quantities, in fragments, were found in the interior and during the excavations for the railway. The operations for the railway also bared on the beach the foundations of a Roman villa, and at Osengall Downs numerous graves of the early Saxon settlers, with which the whole summit of the hill is covered; of these graves nearly 200 were cut through for the construction of the line, which bears an insignificant proportion to those remaining undisturbed. Gleaning from the same authority (*Wright's Wanderings*), we have interesting details of discoveries, in 1847, amongst these graves of the Anglo-Saxons, which are found in rows in the chalk, at about four feet deep. In one were the skeletons of a man, woman, and child, lying arm-in-arm, the mother in the centre, with a large iron spear-head between herself and her husband; under the man's chin was a large amber bead, and towards the waist a belt buckle and a small knife commonly found in the graves of Anglo-Saxons; round the woman's neck was an amber necklace, and near the child—supposed to be a girl of about thirteen—another necklace of amber and glass, a small knife and a pair of bronze tweezers. Another grave contained the skeletons of a man and a woman, with the forehead of the man resting on the cheek of the female; an elegant silver brooch, set with garnets, lay on her breast, and a sword by the side of the man. A pair of bronze scales, with a set of weights composed of Roman coins, was found in another, and in a grave near to it a gold coin of the Emperor Justin, who reigned between the years 518—527, and some sceattas (early Saxon coins).

During these interesting researches two Roman graves were discovered; one was an ordinary one, the other contained a Roman coffin of lead similar to those found at Colchester in Essex, which, Mr. Wright appositely observes, demonstrates that *a Roman and Saxon population lived simultaneously, and probably mixed together, in the Isle of Thanet.* The poet Ausonius, who lived in the fourth century, tells us that his uncle Contentus died and was buried at Rutupiœ, of which his kinsman Flavius Sanctus was afterwards governor. The early Latin writers also well knew this spot, and Juvenal lauds the delicate oysters for which this locality was famous. These references, discoveries, and remains carry us back to the days when England was a Roman province, when the natives spoke Latin, and were well schooled in the manners and customs of the Romans, whose grand naval port was Rutupiœ, defended by the massive fortress of Richborough; that port where, towards the close of Roman rule, Saxon and Roman ships anchored in friendly alliance, lived on terms of amity, and mingled their dead in the same cemeteries.

SANDWICH.

SANDWICH, a name derived from *Sandwic*, the Saxon for *Sandytown*, is ninety-eight miles from London by railway, and thirteen miles from Canterbury; it ranks amongst the principal Cinque Ports, and was formerly one of the most important on the English coast. During the Romans the site of the town was submerged, and part of the bay of *Portus Rupinus*. It is built on the north-east coast of the county, now nearly two miles from the sea, and the sinuous river Stour, on

which it stands, reduced to a stream only navigable for vessels of
light burden.

There is much to interest the antiquarian at Sandwich, for when
Richborough was abandoned by the sea Sandwich rose in importance and became a flourishing harbour. The town was well fortified with a castle on the south side, where Falconbridge, in 1471,
resisted Edward IV. We first read of Sandwich as a port in the
' *Vita Wilfredi* ' of Eddius, wherein he records that Wilfred Archbishop of York landed in the harbour of Sandwich about the year
665. This town and port belonged to the crown until King Ethelred,
in 979, gave them to the brethren of Christchurch, Canterbury. When
Canute, the Danish monarch, had by conquest possessed himself of
the realm, he restored to Christ Church, in 1023, their right and
interest in Sandwich. The port had now gained priority over all
others, and ranked as a hundred within itself, continuing to increase
in importance down to the Conquest. In 1217 the French ravaged
and burned it in part, but, by favour of the king, Henry III., the
damage was shortly repaired.

From the Conquest to Richard II. Sandwich was the royal port
for all fleets, and was constantly visited by the successive monarchs,
who embarked and returned hither from France. At that time there
were 1,500 able seamen belonging to the navy of this port, and in the
reign of Edward IV. the town possessed 90 ships. Sandwich was
plundered by the French in the 16th and 35th years of the reign
of Henry VI., and again in 1457 by Charles VIII. of France, who
landed with 4,000 men and gained possession of the town, which
they nearly destroyed by fire, and put to the sword numbers of the
inhabitants. Edward IV. fortified the town and rebuilt the walls,
contributing £100 annually from the custom dues for their maintenance, which, added to the industry of the inhabitants, soon
restored Sandwich to its former importance. Such enviable prosperity, however, was not of long duration; the waters of the Stour
began rapidly to recede, and, to add to the calamity, a large ship
of Pope Paul IV. was sunk at the entrance of the port, thereby
causing an accumulation of mud and sand with such fatal effect
that, in the reign of Edward VI., the haven was comparatively destroyed and the navy and seamen reduced to insignificance.

On the decline of the port, after the recession of the sea, a new
source of wealth and prosperity arose out of the religious persecu-
tions in Brabant and Flanders, which brought hundreds of the
Walloons to Sandwich, when it became a prosperous *manufacturing*
town, in serges, flannels, and baize, until other localities rivalled
them, and ultimately largely estranged the trade.

Sandwich is united to Stonar and the Isle of Thanet by a bridge,
the centre of which opens for the passage of vessels having station-
ary masts. The river at spring tides is about 150 feet in width,
and in some places 11 feet deep. The town is not considered

healthy, from its contiguity to the marshes. The houses are quaint and primitive, and mostly of an ordinary description; the streets, with the exception of High Street, although well paved, resemble lanes, and are ill-suited for carriage traffic; in Strand Street the house where Queen Elizabeth resided during her visit of some days in 1572, remains, and continues in the occupation of descendants of the original family; an ancient house in the same street has curious wood carving on the front; and in Lucksboat Street is another dwelling, supposed to date from Henry VIII., that contains in a principal apartment some clever carving of whimsical heads on 22 oak panels; there are also other interesting specimens of old street building scattered through the town.

The ancient wall which still surrounds Sandwich has been converted into a pleasing walk, and facing the quay stands ' Fisher's Gate ' with its grey towers, the last remains of its olden fortifications. Canterbury Gate was razed in 1780, and *Sandwich, Wodensborough*, and *New* gates, early in the present century. Sandwich Castle and the adjoining Carmelite priory founded in 1272 are also no more. Here the busy hum of its once crowded streets has lapsed into repose, and the jostlings of active life, lost in painful quiet, sadly contrast with its former glory and importance.

Sandwich was first incorporated by Edward III., as the 'Mayor, Jurats, and Commonalitie of the town and port.' Charles II. granted a new charter, which gave a mayor and twelve jurats, who are, *ex officio*, justices of the peace. All ordinances and decrees emanate from the whole corporate body at a common assembly convened by the sound of a horn. These meetings are held on the first Monday after St. Andrew's day to elect a mayor, and on the following Thursday for choosing inferior officers. The mayor of Sandwich carries a *black* wand as a badge of office, being in contradistinction of most others, who bear *white* wands. The Townhall, or rather Guildhall, is a small Elizabethan structure of two stories. Amongst the relics preserved in the council chamber is a side-saddle of Queen Elizabeth, some mediæval armour, and a scold's ' *ducking stool.*' The market days are Wednesdays and Saturdays, and an annual fair on the 4th December.

Sir Roger Manwood founded a free grammar school for the children of the inhabitants about the years 1564–5. The Carmelite priory of *Whitefriars*, which was founded by Henry Cowfield in 1272, possessed the privilege of affording sanctuary to criminals. The monastery, garden, and meadows, covered an area exceeding five acres, and annexed to it was a cemetery, where, distinct of the friars, many principal inhabitants were buried.

St. John's Hospital stands on the north west side of the corn market. There is no certainty as to its date: the oldest grant, however, was in the sixteenth year of the reign of Edward I., wherein it is called ' *Domus Dei et sancti Johannis de Sandwico,*'

and towards the close of the thirteenth century ' *St. John's Hospitale.*'
The main building was large, with a dining hall, and numerous
apartments for the brethren and sisters, behind which was a range
of rooms called the '*Harbinge*,'—a refuge for travellers and
strangers, who were entertained and comfortably lodged.

St. Thomas's Hospital, between the corn market and New Street,
so named in honour of Thomas à Becket, was founded in the
fourteenth century by Thomas Ellis, a wealthy draper of this town,
who was mayor in 1370, and represented the borough in Parliament. There are eight men and four women on this foundation.

St. Bartholomew's Hospital was founded in 1244 by Sir Henry
de Sandwich, who was Bishop of London in 1262. It stands on
the south of the town, covering about six acres, and was founded
for the support of infirm men and women, '*the brethren and sisters
living under an order of discipline, being maintained at table, and
wearing a uniform habit.*' Their numbers were twelve men and
four women, but at present vacancies are filled irrespective of sex.
The mayor for the time being has the right of presentation when
vacancies occur, and annually, on the festival of St. Bartholomew,
the mayor and jurats visit the foundation in procession as '*Patrons,
governors and visitors.*' The hospital consists of fifteen commodious
dwellings,—a farmhouse, barns, and stables, and pretty gardens for
each of the inmates; the farmhouse was originally the sixteenth
tenement, but is now the residence of the tenant of the lands
belonging to the institution, in lieu of which the incumbent receives
an allowance in money to provide a residence in the town.

This foundation, which is extra-parochial, has an ancient chapel
annexed to the hospital, where formerly three priests officiated, but
at the Reformation, when masses for the dead were abolished, these
chaplains were removed. In 1636 a clergyman was admitted a
brother and celebrated service, after whom the service was monthly,
when a sermon was preached by one of the clergy of Sandwich.
According to the last census, the district of St. Bartholomew's
Hospital contained eighteen houses and fifty-one inhabitants.

Sandwich is within the diocese of Canterbury, and has three
parochial churches dedicated to the Saints Mary, Peter, and
Clement.

St. Mary's parish spreads over 127 statute acres, having a population of 919 persons, occupying 200 dwellings. The church is in
Strand Street, built on the site of a Saxon church destroyed by the
Danes. In 1448 a portion of the steeple fell, when the structure
underwent general repair, and comprised a nave, high chancel,
St. Lawrence chancel, and north and south aisles. On the 25th
of April, 1667, the steeple again fell in, destroying the western
wall, and a large portion of the church, after which it was reconstructed in part, the north aisle and the nave forming the present
edifice. The steeple, which is low, was built over the south porch

in 1718. The base is of stone, with the upper part of brick. The silver and jewellery belonging to this church at the Reformation was estimated at ' 724 *ounces of silver, and ecclesiastical vestments of equal value.*' The monuments are numerous and ancient, and in the churchyard are altar-tombs mostly for leading families long since passed away. The living is a vicarage, valued at £117 per annum. The Rev. E. N. Braddon, the incumbent, was inducted in 1846.

St. Peter's parish has an area of 36 acres only, whilst the houses number 261, and the inhabitants 1,085. The church stands nearly in the centre of the town, and formerly consisted of a nave, and north and south aisles. The steeple, however, fell down in 1661, and destroyed the south aisle, which still remains in ruins, and with it the handsome altar-tomb of Sir John Grove, who lived in the reign of Henry VI., portions of which may yet be seen. The present church is in part the original fabric, reconstructed with Kentish ragstone and flints. The tower is built of the old material to the height of the roof, and upwards to the battlements of brick. In 1504, during the plague, this church was appropriated to the use of Flemish residents—Walloons—for their special worship. In the north aisle are many ancient memorials, including a coffin-shaped gravestone bearing a cross with the arms of Adam Stannar, a priest; a brass for Thomas Gilbert, recording his death in 1597; and in an early English recess, the tomb of Thomas Ellis, the founder of St. Thomas' Hospital, about the years 1385-90. It bears the figures of himself and wife. The living is a rectory, valued at £144 per annum, in the incumbency of the Rev. Horace Gilder, M.A., since 1851.

St. Clement's parish consists of 540 acres, 186 houses, and 889 inhabitants. The church, which stands at the eastern part of the town, is by far the grandest and most ancient structure in Sandwich. The Norman tower, which rises from the centre, is the oldest portion of the fabric, ornamented on either side by ranges of pillars and circular arches; the lowest is a range of six, the second seven, and the uppermost nine arches. The battlements and spire were taken down in the seventeenth century. It is built of Norman stone and boulders, mixed with Caen and sandstone, probably the materials of a former church occupying the site of the present structure. It has a nave, north and south aisles, separated by early English pillars and arches, and three chancels. The roof is of oak, in panels between arched beams, richly carved to represent angels supporting shields, ornamented with roses and foliage. The stalls of the brotherhood of St. George were in the principal chancel. This fraternity, on the annual festival of their patron saint, bore his figure through the town with great pomp. In the north and south aisles were chantries dedicated to the Saints James, Margaret, Thomas the Martyr, and George. The font is of the time of Henry VII., and stands in the north aisle, forming an octagonal basin, supported on a stone pillar. The eight sides are ornamented with roses, shields, grotesque faces, fruits, flowers, and foliage. In this church are numerous monuments and tombs to the memory of early residents, and some brasses, one of the latter being for Elizabeth Spencer, who died in 1583. The churchyard is the supposed site of an ancient cemetery, from the urns and other relics found there. The living is a vicarage in the patronage of the Archbishop of Canterbury, valued at £130 per annum, held by the Rev. E. N. Braddon since 1846, who, as before stated, is also vicar of St. Mary's.

DEAL.

DEAL, anciently *Dale* and Dola, or, according to Domesday, *Addelam,* ' *the low open shore,*' is 102 miles from London by railway. Most historians are unanimous in supposing that Julius Cæsar and his legions landed between Deal and Walmer. Dr. Halley asserts that the cliffs mentioned by Cæsar in his Commentaries were those of Dover, and that the plain and open shore which he next arrived at was that along the Downs here, where he made his landing good. We have, however, no conclusive evidence of the precise spot, although it must have been in this direction; and from the quantities of Roman coins found under the sand banks, mostly of the Emperor Tacitus, A.D. 275, it is evident that Deal was a station early during the Roman occupation.

This is a municipal borough, and a member of the Cinque Ports of Sandwich. It stands close to the sea shore, with a fine open beach opposite the Goodwin Sands, and south of the Downs. It has been computed that 20,000 vessels pass annually through the Downs, and during adverse winds, from two to three and even four hundred ships are sometimes anchored for weeks off Deal. The Deal boatmen, estimated at something exceeding 500, have a high character for intrepidity. Not unfrequently have they put off to wrecks on the Goodwin Sands during the most fearful of storms, and miraculously rescued hundreds that would otherwise have perished.

The town may be described as upper and lower Deal, consisting of three principal streets in lines, facing the sea, with others branching from them into the country. Beach Street, as its name implies, is nearest to the sea, and stretches to the farthest extremity of the town. Thus exposed to the wide expanse of the Downs it contains the elements of health and purity, although frequently threatened with destruction from tempest. The air is very salubrious and dry, and the beach being of shingle the water is beautifully clear and well suited for bathing; many invalids, as well as pleasure seekers, have a preference for Deal, from the animated sea view, its fine bathing and invigorating atmosphere; and although it cannot afford the attractions of more fashionable watering-places, yet its moderate charges and extreme civility are perhaps equivalents.

Deal is decidedly a populous bustling town, largely identified with the shipping interest. Here are large naval and victualling yards, and a custom house, under the superintendence of a comptroller, collector, surveyor, and a staff of active officers. The Deal pilots rank amongst the most skilful of British seamen, and, like the boatmen, have a deserved repute for courage and daring. The Naval Hospital is a large building, with a frontage of 360 feet; the barracks were built in 1795; the custom house, town hall, and naval store-house rank amongst the principal buildings; there are also reading-rooms, and a public library and baths. A handsome pier, extending far into the sea, has just been opened, which will prove of vast importance to the town; the first column was formally fixed on the 8th of April, 1863, in the presence of Mr. Huggessen, one of the Borough Members, and a Lord of the Treasury. It is further proposed to erect a noble harbour and docks, as heretofore, unless in calm weather, communication with Deal was all but impracticable; frequently hundreds of vessels, weather bound for days, and sometimes weeks, have lacked provisions, and although riding off Deal, the nearest market, were necessitated to procure their supplies either from Dover or Ramsgate.

The parochial schools were built in 1853, and the national schools, for one hundred boys and a like number of girls, in 1792. The town is well paved and lighted with gas, and fresh water is abundant, supplied from works erected at the north extremity. Deal was constituted a free town and borough by the charter of William III. in 1699, under the control of a mayor, twelve jurats, and a council of twenty-four, the jurats acting as magistrates, exclusive of the justices of the county. There is a Catholic Chapel, and several others belonging to dissenters of different denominations. The cemetery, in Upper Deal, covers five acres, and is laid out with much taste in shrubs and flowers; it cost £3,000, including two chapels, a keeper's lodge, and the surrounding walls and iron gates.

Henry VIII., in 1539, erected castles at Deal, Walmer, and Sandown, each with four bastions of massive stone-work. In the centre rises a bold round tower, the whole surrounded by a moat, over which was a drawbridge. Deal Castle stands south of the town, and has an imposing appearance. The interior has been re-modelled to form a family residence, to which has been added a suite of handsome apartments stretching towards the sea. The moat forms a plantation, well stocked with shrubs and trees.

Sandown Castle, now a coast-guard station, stands about a mile north of the town, and much resembles its neighbour, Deal Castle, on the south. It was here that Colonel John Hutchinson was imprisoned and died in 1664, who, it will be remembered, was a

Puritan soldier, and one of the regicides who signed the death-warrant of Charles I.

Deal has two markets weekly, and a fair in October for cattle and various merchandise. The parish extends over 1,217 acres, including water. The inhabitants numbered at the last census 7,531, and the houses 1,700.

The town having become very populous in the reign of Queen Anne, a chapel of ease to the mother church was built in 1716 by private subscription. It was consecrated by Archbishop Wake, who contributed £100 towards its erection, and dedicated it to St. George the Martyr. The Rev. H. H. Dombrain was appointed to the perpetual curacy in 1849, at a stipend of £108 per annum. The chapel stands in Lower Deal, having a district containing 2,731 inhabitants. In 1850 another chapel was built in West Street, and dedicated to St. Andrew; this is a handsome structure, built in much better taste than its precursor. It has a district with 2,697 inhabitants. The Rev. M. E. Benson, B.A., has held the incumbency, which is in the gift of the rector, since 1852.

The parish church, dedicated to St. Leonard, is ancient and large, with a tower and turret at the west end, rebuilt in 1684, and largely repaired in 1825. This church has evidently undergone many repairs and alterations, until little of its former character remains; still there are distinct traces of early Norman architecture. The ancient family of Coppice were mostly buried in a vault in the centre of the church called the *Coppice tomb*. The advowson of St. Leonard's was formerly part of the possessions of St. Martin's, Dover, until Henry VIII., when it was given to the Archbishop and his successors, that Primate still being patron of the living, valued at £429 per annum. The rector, the Rev. L. Griffith, whose portion of the parish has a population of 2,103 souls, was appointed in 1862.

WALMER.

THE village of Walmer stands on rising ground half a mile from the shore and one mile from Deal. The pedestrian may enjoy a charming breezy walk from Deal by the sea under the cliffs, but only when the tide permits, otherwise he might be seriously endangered by the rising sea, which lashes the perpendicular cliff on his right at high water. Walmer is considered very healthful, with superb scenery, commanding the Downs and adjacent country; many pretty villas stud the neighbourhood. The beach, which has been levelled, forms a pleasing esplanade, and during the summer months is gay with visitors. Walmer Street is the high road between Deal and Dover. The parish has a population of 3,275 persons, contains 461 houses, and has an area of 1,079 acres, including water.

The manor of Walmer was in remote times part of the possessions of the eminent family of Auberville; a daughter of Sir William de Auberville married Nicholas de Criol, who inherited the manor in right of his wife; their mansion stood near the churchyard, and was a noble structure of stone and flints, with turrets, built in the reign of Edward I. Many stone coffins were discovered in the church cemetery late in the last century, supposed to have been those of this ancient family.

Walmer Barracks, built in 1795, cover an area of 22 acres; they consist of seven blocks of brick buildings for the accommodation of a troop of horse and 1,100 infantry. Walmer Castle, which embraces an uninterrupted view of the Downs and Channel, is now shorn of all its former warlike appliances, save some half-dozen small guns mounted on a platform in a flower-garden, the fortress having been converted into an official residence for the Lord Warden of the Cinque Ports. Here the Hero of Waterloo breathed his last, on the morning of September 14th, 1852. During twenty-three years the late Duke of Wellington, as Lord Warden, spent two months each autumn at Walmer, living in quiet and simplicity, rising when in health at six o'clock, and exercising upon the ramparts; his bedchamber, which is still shown, was little more than three feet wide, furnished to his taste, with merely an iron camp-bedstead, mattress and coverlet, and the simplest of articles. The rooms are mostly small, connected by narrow passages; one is pointed out, about eight feet in width, as the council-chamber where Pitt and Nelson planned their glorious naval operations. In the grounds is the great Senator Pitt's plantation of sycamores, and on the lawn a weeping-willow, planted by the Duke, brought from Napoleon's tomb at St. Helena.

Walmer is supposed to be the spot where Cæsar disembarked his army, fifty-five years before the Christian era; visible marks of entrenchments are still to be found at Hawkeshill, near the castle, and on the Old Down, which accord with Cæsar's description.

The parish church, dedicated to St. Mary, is small, but ancient; it consists of a nave and chancel. The doorways on the north and south sides and chancel arch are Norman, with zigzag and nail-headed mouldings: there are monuments of the Boys, Fogges, and Lisles—the latter descendants from the Lords of Rougemont. The living, valued at £240 per annum, is in the gift of the Archbishop of Canterbury. The Rev. I. B. Harrison succeeded to the perpetual curacy in 1854. A deep circular fosse, or moat, surrounds the churchyard. A chapel of ease to St. Mary's was built in 1848, and dedicated to St. Saviour; the curacy is attached to the mother church.

———◆———

RINGWOULD.

THE parish of Ringwould adjoins Walmer on the south, from whence it is a lovely walk by the seaside along the cliffs, which now tower from two to three hundred feet in height. The parish, which includes the interesting hamlet of Kingsdown, covers an area of 1,710 acres, with a population of 846 souls, occupying 192 houses. The high road from Deal to Dover runs through the village, in which stands the church and parsonage, and from its lofty site commands an extensive sea and land prospect. Ringwould forms a limb of the Cinque Ports, and is a member of the Port of Dover; it must have been a place of some note, as being mentioned in the ancient charters of those ports. The parish is within the ecclesiastical jurisdiction of Canterbury; the church, dedicated to St. Nicholas, is a noble building on a hill, a sea-mark for mariners. The tower was built or—may we say—rebuilt in 1628, of flints, the corners and window-arches being of red brick. The interior presents a mixture of Early English and Perpendicular; it has recently undergone repair and partial restoration. The monuments are simple, and mostly for neighbouring inhabitants; the brasses were for William Avere and his two wives (1405), John Upton (1530), and Elizabeth Gaunt (1580). The living is a rectory, valued at £352 per annum. The Rev. C. V. H. Sumner, chaplain to the Queen, and vicar of West Cliffe, succeeded to the appointment in 1853. Bearing to the right across the meadows we reach—

KINGSDOWN,

A PRETTY little village, with its houses in a line at right-angles to the beach. Like Ringwould, it must have been of some repute, from being included in the ancient charters of the Cinque Ports, and described as ' *the Ville and Hamlet of Kingsdowne;*' although now a fishing-hamlet, and, from the craft of the inhabitants, commonly called ' *Kingsdown boats.*' Mr. Pemberton Leigh, now Lord Kingsdown, owes the title of his barony, created in 1859, to this place. On the beach is a modern corrugated iron building, erected for naval volunteer coastguard practice, with targets and breastworks. On the side of a rising lane, richly wooded, stands a pretty little new church, vested in trustees, dedicated to St. John the Evangelist; on the opposite side is the parsonage. The living is a perpetual curacy, to which the Rev. Edwin Badger was appointed in 1862.

After passing the village of Kingsdown, and keeping by the shore, the cliffs stand out in majestic proportions, thus graphically described by Mr. Wright: '*The chalk cliffs become bolder, rising to an elevation of from two to three hundred feet, and, the face being quite perdendicular, they appear like the walls and towers of some gigantic fortress. This effect is heightened by the parallel lines of dark flint, which look at a distance not unlike the brick bonding-courses of the Roman masonry. These lofty perpendicular cliffs continue for several miles, and afford a continued variety of grand groups, until we reach St. Margaret's Bay.*'

ST. MARGARET'S-AT-CLIFFE,

SOMETIMES called *St. Margaret's near Dover*, and in Domesday *St. Margarita*, stands high on the chalk cliffs, with the South Foreland at its western extremity. The cliffs rise from the beach, nearly perpendicular, to an altitude approaching 400 feet, upon which are the village and church a quarter of a mile from the brow. On the beach is a fine spring of fresh water, with several others from this to Dover, which flow abundantly on the decrease of the tides. Lobsters of the finest flavour are caught in the bay, which during the time of Archbishop Morton, who lived in the fifteenth century, had a small jetty built by one Thomas Lawrence for the convenience of the resident fishermen.

The parish, which has an area of 1,924 acres, with 152 houses, and 831 inhabitants, is within the ecclesiastical jurisdiction of Canterbury: but the church, dedicated to St. Margaret, is exempt from the control of the archdeacon. St. Margaret's Church is a large Norman structure, having a massive tower at the west end, and formerly small turrets at each angle: these, however, were taken down in 1711, after the one to the west had fallen. The roof rests on semicircular arches with elaborate mouldings, supported by noble columns and sculptured capitals, further elaborated by rude heads, forming four bays on either side of the nave; handsome arches span the lofty chancel and western entrance, richly ornamented with grotesque heads; the windows have mostly circular heads, and the clerestory windows range between external arches with considerable effect. May we hope the time not distant when this ancient structure shall be faithfully restored? The living is a vicarage, valued at £160 per annum, in the gift of the Archbishop of Canterbury. An old Norman custom is still observed in this isolated village—that of the curfew bell (*couvre fue*); a shepherd, who was killed in 1696 by falling over the cliffs, having given a piece of land for that purpose.

A short walk westward and we arrive at West Cliffe, on which stand—

DISTINGUISHED as the *high light* and the *low light.* The lantern-towers rise from the centre of neat houses resembling villas, with gardens walled in; the high light is on a rock not less than 250 feet above the sea. From the gallery of the tower, which is 30 feet high, Calais lighthouse may be seen, and in clear weather the lights of Boulogne and Dunkirk are most distinct. The upper light, which may be seen 25 miles distant, is disseminated on the dioptric principle, the illumination being refracted by a number of prisms, whilst the lower light is by parabolic reflectors—both lanterns being surrounded with plate-glass.

Leaving the South Foreland, we journey westward for Dover, and pausing on the hill near the Preventive Station, contemplate the view before us. On the left, the immense expanse of sea; beneath, bold projections of cliff broken into picturesque masses; beyond, Dover stretching to the pier, Dover Castle peering above the Downs, the lofty headland of Shakspeare's Cliff, and the summits of hills near Folkestone. The walk across the barren downs, although the nearest, is dreary, with scarcely an object to attract; for, excepting the little wooded vale of Oxney, barely a tree is to be seen. About a mile short of Dover stands the '*lone tree*,' in the middle of a dreary waste, to which a legend attaches, thus told by Wright: '*In the days of the Commonwealth, two soldiers of the garrison of Dover Castle were jealous of each other on account of a woman, and, chancing to wal: thus far together, one suddenly slew the other with a thick staff which he had in his hand. Horror-stricken at the crime he had committed, the murderer threw the weapon from him violently, and hastened from the spot. But the staff, falling in such a manner as to stick upright in the ground, immediately took root, and grew into the solitary tree which still remains as a perpetual testimony of this sanguinary deed.*'

DOVER.

DOVER—the *Dubris* of Antonius, called by the Saxons *Dorfa* and *Dofris*, and written in Domesday *Dovere*—stands at the extremity of a spacious valley bounded by '*Albion's earliest beauties*,' the white cliffs of '*Old England.*' Between this chain of eminences lies the town and harbour; on the north side, crowning one of these stupendous cliffs, stands Dover Castle, the buildings alone covering six acres, and its dimensions within the area (according to Hasted) thirty-five acres of ground, with the citadel in the centre, and formidable fortifications encompassing its walls. The cliff, or rather rock, on which stands the castle is rugged inland, but facing the sea presents a perpendicular face, rising 320 feet from the beach.

We have no certain information as to the first inhabitants of Dover. Their mode of warfare was not that of either the Gauls or Germans, which has long been a problem, whence a rude people, whose knowledge of the arts having only advanced to the building their boats of osiers covered with hides, had acquired the art of managing war-chariots, even to elicit the surprise of Julius Cæsar nineteen hundred years since, when he found a formidable host of warriors ranged on the cliffs around Dover to oppose his landing, and of whom he quaintly remarked that in their mode of warfare with chariots '*they possessed the swiftness of horse, and the stability of foot.*'

Dover Castle is remarkable for its strength—the Gibraltar of England—called in the reign of Edward the Confessor the lock and key of the whole kingdom—a marvellous mass of fortifications of every age, Roman, Saxon, and Norman, down to the present century. There are barracks for 2,000 men, excavated in the solid rock, and others above the town, in direct communication by a military shaft. It may be observed that under the Romans its importance as a fortress was by no means eminent; their stronghold was Richborough, then Rutupiæ. The Roman Pharos, or lighthouse, a massive octagonal tower, still remains. It is said to be the most ancient of Roman architecture in regular masonry existing in Britain, and forms not only a picturesque object inland, but has been a landmark during eighteen centuries. The walls are ten feet thick; the interior is square, and fourteen feet in diameter.

Nearly adjoining the Pharos is the Church called *St. Mary-in-Castro.* Some historians attribute its foundation to Lucius, a British king by Roman courtesy. If correct, which is doubtful, this church dates from the second century. It is built in the form of a cross. The central tower, 28 feet square, is supported by lofty arches, the north and south pilasters being of squared stones. Roman tiles appear in all parts of the structure, which has undergone every variety of alteration. The first roof was flat, the next was considerably raised, and a third roof less elevated than the second, their respective heights and forms being still apparent from marks remaining on the tower.

King Ethelbert after his conversion to Christianity gave this church to Augustine, who dedicated it to St. Mary. Eadbald, his son, founded a college for ecclesiastics, which he annexed to the church. The college was removed into the town in 696, but the church retained three chaplains, who, wearing the prebendal vestments, each in turn chaunted early matins privately before morning service. The principal chaplain celebrated Mass to the governor of the castle at the high altar ; a second to the marshalmen and officers, at ten o'clock, at the altar of the Virgin Mary; whilst the third chaplain performed like offices to the soldiers at nine, before the altar of relics.   Sir Robert Asheton, chamberlain to Edward III., and many other celebrities of remote times, were buried in this church, but most of the memorials have perished.   Henry Howard, Earl of Northampton, and Lord Warden of the Cinque Ports in the reign of James I., who died in 1614, was also interred here, and a superb monument erected to his memory, at a cost of £500.   The monument, with his remains, were removed in 1696 to the chapel of Greenwich Hospital.   Within a few years, according to *Chambers*, this grand ecclesiastical relic has been restored, so far as possible, and now forms a garrison church for 600 men.

On the departure of the Romans, the Saxons extended the castle, built massive walls, which they fortified by numerous towers, excavated fosses, and strengthened the Roman works.   The entrance to the Saxon fortifications was by a narrow path cut through a bank south-west of the Roman fortress, at a point where the hill is most difficult to ascend, thereby rendering it all but impregnable if attempted by a besieging army.

When the Danes had widely spread desolation over the coast of Britain in the ninth century, the Saxons further strengthened this fortress, fortified the bridges over the ditches, defended the passes by gates, and built other towers.   We fall back on *Hasted* and *Ireland* for interesting descriptions of several of the towers, few of which remain :—

GODWIN'S TOWER took its name from the famous Earl of Kent. He enlarged the entrance into the Roman fortress by removing the Colton and Arthur Gates, formed a vallum on the opposite side, over the ditch, raised the wall within the parapet round the Roman works, which was continued across the vallum to a gateway in the wall, where he built the tower bearing his name.

CLINTON TOWER, of which there are no remains, stood near the vallum of Godwin ; this tower was square, and named after Jeffery Clinton, who was Lord Chief Justice of England, Chamberlain and Treasurer to Henry I. (twelfth century), and in command of this tower.

VALENCE TOWER was circular, and south-east of the Roman fortress.   William Valence, after whom it was named, was allied to Henry III. ; his mother was Isabella, widow of King John, whom his father married.   He rose to great honour, but was slain in battle at Bayonne.   A noble monument was erected to his memory in Westminster Abbey.   Valence Tower was destroyed many years since.

MORTIMER TOWER.—Ralph de Mortimer, who commanded this tower, was allied to William the Conqueror.   He defeated the Earl of Shrewsbury, and in reward for his bravery was granted the Earl's castle of Wigmore and all his forfeited lands.   Mortimer Tower was quadrangular in form; a few traces of the foundations, sunk several feet in the solid rock, are the only remains.

COLTON GATE AND SQUARE TOWER were built over the original entrance of the Saxon works; they were strengthened and repaired after the Conquest, and then confided to Fulbert de Douvre. In the early part of the fourteenth century Lord Burghersh was commander of this tower; his armorial bearings may still be seen on a stone shield in front.

HARCOURT TOWER was built over two parallel walls forming a passage from Peverell's Tower; the sides were supported by arches, which led to a subterranean gate, and by a flight of steps to the Suffolk Tower. The whole have disappeared, even to the foundations, which were razed in 1797.

WELL TOWER AND GATE, so named from a well 380 feet deep within its precincts, have few remains left.

THE ARMOURER's TOWER formed the manufactory for weapons of warfare, and the repairs of arms for the garrison; it was taken down during extensive alterations in 1795–6.

KING ARTHUR's GATE, which led through the area before Palace Gate into the Roman fortress, has been demolished, and most of the Roman fortress levelled with the quadrangle.

PALACE GATE was the entrance to the Saxon keep, in front of the Roman camp; it was so called from leading to the royal apartments.

SUFFOLK TOWER was converted into a stately mansion by Edward IV. for his brother-in-law, the Duke of Suffolk, whose father was beheaded by a common seaman in Dover Roads.

THE OLD ARSENAL TOWER was, from a remote period, the depository for war implements and machines for the defence of the castle.

THE KING's KITCHEN AND OFFICES occupied the entire space between the old magazine and the eastern angle of the keep; they were fitted up in the thirteenth century, probably for Edward I., who frequently resided at the castle. These buildings were removed in 1795, and barracks now cover the site.

KING ARTHUR's HALL stood on the north-eastern side of the KEEP, in front of three towers; it was removed, and a messroom, kitchen, and barracks erected on the spot.

GUINEVER's CHAMBER, also called Arthur's Private Hall, or his Queen's bedchamber, stood between Gore's Tower and Palace Gate. Henry VIII. made this a storeroom for provisions during his residence with Anne Boleyn at the castle.

The KING's GATE was defended by a strong outwork enclosing an area before the principal gates. The gates, opening from the area into the KEEP, were defended by a portcullis, having towers on either side, where archers could command the whole extent of the vallum.

MAMMINOT'S TOWERS stood south-west of the KEEP; this was also a fortress for archers, and named after the Marshal who held certain lands for erecting and maintaining towers on the exterior walls.

THE KEEP is by far the grandest structure of the ancients in Dover Castle. It is a large square massive tower built in the centre of the quadrangle: the sides, on the east and west, measure 123 feet, the north wall 108, and the south 103 feet. The turret on the north side rises 95 feet from the cliff, and above low-water mark upwards of 460 feet. The foundations, which are 24 feet in thickness, were supposed to have been laid about the year 1153 by the son of Henry I. It is built in solid masonry, after the plan of Gundulph, Bishop of Rochester, who probably superintended the works. Light and air were admitted by loopholes in the massive walls, perforated for the discharge of arrows and other missiles. On the south-east side is a steep flight of steps starting from a contracted arch widening upwards. In the centre of the ground-floor is a space fifty feet square, divided by three large arches into two aisles; on the south-west ran a passage fifty-two feet long and twelve wide, used of late years as a magazine; on this floor were also two large prisons, one thirty-eight and the other thirty feet long, lighted by small apertures in the wall.

Ascending a flight of steps on the south-east side, we reach the next floor, having two large rooms in the centre, a guardroom and the interesting Norman chapel, richly ornamented and in tolerable preservation; this was the King's chapel, or in his absence appropriated to the Governor. A grand flight of stairs, strongly defended, leads to the upper floor, or royal apartments. At the foot of the staircase was a large archway, fortified with a portcullis, and in the walls on either side concealed galleries for archers. The principal rooms were sumptuously appointed for the King and Royalty, and at the entrance is a famous well 400 feet deep.

This noble fortress is in excellent preservation. In the year 1800 bombproof arches were built over the summit, and subsequently a traversing platform constructed, mounted with guns of large calibre. Our space will not admit of further mention of the numerous gates and towers with which Dover Castle abounds; suffice it to say, that every part of the castle is being repaired, and colossal works erected; while it stands, in the full majesty of all its historical grandeur, a gigantic and formidable fortress, passive in the perfection of modern warfare, but, as a type of the 'BRITISH LION,' not to be roused with impunity.

Upon the cliff stands a curious piece of brass ordnance twenty-four feet long, commonly called ' Queen Elizabeth's pocket pistol ;' it was cast at Utrecht by James Tolkys, A.D. 1544, and presented by the States of Holland to that Queen.

DOVER HEIGHTS, from their great elevation, overlook the castle, and flank the valley on the south-west. In 1800 an Act of Parliament authorised the expenditure of £250,000 for the defences of Dover; of that sum £100,000 was to be expended on the castle, and £150,000 on the western heights. These heights are covered with every appliance of military art—a citadel defended by ditches, a grand redoubt, barracks, messrooms, masked batteries, and lines of cannon, as well as formidable works of every description, both offensive and defensive, now in progress of construction. A spiral staircase, called a *military shaft*, rises through the chalk cliff, *Chambers* says, of 199 steps, but *Measom* describes the shaft as containing ' *three spiral flights of* 140 *steps each.*' A handsome gothic chapel school, of brick and stone, has been recently built, with a residence for the schoolmaster adjoining, where the soldiers and their children are carefully educated : as a chapel, it affords seat accommodation for 800 adults. There is also another new gothic structure for the families of married soldiers, fitted up with special care, and replete with domestic comforts ; here fifty-four families reside.

Everybody has heard of Shakspeare's Cliff, 576 feet high, and perhaps read the immortal bard's description ; but all may not know that the South-Eastern Railway has a tunnel four-fifths of a mile long pierced through it in two distinct apertures thirty feet high, ventilated by lateral outlets to the sea, and perpendicular shafts to the surface ; altogether this is a grand triumph of engineering science.

DOVER HARBOUR may be said to date from the fifteenth century, when Henry VII., after Sandwich Haven was destroyed through the recession of the sea, commenced a port at Dover ; but Henry VIII. in 1533 built a pier of stone, which after his death was neglected, until Queen Elizabeth, on the representation of Raleigh, resolved to resume the works out of funds to be raised by a tax on all vessels passing Dover. Until within a few years a formidable bar of shifting shingle gathered at the mouth of the harbour, which not only caused an accumulation of sand within the harbour, but was in itself dangerous to be crossed except at certain phases of the tide. We well remember some thirty-five years since returning from Calais by the mail-packet, and being unable to cross this bar, with a tempestuous sea rolling most fearfully—the hour midnight—every passenger ill, even to the *pet poodle* of a lady ; and being told by the captain, to the dismay of all, that we must be content to lay off some four hours, unless any had courage to be tumbled into a twelve-oared boat then putting off from the shore. We recall the boat coming alongside, one moment rising even with the deck, the next sunk deep in the angry trough of the sea, and our feelings when cleverly snatched from the deck by daring boatmen to fall into their fragile craft as she plunged downwards into the foaming hollow beneath: now, however, those difficulties have been removed, and vessels may with safety enter the port in all weathers. Dover

Harbour has an outer basin, with an area of $7\frac{1}{2}$ acres, and an inner basin of $6\frac{1}{4}$ acres, distinct of a wet-dock, a graving-dock, and the pent, or breakwater, covering $11\frac{1}{2}$ acres ; the pierheads are of masonry and substantial brickwork, with an opening of 110 feet.

A *Harbour of Refuge* is being constructed, at an estimated cost of £2,500,000, to enclose upwards of five hundred acres of water-space; it was commenced in 1847, and, if carried out as planned, will consist of three piers, measuring respectively 3,500, 2,500, and 2,000 feet in length, with an entrance from the east 750 feet wide, and another on the south of 700 feet. This gigantic undertaking will be the work of many years—necessarily so, from the formidable difficulties to be surmounted, as well as from interruptions, conse-quent on stormy weather, by the occasional displacement of large blocks of solid masonry. The foundations are ninety feet thick, and forty feet below low-water mark. The first portion of this national undertaking was finished in 1854, and consists of 800 feet, called the Admiralty Pier, which was seven years building ; on its completion, a second contract was effected for 1,000 feet, to be finished this year. The harbour is to be defended by military fortifications, as suggested by the Royal Defence Commissioners.

Dover was the first of the Cinque Ports incorporated by charter, under the title of the *Mayor and Commonalty*. The corporation seal, which is of brass, was engraved in 1305 ; upon the obverse is represented an antique ship, and on the reverse St. Martin on horseback, supporting himself on a crutch whilst dividing his cloak with a sword to clothe a half-naked mendicant. The town has un-dergone vast improvements and extension within a few years ; the older portions, which were narrow and dirty, have been widened, paved, and well lighted. There are now handsome lines of streets and terraces, imposing shops, and commanding dwellings in front of the sea, for fashionable and middle-class visitors ; those on Waterloo Crescent, Clarence Lawn, the Marine Parade, and their continuations, form a noble range of buildings between the North Pier and Castle Cliffe. Hotel accommodation has also made a stride ; the ' *long, long bills*,' for which *Byron* gave Dover credit, have un-dergone revision, and no longer justify the unfavourable appellation they once merited. A company has been formed for the building of a grand hotel on the Marine Parade, to cost £75,000.

The Priory of St. Martin at Dover, founded in 1132 by Arch-bishop Corboil, demands especial notice, as being identified with the earliest of monasteries in England. *Hasted*, in his ' History of Kent,' after referring to the College for twenty-two secular canons within the precincts of the castle, tells us—' *That King Withred, finding a religious community inconvenient near a fortress, had them removed into the town, where he built a priory and church about the year* 696, *which remained until the time of Archbishop Corboil. That primate found the canons demoralised, and guilty of grave misconduct, when he at once expelled them the foundation and erected the Priory of St. Martin for canons from Merton Abbey; his successor, however, who completed the monastery in 1139, introduced Benedictine monks. The brew-house and bakery were built in 1231, and the gateway about 1320.'* Many of the ruins remained until the year 1844, when considerable quantities were removed and new streets built on their site. There still, however, exists the Early Decorated gateway, the refectory, and the dormitory. The gateway is in good preservation. The refectory, 100 feet long, has been used as a barn, on the walls of which are traces of frescoes. Columns and arches rise nearly to the roof, 26 feet high, having small windows in the gable, and traces of others. The original doorway at the south-west is blocked up. Some remains of the dormitory stand west of the gate, consisting of buttresses and parts of the walls.

St. Bartholomew's Hospital was founded about the year 1150, by two monks of Dover, for poor lepers. The building stood west of the London Road, and opposite to where the Wesleyan Chapel now stands. There were ten brethren and the same number of sisters on the foundation, but the funds becoming impoverished, their numbers were reduced to eight of either sex. This hospital was suppressed in 1535, and the building, with the chapel, wholly destroyed.

The Hospital of Maison Dieu ('*House of God*') was erected and endowed by Hubert de Burgh in the year 1227, the eleventh of Henry III. The master, brethren, and sisters on the foundation were specially enjoined to welcome with every hospitality all strangers of either sex. Snbsequently many bequests were conferred on this institution. Two sisters gave lands and tenements to provide a priest; but as there was no chapel, his offices were, of necessity, celebrated in St. Mary's Church, whither few of those receiving temporary assistance repaired. To meet the inconvenience, Henry III. undertook to build a chapel adjoining the hospital, in consideration of Hubert de Burgh resigning to the king the patronage and all his interest in the foundation. Simon de Wardune gave lands and rentals. Henry III. granted '*tithes of the passage*,' and ten pounds annually out of the port dues. Edward Prescot, under his will dated 1482, left certain sums to the priests and novices, '*to sing masses on the day of his death, and monthly afterwards*.' William Warren gave £4 annually for ever for an *obiit*. This hospital afforded temporary residence for Kings Edward II., Edward III., and Richard II. Here also the officers of state were lodged and maintained when the king resolved on a continental voyage. After the suppression of religious houses by Henry VIII., it was used as a storehouse for grain, flour, and biscuits, a brewery, and bakehouse, and subsequently as a victualling depôt for the Royal Navy until the peace of 1815.

In 1834 the Corporation of Dover purchased the remains of this highly interesting hospital, and at considerable cost rendered it available for municipal purposes: one portion has been converted into the guild or town-hall, and now contains some good paintings and figures in stained glass ; amongst the paintings are those of Charles II., James II., Queen Anne, George I., and the late Duke of Wellington.   A handsome window at the west end was filled in 1858 with rich painted glass. in four compartments, representing the figures of the founder (Hubert de Burgh), Edward III., Henry III., and Richard II.   The town-gaol is under the hall, and contains some ancient axes, halberts, and other warlike implements; whilst another interesting portion of this relic of the thirteenth century has been remodelled, and forms a convenient session-house.

Nearly opposite to the hospital, on the other side of the road, was a Saxon cemetery ; many graves were opened while excavating in the chalk, which contained spearheads, swords, beads, and other trinkets.

The early Kentish historians positively declared that the KNIGHTS TEMPLARS had a church at Dover; Lambarde even named the site as being near the Roman Pharos.   Later authorities, however, denied the existence of any such building at Dover; but a discovery made on the Heights, in 1806, whilst constructing a new road, laid open the foundations of a very ancient circular stone building, thirty-two feet in diameter.   The walls were thirty inches thick, and from four to five feet high, ornamented by pilasters and niches, with a square vestibule eastward, measuring twenty-four feet by twenty.   These foundations were upon the highest ridge of the hill, and fully corroborate Lambarde's assertion, as being *near the Roman Pharos*; and it is an interesting fact that the Templars' church in London, known as the *Temple Church*, corresponds to the ruins in question —a circular structure, in imitation of the Holy Sepulchre at Jerusalem.

Dover is a bustling town, and has some popularity for sea-bathing ; the water is beautifully clear, but the beach rather coarse and full steep.   Wellington Hall is the fashionable resort for balls, concerts, and public meetings, adjoining which is an extensive repository for every sort of fancy articles, including music and musical instruments.

The Sailors' Home in Blenheim Street was built in 1855–6 ; it is a noble institution, founded for the relief and shelter of distressed seamen, provided with a library and reading-room, refectory, baths, a smoking-room, and dormitories fitted with forty beds ; in front of the institution stands a Russian mortar, captured in the Baltic. Here is also a large military hospital and a dispensary, joint-stock banks and a bank for savings; the Custom House is near the harbour.   The Theatre, a neat structure, was built in 1790 ; the Museum, formerly deposited in the *Old Court Hall*, has been re-arranged in a commodious building near the Post Office, and contains many interesting local antiquities, Roman coins, arms, fossils, and an array of curiosities well deserving minute inspection. In Camden Square is a granite and bronze monument to the memory of the brave men of the 60th Rifles who fell in the Crimea.

Education is certainly not neglected in Dover: here are large Government and private schools, industrial and infant schools, distinct of Sunday-schools, that alone afford religious instruction to between five and six thousand children. The Dissenters have also numerous chapels, the Roman Catholics a church, and the Jews a synagogue.

The town and port of Dover is within the ecclesiastical jurisdiction of the diocese of Canterbury, and formerly contained six parochial churches, dedicated to St. Nicholas, St. John, St. Peter, St. Martin-le-Grand, St. Mary, and St. James; of these six churches only those of St. James and St. Mary remain.

The Church of St. Martin-le-Grand, with the exception of St. Mary-in-Castro in the Roman fortress, was the most ancient in Dover; it occupied a considerable portion of the old market-place, and although many of the ruins exist, they are so mixed up with houses of which they are made to form parts, as to be scarcely distinguishable.

St. John's Church, which stood at the upper end of Biggin Street, at the entrance to the town from Canterbury, was taken down in the year 1537; not a vestige remains to mark the spot.

The Church of St. Peter was situated north-west of the old market-place, now represented by a row of houses; it was a rectory in the patronage of the Crown, and had a cemetery adjoining. The mayor and borough members were chosen in this church down to 1583, and divine service was celebrated as late as 1611, when John Gray was rector, after which the parish was united to St. Mary's.

St. Nicholas' Church stood in the centre of Bench Street: service was celebrated here until 1526, when it was partly converted into a stable; in 1796 the porch was taken down. At that time Mr. Ashdown, a Baptist minister, had the tower for his parlour, and other apartments adjoining, and an angle of the churchyard for his garden; the church was taken down in 1836.

The Church of St. Mary-the-Virgin, built in 1216, has recently undergone extensive restoration, at an outlay of £6,000. The square tower at the west end has a spire covered with lead, and on its summit a large leaden cross until 1634, when it was removed, and a lighter one of wood and iron substituted; in 1724 the bells were recast, and increased from a peal of six to eight bells. The west front of the tower is elaborately ornamented by Norman pillars and arches in four tiers. The interior consists of a nave, north and south aisles, and chancel: the roof, supported by two rows of massive pillars and arches, has a curious effect, from the variety displayed in the bases and capitals of the columns, and

190 JOTTINGS OF KENT.

the style of the arches, the latter especially—s
others elliptical and pointed, whilst the int
columns range from seven to thirteen feet. Am(
is a tablet to Samuel Foote, the comedian and d
at the Ship Inn, in this town, October 1777; a
Poet Churchill. The living is a perpetual curac
parishioners, who, upon a vacancy, invite candida
is subjected to a course of probation, when the p
to an election. The present incumbent, the]
M.A., surrogate and rural dean, was electe(
parish has a population of 6,424 persons.

St. James's Church, another ancient structure
of Castle Hill; it consists of a nave, aisles, and c
embattled tower, supported by massive pillars
the north aisle, and contains a peal of six b(
Lord Warden held his courts of *chancery and ad*
aisle, near the chancel. These courts are still op
but the business is at once adjourned to th
Amongst those buried within its walls were Jol
1485, '*before the image of St. James, near that o/
choir*;' Elizabeth à Wodde, in the year 152:
'*half a sheet to the high altar, a kercher to cover i
coverlet to be laid before the altar for poor child
cloth of drap to make two towels, one for St. Jam(
the Cross.*' John Broke, buried in Our Lady's C
£40 for '*a complete suit of vestments to obtain the 7
for ever.*' There are 4,122 inhabitants in this p
valued at £245 per annum, is in the patronage o
Canterbury, to which the Rev. W. E. Light, M.A.

Trinity Church is a handsome modern structu
mented English style of architecture, between
at a cost of £8,000. This is a perpetual curac}
Archbishop of Canterbury, with a stipend of £
a population of 4,490 souls. The Rev. H. Ham(
to the curacy in 1863.

Christ Church (Hougham in Dover), a small
1844, has a district with 1,803 inhabitants. Th(
ing is Early English, and the patronage of the i]
in trustees. The Rev. R. Glover (surrogate) was
curate in the year 1862.

The population of Dover, within the municip;
limits, amounts to 25,325 souls, occupying 4,1
area, houses, and population of the entire Cou:
census of 1861, were—

Statute acres .	. . . .
Houses .	. . . .
Population .	. . . .

Our task is now finished. With Dover we close our simple sketches, desiring to thank our readers for their companionship whilst cursorily tracing the ancient history of this remarkable county. We have meditated over ruined grandeur in mouldering temples and ancient fortresses ; peered into cities and towns, villages and hamlets, to learn of men and manners, governments and institutions ; and we have rambled amongst Nature's choicest beauties, to feast on gorgeous landscapes not to be surpassed.

They were written from motives wholly irrespective of personal advantage, simply as a freewill offering to the people of Kent, who have so magnanimously figured in the early history of our country ; and as the pleasurable occupation of many winter evenings by our own fireside, when the blast without gives an additional charm to the family circle, and when, with our beloved wife and dear children clustered round the blazing hearth, we have gossipped and written of wanderings in Kent on bright summer days, 'midst the joyous melody of birds and the rich perfume of gay flowers ; or, on winged fancy, been transported to Gravesend on an autumn evening, watching large merchant steamers as they glide by Tilbury, illuming their course in colours of red and green ; or the rush and excitement for the railway boat, now furrowing and foaming from the pier with her living freight for the up-train : when silvery moonbeams play on the rippling Thames, and twinkling lights from yon anchored ships sparkle on its bosom like distant meteors.

With a sincere grip, we again take leave of our many friends at the season of fireside festivities, when Holly and Mistletoe deck English homes, from the mansion to the cottage—when families, gathered from distant points, meet in happy conclave to enjoy the blessings of Providence—when Pater revives memories of boyhood, and when Mater lovingly rehearses recollections of early life, reminding us of how much we have to be thankful for: the season when friends delight to mingle in social gatherings, realities of choice fare in poultry, Old England's roast beef, plum-puddings, mince-pies, with every other luxury—not, however, forgetting those whose privations claim our generous sympathies.

At no more appropriate season, we feel, could we say to all who have followed us through these desultory JOTTINGS—

WE WISH YOU A JOYOUS CHRISTMAS, A HAPPY NEW YEAR, AND A HEARTY

Farewell !

INDEX.

o

——:::——

GRAVESEND: PRINTED BY T. HALL, 4*a*, WINDMILL STREET.